THE RURAL ELITE IN AN INDIAN STATE

A Case Study of Rajasthan.

Iqbal Narain

K. C. Pande

Mohan Lal Sharma

South Asia Books

Published in the United States of America by

South Asia Books

Box 502

Columbia, Mo. 65201

1976

by arrangement with

MANOHAR BOOK SERVICE

2, Ansari Road, Darya Ganj,

New Delhi-110002, India

ISBN—0-88386-761-3

Printed in India

at Vishal Printers, 2/34 Roop Nagar, Delhi-110007

THE RURAL ELITE IN AN INDIAN STATE
A Case Study of Rajasthan

PREFACE

We have great pleasure in placing in the hands of the readers our study of the emerging *Rural Elite in an Indian State*. It is a field report on Rajasthan, one of the 22 States constituting the Indian Union. Rajasthan as an amalgam of erstwhile princely states has its own backlog of socio-economic, political and even psychic backwardness, and yet it is stealthily feeling its way towards modernisation and development. The rural elite are both an embodiment of the personality of the state and a catalyst of change. The situation that obtains in Rajasthan and the profile of its elite are not unique; they have many counterparts in several states of India. This perhaps makes the study worthwhile from a comparative angle also.

Let us begin with a word on our theoretical concerns. In the study of community power-structure, the theory of the elite has evoked mixed reactions. It has aroused both appreciation and apprehension. At the hands of Pareto, Mosca, and a few others among their contemporaries the theory became not only a counter-proposition to refute Marxism, but also a plea for a realistic appraisal of the functioning of democratic institutions by questioning the basic premises of the Utilitarians and the Idealists that human nature is imbued with the element of reason. Schumpeter cleared the decks for work in this direction. Michels with his "iron law of oligarchy" has been another source of inspiration. But it was left to C. Wright Mills to shake the very foundations of democratic thought. The author of *The Power Elite*, crediting the trinity of political, corporate and military elites with the responsibility for "core" decisions, illuminated the glaring inequalities in the distribution of power in the struggle for valued goods. The somewhat stark and alarming findings of the study did make social scientists interested in community studies sensitive to the dimension of power and its constituent elements. But, unfortunately, most of the community power studies did not go beyond polemic writings. Of course, there are books like *Who Governs ?* that cannot just be dismissed as mere polemics. But then it cannot be said that Robert Dahl, pluralist as he is, can be completely absolved of the change of having a blinkered approach and exhibiting a "mobilization of biases" for which Mills has also been subjected to severe criticism. In fact, the pluralist theory itself has been under attack in the wake of the failure of the national elite even in the U.S.A. where it has held its sway for long. The objective of our study has neither been to delineate the concept of the elite *de novo* nor to probe into its rationale. We have referred to theorists of the elite just in order to identify our theoretical framework and define the concepts that we are using. Having done that, we have allowed the elite structure in rural Rajasthan to speak for itself without any constraints in terms of an *a pirori* bias in favour of or against the theory of the elite.

In fact, the basic assumption has been that the interests of the elite can be harmonized with the needs of development. But the assumption only visualizes a possibility. In fact, beyond the four walls of this assumption, value-neutrality can be claimed. We have also not taken any position between the claims and counter-claims of what are known as conservative and radical theorists of stratification on the issue that the exercise of power is functional or dysfunctional to development. Both the viewpoints can at least be credited with at least partial truth. The functionality or dysfunctionality would depend,in the ultimate analysis, on the character of the elite and upon the milieu within which it operates. Nevertheless, the 'veto' group theory carries some weight even if the conflict between the "ins" and "outs" is conceded.

We may also add that we have not adopted the decision-making approach because, in our view it fails to provide a meaningful perspective for the study of *potential* power or what James March calls the "power of power". Naturally we have tended to lay greater reliance on the "positional' approaches used by Mills and some other elite-theorists. To some extent we have tried to supplement it by the "reputational" approach adopted by Hunter. But we have taken from these scholars only the basic framework of their approaches. We have, however, applied them in a way that suits the demands of the study and the exigencies of the Indian situation.

A few words about the context and scheme of the study

would also not be out of place here. The present study was
sponsored at a time when there was a mood of revaluation
about the performance of panchayati raj. Panchayati raj politics has come to be identified, rightly or wrongly, with rural
politics and consequently with the rural power-structure. At
a seminar in Delhi, M.N. Srinivas had expressed regret that
studies of the rural areas are as are no more than the study of
panchayati raj and politics within them. To a large extent the
two are inseparable, as the panchayats are a key institution
today in the village system and encompass the greater part
of village life. It should, therefore, not be surprising if pacha-
yati raj becomes a key focus and one of the critical indices for
the study of rural politics. Therefore, one of the objectives
of our study has also been to find out to what extent the
profile of the emerging rural elite is compatible with the needs
and demands of development as envisaged in the mechanism
of panchayati raj. We are conscious of the fact that, owing to
this self-imposed limitation, we have not succeeded in capturing a total view of rural power structure. But then our
resources set a limit on our academic pursuit.

We also do not agree with the view that the concept of rural
elite is itself a misnomer. The village system today, with panchayati raj as its power nexus, and linkage politics as its operational milieu, certainly has the potential to throw up a rural
elite, who are already in the offing.

Finally, the scheme of our study has been quite ambitious
and it is, therefore, possible that we may not have always
succeeded in doing justice to each of its many facets, all the
more because we have not been able to use all our data in the
report because of paucity of time and resources.

If the study, in spite of its many limitations, of which no
one is more conscious than its authors, succeeds in generating
even descriptive hypotheses for future research, the authors
would feel amply rewarded in their efforts.

Jaipur
March 1, 1976

Iqbal Narain
K. C. Pande
Mohan Lal Sharma

ACKNOWLEDGEMENTS

The present study is not, and could not have been, the work of a single individual. It is a co-operative academic effort in which several persons, academics and administrators, have contributed. We are as such indebted both to institutions and to individuals.

Our thanks are primarily due to the University Grants Commission which has been quite generous in financing the study. The grant made by them enabled us to meet the entire expenses involved in field work and processing of the field data. We would also like to express our gratitude to Dr. Yogendra Singh, now Professor at the Centre for the Study of Social Systems at the Jawaharlal Nehru University, New Delhi, for allowing us to draw generously on his conceptual and methodological insights in the planning of the study. We are also thankful to Dr. D.B. Mathur, Department of Political Science, University of Rajasthan, Jaipur, for going through the first draft of the report and offering valuable comments and suggestions which went a long way in helping us to crystallize and refine our ideas and their presentation. We are also thankful to Dr. K.L. Sharma, Assistant Professor at the Centre for the Study of Social Systems at the Jawaharlal Nehru University, New Delhi and Mr. P.C. Mathur, Research Associate, Department of Political Science, University of Rajasthan, Jaipur, for assisting us in attempting the survey of literature and in refining our conceptual tools.

I have no words to express my gratitude to my co-author. Mr. K.C. Pande, Senior Research Associate, who has played a pivotal role in the project from its inception to the report writing stage. Whatever academic merit can be attributed to this work is largely due to his insightful contribution both in substantive and methodological terms. I am equally indebted to

Mr. Mohan Lal Sharma, Research Associate, who prepared the first draft of the report. His interest in empirical theory, his conceptual insights and passion for methodological rigour have left a positive imprint on this work.

Equal credit is due to the energetic and enthusiastic band of research assistants constituting the field survey team. The rural background of the field staff, imbuing them with a sense of informality, contributed in good measure in getting over the barricades between them and the villagers which are a common experience in village surveys. It was largely because of this that complaints of non-cooperation from the sampled population were almost nil except during the first few days in Bhilwara district. More importantly, an attitude of complete identification, sense of professional stake, integrity, and infinite capacity for hard work characterised the survey team. To them we really owe our modest success in good measure. Our sincere and grateful thanks in this regard are due to Messers Gulkand Regar, Laxmi Narain, Manohar Singhvi, Narendra Pandhaya, Prabhu Dayal Sharma, Dr. Ravindra Prakash Sharma, Satya Deo Bareth and Dr. S. L. Srivastava.

A word about the guidance and help that we received from the officials will also not be out of place here. We have pleasant recollections of the fact that from the initial stage of planning through field work and final report writing, the officials at all levels extended full co-operation to us. If the Development Commissioner came to help at the planning stage, the field staff gave us all support and cooperation at subsequent stages. But for their assistance neither the planning of the study would have been insightful nor survey work and *rapport* in the field possible. We take this opportunity to offer our grateful thanks to them.

We would be failing in our duty if we do not record our appreciation of the satisfying response that the survey team received from the citizens and the persons of the elite. After the initial inhibitions were overcome, lodging and boarding facilities were made available in the various villages where the field work was conducted and the respondents would do their best to create favourable conditions to help out the survey team. However, some difficulty in this regard was experienced in Bhilwara district in initial stages, where it took some time to convince the people concerned that the investigations were bona fide and the field staff had only an academic interest in the job. But the research staff in the field expected spells of initial inhibition and they were, in fact, forewarned to that effect during their training at the headquarters, and also by the samiti officials. The latter informed the research team in Bhilwara that both officials and non-officials had exploited the ignorant and innocent people of the area in the past. However, when influential persons in the area were contacted, they were only too glad to help. Once the people were convinced that the survey team was pursuing a genuinely academic quest, no trace of inhibiting suspicion was left. It would also be worthwhile to add in passing that it was quite a trying job to explain to several of these well-meaning people in Bhilwara and elsewhere what a team from the University meant and what it was doing there. But aside from these understandable inhibitions and that also in the initial stages of our enquiry, the respondents were both cooperative and frank and the present study is, in fact, a living tribute to their willing response, for which we would ever remain indebted to them.

We would also like to record our appreciation of Shri O.P. Varma, who typed five hundred and odd pages neatly, with interest, skill and dexterity in spite of the fact that the drafts given to him for final typing were none-too-clean; they were, in fact, overlaid with corrections of all sorts.

We have no words to express our gratitude to Dr. S.P. Varma, former Professor & Head of the Department of Political Science, University of Rajasthan, Jaipur, and now National Fellow, Indian Council of Social Science Research, whose academic leadership has created an environment of research in the department which, in turn, has made the present study possible.

We are also grateful to Dr. R.N. Mookherjee of the Department of English, University of Rajasthan, Jaipur, for his thoroughly revising the MSS from the point of view of style and language in the light of the valuable comments of the reader to whom the MSS was sent by one publisher for opinion and suggestions. We are equally thankful to the anonymous reader

xii

whose suggestions have gone a long way in improving the quality of the book.

Finally, our grateful thanks are also due to our publishers for bringing out the book with creative interest and within record time.

Jaipur   Iqbal Narain
March 1, 1976

CONTENTS

CONTENTS

1

INTRODUCTION

THE PRESENT STUDY of the emerging rural elite has been undertaken in the specific context of Rajasthan, and in the wake of the changes brought about by panchayati raj and community development programmes. The objectives of panchayati raj are democratization, development, and social change; and the institutional leadership under its aegis forms the nucleus of a new emerging elite in rural India. It is only natural to expect this new elite to justify itself as the end-generating catalyst of a new tranformation in terms of the objectives of panchayati raj. It is, therefore, relevant to enquire who are the elites in the changing social milieu; in what way they acquire power; and with what motives they wield it. Further, the primary objectives of the study are to discover to what extent the emerging elite differs from the traditional elite; to what extent the values of the political system, with special reference to panchayati raj, have been imbibed by it; and to what extent it can be expected to act as an agent of democratization, development, and social change.

With these ends in view, the survey deals with the socio-economic background, levels of political consciousness, the patterns of political affiliations, role perception and behaviour, and, finally, the development orientation of the emerging rural elite in Rajasthan. Special attention has been paid to institutional leaders under panchayati raj, since they constitute the core of the emerging rural elite.

Theoretical Framework and Methodology

In the realm of the social sciences, the term 'elite' is placed in a specific context. One is treated as a member of the elite strata in that particular field or branch in which one is better placed *vis-a-vis* the rest of one's companions. The specification is relative : one might be considered as a part of the elite strata in a particular sphere—academic, professional, vocational and the like; yet in another walk of life one might not be so placed and, as such, rated among the masses. In addition, the term has a cultural context also. With changes in a given value system, elite fixations are likely to vary. For example, in a congregation of a theocratic nature, a priest may hold a position among the elites, which he will lose if placed in a group of atheists. Also, though the entire discussion of elites concerns the realm of inequality, the core of the argument relates to institutionalized inequalities, which are being taken here both in the sense of ascribed and achieved status.

Emphasizing the inequality of individual endowment in social life, Pareto[1] defines a member of an elite group as one who secures the highest scores in a specific branch; by specifying the degree of individual endowment, one may be said to belong to a lower stratum or a higher stratum. He further classifies elites as governing and non-governing. Obviously, Pareto is conscious of the coincidence of economic and political power and talks of the primacy of the political elite or the ruling elite. Mosca[2] explains, in a similar vein, that the elite consists of an organized minority which rules over the unorganized majority. Mosca, however, goes beyond Pareto who concentrated on psychological attributes in the emergence and dominance of elite persons and said that the study of dynamics of social forces is equally important. Bottomore[3], who more often than not appears to be attempting a summary of the thought of Pareto and Mosca on the subject, maintains that the minority which rules over the majority consists of those who occupy posts of political command. The ruling minority, he further contends, is replaceable. Pareto termed this 'circulation of elites'. Bottomore applies the term 'elite' to functional, mainly occupational, groups which have high status in society. For Lasswell,[4] political

1. Pareto, V., *The Mind and Society*, English translation by Bongiorno and Arthur Livingston (New York : Harcourt, Brace & Co., 1935), Vol. III, pp. 1422-23.
2. Mosca, Gaetano, *The Ruling Class* (New York : McGraw-Hill, 1939), pp. 50-53.
3. Bottomore, T. B., *Elites and Society* (Penguin Books, 1968), pp. 7-23.
4. Lasswell, H. D., *et al.*, *The Comparative Study of Elites* (Stanford : Hoover Institute, Series B. Elites, No. 1, 1952).

elite, as distinct from other type of elite, comprise the power holders of a body-politic, but he adds that the power positions include both leadership positions and social formations from which leaders emerge and to which accountability is maintained during a given period. Raymond Aron[5] has held a pluralistic view of elites. He, however, makes a distinction between elites and classes and examines the relationship between the intellectual elite and the power structure. Like Pareto and Mosca, Mannheim[6] attributes actual policy-making and implementing roles to the elite. He also holds that the two concepts of democracy and elite are not necessarily incompatible. In Marxian thinking, particulary the classical one, the concept of elite is somewhat of an anathema. However, the ruling class of their view which maintains political hegemony because of its control over means of production, maybe treated as constituting ruling strata. The neo-Marxists have made an attempt to reinvigorate the concept, discarded both in Marxian and pluralistic[7] thought by according it central place in the understanding of contemporary reality. C. Wright Mills, one of the most prominent theoriests in this respect, holds that power elite, a tiny and oligarchic group, is the main driving force of the contemporary society. The power elite is singular because it is composed of closely knit military, economic and political forces.[8]

An overview of these definitions of 'elite' yields the following substantive issues which form the pivot of our enquiry :

1. The political domination of a few over the many has

5. Raymond, Aron, "Social Structure and the Ruling Class", Part I, *British Journal of Sociology* I(1), 1950. See also his work, *The Opium of the Intellectuals* (London, 1957).

6. Mannheim, Karl, *Ideology and Utopia* (London : Kegan Paul, 1936), and *Essays on the Sociology of Culture*, London : Routledge & Kegan Paul, 1956).

7. For a representative view see, Dahl, Robert "A Critique of Ruling Elite Model", *American Political Science Review* LII (2), June 1958, 463-69.

8. Mills, C. Wright *The Power Elite*, (New York : Oxford, 1956). He draws his data from the study of American elite. For an interesting discussion of elite formation in the socialist system particularly the Soviet Union see Djilas, Milovan *The New Class*, (London; Thames & Hudson, 1957).

been a key consideration in the concept and analysis of elites, though the actual sources of dominance may differ. There are different categories within the elite, and it is assumed that the political factor offers leverage to all members of the elite group and they, in turn, can also influence politics. Hence members of the elite group are said to belong to the 'ruling class'.

2. An elite position does not necessarily carry with itself the element of effectivity. But the elite is superior to the majority in a given field. This superiority of status, more often than not, enables the elite to influence others.

3. Finally, different elites constitute respective hierarchies in different arenas. This is a relative phenomenon and can be judged in terms of 'high' and 'low' level elites.

The member of an elite group is thus a person enjoying a superior position in relation to other persons in a particular field. In any discussion of the elite, therefore, the nature and bases of its superior position and not so much the incidence of its effectivity are the focus of the enquiry. This is done so in this study. In contrast, leadership is essentially a sum total of the degree and extent of influence to which the rest of the members of a group are amenable. A leader's guidance and directions are supposed to be accepted by the rest because they consist of various factors such as force, charismatic appeal, a sense of common good, influence, coercion, and so on. Thus leadership is a function exercised in relation to group-followers[9], while elite status is a relative position reflecting superiority. Both may be held by the same person and yet they require different traits for an effective maintenance of the two positions. While a member of an elite group has to establish and exhibit his excellence in a particular field, a leader has to prevail over the group members with or without the factor of excellence. Thus elite status is hierarchical in character, while leadership is essentially relational and inter-actional in nature. It is often thought that being a leader makes one part of an elite in one respect or the other; the reverse is not always true. We are concerned more with the analysis of elite status in our study, even with regard

9. For discussion of the point, see Nagpaul, Hans, "Leadership : A Frame of Reference" in Vidyarthi, L.P., (ed.), *Leadership in India* (Bombay, Asia Publishing House, 1967), Pp. 58-65.

to panchayati raj functionaries, than with the delineation of the leadership profile of members of the elite group though some overlap is perhaps both natural and unavoidable.

MAJOR HYPOTHESES

The major hypotheses and the sub-hypotheses of the study can now be listed below for ready reference :

1. The emerging rural elite in general, and in the specific context of panchayati raj, is not different from the traditional rural elite. This major hypothesis has been split up into the following sub-hypotheses :

(a) education has yet to acquire a decisive role in the making of the rural elite;

(b) higher social and economic strata continue to be the basis of elite status;

(c) the older male age group is the main source from which the elite emerges; and

(d) there is marginal political mobility from lower to higher echelons of power.

2. The elite under panchayati raj is 'civic-amenities-oriented' rather than production-oriented. This hypothesis admits of the following sub-hypotheses :

(a) the elite person in the older age group is more 'civic-amenities-oriented' than his counterpart in the younger age group; and

(b) elite persons with less education are more 'civic-amenities-oriented' than the elite persons in relatively higher educational categories.

3. The rural elite under panchayati raj is more interested in politics than in the fulfilment of developmental obligations. The sub-hypotheses here are :

(a) the member of the elite group uses power to serve his own interests and better his own social status;

(b) the member of the elite exercises power to enhance his influence and strengthen his position by rewarding his loyal camp followers and punishing his adversaries; and

(c) the power and influence of the elite in rural society is more conducive to a *status quo* situation than to social change.

4. It is not the involvement of the rural elite in local politics which hinders the healthy growth of democracy at the grassroots level; the malady lies in the political linkages of the rural elite with district and state level elites. The breakdown of this hypothesis in terms of sub-hypotheses is as follows :

(a) the defaults of the political elite at the rural level are overlooked by those who are in higher echelons of political power; and

(b) political elites at higher levels support their counterparts at the rural local level to build up their own support structure, irrespective of the interests of the local rural constituents.

5. There is maladjustment between political representatives and officials under panchayati raj. This, in turn, admits of the following sub-hypotheses :

(a) the contempt of officials for the elected representatives is the hangover of a feudal administrative tradition;

(b) the officials are averse to the idea of sharing power with elected representatives; and

(c) the elected representatives, owing to a low level of education and lack of administrative experience, fail to assert themselves against the officials.

6. There exists a wide gap between the elite and the masses in terms of levels of political consciousness and economic status which, in turn, admits of the following explanatory sub-hypotheses :

(a) there is wide gap between the literacy status and the levels of consciousness of the elite and the masses; and

(b) there is lack of meaningful communication between the elite and the masses.

7. The emerging rural elite in Rajasthan by its temper and training is unsuited to become a catalytic agent for social change.

SELECTION OF THE SAMPLE

The following table 1.1 gives a comparative overview of the five districts treated as representative of the regions and sub-regions in our enquiry:

One panchayat samiti in each district was selected using purposive criteria. It was conceded that the samitis should reflect the district averages. Besides, preference was given to a samiti where some developmpent works had been carried out. As it will be seen in Chapter 3, most of earlier studies sought to establish a correlation between the incidence of development and the extent of transformation of leadership. Since the present study also centres round the emerging pattern of elite status in rural society, the developmental variable was naturally assigned an important place.

TABLE 1.1

Broad Socio-political Features of Selected Districts

District	Level of Development	Traditional Pattern of land management	Political affiliation*
Ganganagar	High	*Khalsa* and *Zamindari*	Congress
Nagaur	Low	*Jagirdari*	Non-Congress (Swatantra)
Bharatpur	Middle	*Khalsa* and *Zamindari*	Non-Congress (S.S.P.)
Jhalawar	Low	*Khalsa*	Non-Congress (Jana Sangh and B.K.D.)
Bhilwara	Low (but endo-wed with a deve-lopment potential)	*Jagirdari*	Congress

*Discerned from the results of 1967 elections.

Similarly, one panchayat was selected from each of the five selected panchayat samitis. The basic categorization of panch-ayats was done in keeping with the population and number of villages. Thus a dominant cluster would emerge and the aver-age panchayat of the dominant group was selected; this was not necessarily in conformity with the mean average of the panchayat samitis. This was done with a view to find out how the size of a panchayat limits the interactional and relational patterns of the elite *vis-a-vis* the people on the one hand and the higher level leaders on the other.

It is assumed that in view of the purposive nature of the sel-ection of areas in the present study, the resultant characterisa-tion of the emerging rural elite is expected to be a dominant rather than a representative one, when viewed from the point of view of the state of Rajasthan. Secondly, the study does not postulate a static view of the present but a dynamic one. We have thus not been content just with a description of the state of affairs as it is but have also tried to project the shape of things which is yet to emerge. This becomes relevant in order to assess the extent of the elite-mass gulf, reported to be widening even in the midst of present-day social change, and its consequences. This may also provide an insight into the labyrinth of tensions building up in the rural social structure, the significance of which cannot possibly be underrated today in any study.

As stated elsewhere the focus of our survey centred on a study of panchayati raj leadership in particular and members of the reputational elite strata of the area in general. At the village level, the reputational elite and elected representatives to panchayats were taken to constitute the elite of the area; while at samiti and zila parishad levels, only representatives elected to these bodies were included. M.L.As associated with the panchayat samiti were also included in the sample. In addition, up to forty villagers from each of selected panchayats were interviewed. The villagers interviewed were selected by a process of systematic random sampling.

At the panchayat level, all panchas and sarpanchas together with all the former sarpanchas were included in the sample. To select the reputational elite, a different method was devised. Elected representatives as well as villagers were asked to indicate the persons who in their respective areas enjoyed a position of influence in the elite group. The names of persons nominated were arranged, by frequency of references in descending order. The top five were selected for interview. Apart from members of the institutional and reputational elite groups, two progressive farmers, whose names were ascertained from the sarpanch and the V.L.W. of the concerned panchayat, were also interviewed.

In addition, at the panchayat samiti level, those interviewed included: chairman of all the standing committees, members coopted to various standing committees, two sarpanchas of the developed panchayats, and M.L. As associated with the samiti under study. At the zila parishad level, the elite included four pradhans (one from the most developed samitis, two from average samitis and one from one of the stagnant samitis).

Similarly, panchayati raj officials, who were interviewed with the help of an interview guide, included the deputy district development officer (Dy. D. D. O), vikas adhikari, extension officers and the village level worker (V.L.W.) concerned.[10]

SURVEY TECHNIQUES

For purposes of this study, the following techniques were used :

1. *Interview:* Members of the elite group as well as villagers were interviewed using a formal schedule in order to ascertain views from both ends of the spectrum about the bases of elite status and the nature of elite-mass interaction. In addition to the members of the elite group and villagers, officials associated with panchayati raj institutions were also interviewed. This was done informally, but guidelines were provided.

2. *Observation:* To supplement the facts obtained and to make a meaningful interpretation of the data ascertained through the interview method, it was decided to observe the interactional pattern that prevailed between the elite (both formal and informal) and the people, by moving around with them and attending meetings of panchayati raj institutions. The points under observation were : to what extent persons of the elite strata in their behaviour reflect a democratic/authoritarian, universalistic/particularistic and secular/communal out-look. For this aspect of the research project, investigators maintained daily diaries with indices covering these points. They later submitted exhaustive reports on the basis of these diaries.

3. *Collection of Secondary Data:* For an ecological survey of the panchayats under study, a census of villages covered by a panchayat was undertaken with the help of a village schedule. Through this schedule, data were collected regarding location of villages; distance from the nearest centres of communication and administration; caste composition; literacy status; distance from social service centres and frequency of contacts with these centres; and the extent of developmental activities.

10. The information thus collected has been used only for comparative purposes and that also mostly in footnotes.

PLANNING THE SURVEY

The field work for the study was spread over ten months (March 1970—December 1970). The interviews were held in the course of visits of the survey teams, which consisted of four research investigators and whose stay in each district was spread over 30 to 40 days, depending upon the season as well as the availability of transportation facilities. In each district, nearly half the stay was taken up by completion of the survey at the level of the panchayat picked up for detailed study (henceforth referred to as the base panchayat). The remainder of the stay was devoted to interviewing members of the elite group at panchayat samiti and zila parishad levels.

The completion of the interviews of members of districtlevel elite group took much more time, owing to their mobility. In some cases, the research teams could not easily find some pradhans, many of whom had to be approached more than once. Some pradhans were found to be in a great hurry, and even when prior appointments were made, did not keep them. There were others who had promised to fill in the schedules, which were to be delivered by post, but which never reached us. It was a trying task for the investigators to locate the M.L.As. They were attending assembly sessions or committee meetings; or looking after their constituencies or were otherwise pre-occupied. Soon after the Lok Sabha elections were announced, it became absolutely impossible to locate the M.L.As. The narrative of trying conditions should explain the poor response from the elite in some of these categories. This difficulty was faced at panchayat samiti level also, though in smaller measure. Still, there the respondents could be located at their home addresses, or at least at panchayat samiti headquarters, as many of them paid frequent visits there. This was made possible by the cooperation of the samiti officials.

Lastly, a word about the individuals manning the survey team. A study of this sort gets enriched by pooling the potential of inter-disciplinary talent. The Senior Research Associate, an economist by training, has been actively involved in a large number of research projects. He helped, in an honorary capacity, the four members of the research team—two from the field of Political Science, one Sociologist, and still another a student of Social Work—who all held Master's degree in their respective disciplines. The short-term replacements (which were made necessary when some members of the original team left the project) came from the field of Political Science.

OUR FIELDWORK SUFFERED FROM LIMITATIONS

First, owing to paucity of resources, the time allocated for the study in each district had to be rationed to four to five weeks. This short period did not allow for exhaustive analyses, especially because the observation method could not be carried too far. The survey team, therefore, did not come across many important occasions which could provide insight into the patterns of elite behaviour and elite-mass relationships. The occasions which usually bring these into bold relief are crisis periods, such as drought, intense intra-village or inter-village feuds, and formal occasions such as panchayat or gram sabha meetings. No meetings were held during the time the survey teams were at work, and no crisis occurred. The paucity of resources also limited the study both in terms of area and sample. As the number of districts was raised from three to five, we had to give up the original proposal of studying two panchayat samitis within a district. Thus the study does not reflect intra-district variations. Further, as already explained in the discussion of the criteria of selection, the survey results reflect dominant rather than representative trends.

Second, as members of the elite group at the upper level could not be interviewed in sufficient numbers, their views are not proportionately represented for comparative purposes.

Finally, there was discernible antagonism, despair, and anger among the respondents because they thought that the panchayati raj institutions had failed to deliver the goods. They were also critical of the postponement of elections to these institutions; of factionalism leading to indifference to institutional obligations; and of wide spread wastage of resources and talent. However, it would not be an exaggerated inference that perhaps many of them exhibited despair without weighing the large-scale utility and services, opportunity and hope, ensured by panchayati raj institutions to people in village India[11]. This digression apart, the changing attitude towards panchayati raj, made the task of enthusing the people about the enquiry somewhat difficult.

Survey of the Literature

Traditional studies in the rural context sought to lay emphasis on 'system-maintenance'—*i.e.*, on the regularization of various forces and ascribed roles to ensure the *status quo*. In such a value system, it was natural that a position in the elite group would be acquired by those whose ascribed role was held superior or dominant in terms of inter-segmental relationships. Thus the priests and the governing class (*Jagirdars* and *Patels*) were treated as the topmost elite.[12] Immediately below them were moneylenders, who owed their dominant position to their capacity to make money available to those who desperately needed it. From the intra-segmental point of view, the elite happened to be the one who excelled in his profession. Thus, among *Brahmins*, those devoted to learning, were placed at the top; those confined to priestly activities were placed in-between; and those who took to other professions were ranked low.

11. This was interestingly confirmed during informal and cordial discussions with several sarpanchas and other village leaders at many centres, who were normally not our respondents. The sarpanchas of Raisinghnagar, to begin with, were absolutely hostile and asked for the immediate abolition of panchayati raj institutions. With quiet consideration and patience, as the survey team kept on reminding the group of the immense services rendered and the potentials of panchayati raj, it was found that even the most hostile among the group settled for a sober and balanced assessment and conceded that panchayati raj alone could make the common man fearless; it alone could ensure a democratic system; it alone could ensure a responsive machinery of administration; and, above all, the mechanism of development and progress could not be made end-generating without the extended benefits of panchayati raj institutions.

12. For a discussion of *Brahmin* elite, see Daniel, Ingalls, "The Brahmin Tradition," in Singer, Milton (ed.), *Traditional India : Structure and Change* (Philadelphia : American Folklore Society, 1959). For the position of the governing class, see Hitchcock, John T., "The Idea of the Martial Rajput" in the same book.

A review of the literature dealing with the traditional socio-economic system would also reveal that the elite structure was, by and large, static, in the sense that there was little room for mobility, change, innovation or improvisation. The existing value system prevented one class or group from changing over to another profession. For instance, moneyed classes or groups could not possibly enter other more productive activities such as agriculture, handicrafts, etc. and so these activities got caught up in stagnation. Similarly, groups involved in agriculture, handicrafts, etc. could not be encouraged to innovate—and hence stayed static. Consequently, the elite structure survived without becoming an instrument of change in the socio-economic system, nor did it permit others to bring it about. The situation did not help the processes of modernization, particularly in rural India, where the elite served as a 'reference group' in relation to the masses.

It is also worthwhile to recall in this context that certain forces and factors have been at work, particularly since independence, which have had the potential to change the ecological perspective. Some of these are :

1. A revolution in the means of transportation and communication exposed insulated villages to the outer world.

2. Industrial growth and consequent changes in the modes of production had the potential to cause changes in the traditional economic structure.

3. The secular educational system had the capacity to change traditional attitudes and value systems.

4. The adoption of universal adult franchise, the emphasis on a revival of the panchayat system, and finally, the introduction of democratic decentralisation churned the rural psyche from within and made the villagers develop new yearnings and aspirations.

5. Finally, the growing emphasis on rural development, particularly in the context of community development (CD) programmes, could serve as an earnest for the acceleration of the modernizing processes.

All these, cumulatively, were enough to create a ferment in rural society which would naturally not leave the elite structure untouched. It is around the broad foci of rural ferment as part and parcel of the initial thrust of the processes of modernization, and its implications for the elite structure in rural society, that we propose to survey the more important village studies in this chapter.

VILLAGE STUDIES

Hitherto, rural studies have tended to be wholistic and general. These studies treat rural life as an organic whole, and different aspects of contemporary rural society, such as caste, religion, beliefs, leadership and the like, as functionally inter-dependent. They usually lack an evolutionary perspective. More often than not, they offer just structural-functional profiles of rural life, which they do not usually treat as a process. These studies, as such, do not throw light on the patterns of conflicts and social mobility in rural India. Leadership studies, to begin with, were part and parcel of these wholistic studies. They were confined to leadership patterns and attributes and were not delineated against the dominant elite structure and the pattern of its relationship with the masses. However, as leaders invariably constitute an elite in society, though not the only elite, an initial review of these studies would still be worthwhile here.

Among pioneering studies of this type may be included those by Oscar Lewis[13] and H.S. Dhillon.[14] These studies have dealt with the varied roles of caste and kinship factions in the decision-making process in rural India. However, these studies do not adequately cover the dynamism and mobility pattern among leaders. Yogendra Singh provides useful insights in this regard. While examining the nature of the power structure in six villages of U.P., he has also discussed the patterns of traditional and emerging leadership.[15] *Leadership*

13. Lewis, Oscar, *Village Life in Northern India* (Urbana : University of Illinois Press, 1958) and "Peasant Culture in India and Mexico: A Comparative Analysis" in *Village India* (ed.) Marriott, McKim, (Chicago : University of Chicago Press, 1955), pp. 145-70.

14. Dhillon, H. S., *Leadership and Groups in a South Indian Village* (New Delhi: Planning Commission, 1955).

15. Singh, Yogendra, "Changing Power Structure of Village Community : A Case Study of Six Villages in Eastern U. P." in Desai, A.R. (ed.). *Rural Sociology in India*, (Bombay : Popular, 1969) pp. 711-23.

and Political Institutions in India, edited by Park and Pinker, includes some articles exclusively devoted to leadership studies, especially in the context of the changes brought about by panchayati raj and the community development programmes. Baij Nath Singh in his study of Etawah district (U.P.) has identified the emergence by the late forties, of a new and young leadership. According to him, the transformation came in the wake of land reforms, education and democratization. This new leadership, he found, was adequately interested in community development projects and was keen to ensure that these be developed as a people's programme with government participation. The sources of recruitment of the new leadership were also wider, not confined to traditionally entrenched land-lord village chief and a few caste Hindu families.[16] Evelyn Wood is of the opinion that aristocratic leadership has been supplied by Brahmins and Rajputs. Still the author has conceded that paternalistic and lineage based leadership has been vanishing.[17] Similarly, John Hitchcock in his study of leadership in a north Indian village, has held that caste as a basis of leadership has been continuing, though among lower castes there is growing consciousness of the need for economic reforms. Secondly, he finds present caste leaders to be more educated and development-oriented.[18] Henry Orenstein's study presents aspects of leadership behaviour in a village in Poona district. The author has observed that though persons of high repute and status are elected to formal positions in the newly established panchayats, they tend to embody the functional roles more in their personal capacity than make efforts to institutionalize it. Perhaps this is so because the formal and legal structures do not permit solution of disputes and problems using a sliding scale of values (a traditional value system according to which not all people are considered equal). However, under pressure

16. Singh, B. N., "The Impact of the Community Development Pro-gramme on Rural Leadership",in Park, R.L.,and Tinker,Irene,(ed.) *Leadership and Political Institutions in India* (Oxford University Press, 1960), pp. 358-71.
17. Wood, Evelyn, "Patterns of Influence within Rural India", in Park & Tinker, (ed.,) *Ibid.*, pp. 372-90.
18. Hitchcock, John T., "Leadership in a North Indian Village" in *Ibid.*, pp.395-414.

of the declared objectives of the Congress party, with which the leadership is affiliated, the elite tries to maintain a facade of equality.[19] Alan Beals, in his study of a Mysore village has also found that while traditional leadership is losing its influence, no clear trends about the new leadership are noticeable.[20] Authors of the studies of Andhra[21] and Karnatak[22] villages have also observed that traditional bases (such as caste and money) still continue to be of consequence. These studies, on the whole, seek to point out that traditional bases, such as kinship, caste, wealth and the like, continue to be effective, though, the degree of their influence has varied from area to area.

Two Sociologists, M.N. Srinivas[23] and S. C. Dube[24], have made specific contributions to the study of leadership, both in terms of concepts and methods. Srinivas regards the concept of dominant caste as crucial for the study of leadership. He observes that the dominant caste is functional for the maintenance of village community and also works as a reference point for the lower castes to improve their position, both social and economic. On the other hand, Dube feels that the concept of dominant caste is not of much help, since only a handful of individuals or families in a caste hold the prestige of status symbols, financial resources, and position of influence within and outside the caste group which gets further weakened in the wake of village factionalism.

A study by Wisers may also be included among the early studies of leadership. They have observed that "if caste precedence and economic power rest in the same men their leadership is assured. If the two qualities are separate, villagers follow the man who can grant or withhold their daily

19. Orenstein, Henry, "A Bombay Village", in *Ibid.*, pp. 414-26.
20. Beals, Alan, "Leadership in a Mysore Village" in *Ibid.*, pp. 426-37.
21. Bachenheimer, R., "Elements of Leadership in an Andhra Village", *Ibid.*, pp. 445-52.
22. Harper, Edward B., & Louise G. Harper, "Political Organization and Leadership in a Karnatak Village", in *ibid.*, pp. 453-69.
23. Srinivas, M. N., "The Dominant Caste in Rampura" in *American Anthropologist*, 61 (1), February 1969, pp. 1-16.
24. Dube, S. C., "Caste Dominance and Factionalism" *Contributions to Indian Sociology*, New Series No. II, December 1968, pp. 58-81.

bread. Ordinarily we find this power resting with the twice-born."[25] That is symbolic of a congruent elite structure. Another study of emerging leadership in rural India resulted from a seminar held at Ranchi University in 1962.[26] The papers dealing with the leadership pattern in U.P., Bihar, Rajasthan and Punjab are important in this regard. It emerges from these papers that the role of traditional factors is on the decline, but money still remains of the most important bases of leadership. To some extent education is also believed to be playing a vital role in the make-up of village leaders.

An important landmark in clarifying the concepts and methods in rural leadership studies in the light of field researches in South Asia has been the organization of an International Round Table on *Emerging Patterns of Rural Leadership in South Asia (1963)* and publication of its proceedings.[27] Besides the papers of S. C. Dube and Lila Dube, dealing with methodological problems and a survey of contemporary literature on the subject, papers on the results of similar studies undertaken in Pakistan, Ceylon, Indonesia etc. have also been included. Rajni Kothari does the summing up, in which he sets the emerging trends against a cross-cultural comparative perspective. The papers in the volume cover structural/functional and behavioural aspects of emerging rural leardership in the region and their importance lies in this wholistic view.

These studies, conducted mainly by sociologists and anthropologists, over-emphasize the attributes of rural leadership in terms of ascription and achievement and discuss the nature of leadership in terms of formal and informal, and faction-oriented and unified leadership patterns. These are not studies of rural elite in all its aspects. Not much light is thrown on how the leaders stand as a reference group elite in relation to

25. Wiser, W.H. and Wiser, C.V., *Behind Mud Walls: 1930-60* (Berkeley: University of California Press, 1964), pp. 18-19.
26. Vidyarthi, L.P. (ed.), *Leadership in India*, (Bombay : Asia Publishing House, 1967).
27. Dube, S.C. (ed.), *Emerging Pattern of Rural Leadership in Southern Asia* (Hyderabad : National Institute of Community Development 1965).

the villagers, on what patterns of horizontal and vertical linkages are developing among them, on how they communicate, behave and function.

PANCHAYATI RAJ STUDIES

Some studies were undertaken in the early sixties to investigate the changes brought about after the introduction of democratic decentralisation as recommended by Balwantrai Mehta Committee Report. Some of these surveys have had a wider scope. They dealt with the overall functioning of panchayati raj institutions, covering such aspects as their constitution, finances, functioning, and the extent of people's participation in them. The foci of study also included the role and bases of leadership of those who came to man these institutions. A particular mention may be made here of the five studies sponsored by the National Institute of Community Development, Hyderabad, for the review of panchayati raj as operating in Andhra Pradesh, Rajasthan, Gujarat, Maharashtra and Madras (now Tamilnadu).[28]

The Maharashtra study seeks to show that the democratic functioning of panchayati raj institutions depends upon the calibre of rural leadership and that talented leadership is coming up. This leadership appears to be concerned with expectations for community welfare and shows awareness of the need for social change. The Gujarat study corroborates the findings of the Maharashtra study. Paradoxical as it may seem, both studies note the emergence of leaders drawn from the landed classes, who subsequently rise to man the institutions of panchayati raj. The Rajasthan study provides a different picture. It shows that though comparatively young and better educated leadership is in the offing, caste, in terms of rank and strength, family status and capability to lend money continue to be its effective bases. Looking at orientations, the study finds that elected panchayati raj representatives are not conscious of their responsibility for cultivating enlightened public opinion and, as a consequence, fostering effective

---

28. For summaries of these studies see, Jacob, George (ed.,) *Readings on Panchayati Raj* (Hyderabad : N.I.C.D., 1971). The book also includes a study on Mysore by K.S. Bhat.

socio-economic awareness and conscious concern for change in traditional order. Likewise, a hangover from the feudal order is discernible in the bases of leadership and its functioning in one of the two panchayat samitis selected for study. The leadership is neo-traditional insofar as one of its new secular bases has been the capacity to bring benefits of development to the village. It is also trying to reconcile the competing claims of power and development. In Andhra, again, the leadership is not progressive in outlook, though it has taken a keener interest in developmental activities. All these studies bring out two common trends : first, comparatively speaking, the new leadership emerging in the wake of panchayti raj is less tradition-oriented than the vast majority of their fellow-citizens in rural India; and second, political linkages and party affiliations are not well established at the village level, though some traces may be seen at samiti and zila parishad levels, as in Rajasthan.

The findings of S.C. Jain[29] are as distressing as they are sharp.. It is revealing that people with little education are getting elected to various offices under panchayati raj. But "a further disturbing feature of the leadership situation in the panchayati raj is the capturing of organization by unprogressive and irresponsible leadership and the big gap between the leaders and the led . . . The middle class leadership (such as lawyer, doctor, trade unionist) which could provide necessary mobility without jeopardising the stability, is conspicuously absent."[30] The fact that feudal chiefs and jagirdars are coming to occupy positions of power in Rajasthan has also been noted by O.P. Sharma.[31] In explaining the phenomenon, he quotes B.R. Chauhan : "their [feudal chiefs'] intimate familiarity with the existing social order of rural Rajasthan in conjunction with forced changes in the earlier feudal structure constrained them to attempt their re-entry into the system

29. Jain, S.C., *Community Development and Panchayati Raj in India* (Delhi : Allied Publishers, 1967). See especially the last chapter, "Caveat Actor", pp. 611-27.

30. *Ibid.*, p. 622.

31. Sharma, O.P., *The Emerging Pattern of Rural Leadership in India*; unpublished Ph.D. thesis, Department of Sociology, Indiana University, 1966, (Mimeographed).

through the legitimate and institutional procedure of panchayati raj."[32] His findings ccrroborate the contention of S.C. Jain that the emergence of this group has adversely affected the functioning of panchayati raj and contributed to the failure of the scheme to reach either its ideological or practical goals.[33]

In his study[34] of a village in Tanjore district of Tamilnadu, Andrè Bèteille has observed the bases and behavioural pattern of the rural elite. His finding is that, while the traditional leadership was provided by the high caste Brahmins, who simultaneously happened to be landlords as well as power-wielders, there is a process of differentiation at work in the bases of present-day leadership. With the technological revolution in agriculture and land reforms, the middle castes are also assuming leadership positions on the basis of their numerical strength and their newly acquired wealth. In fact, the new peasant proprietor class now wields political influence. Bétéille's observations are similar to those of S.C. Jain and O.P. Sharma in that they show that the present-day elites are modernistic rather than modernizing so far as their social obligations are concerned. Further, Bétéille holds that lower castes will not acquire a position in the elite group until the agrarian structure is thoroughly transformed. Somewhat different trends have been noticed, so far as the bases of leadership are concerned, by K.S. Bhat[35] and Paul Karipurath[36] in their separate studies on the emerging pattern of rural leadership in Mysore State. Both these studies point to the emer-

32. *Ibid* , p. 210.
33. *Ibid.*, p. 206.
34. His studies are to be found in his books, *Caste, Old and New; Essays in Social Structnre and Social Startification* (Bombay, Asia Publishing House, 1969) and *Caste, Class and Power : Changing Patterns of Stratification in a Tanjore Village* (Bombay : Oxford University Press, 1966).
35. Bhatt, K.S., *Panchayati Raj in Mysore* (Unpublished Ph. D. thesis) Bombay, University of Bombay, 1966. Also see an article (based on the summary presentation of the findings) entitled "Emerging Pattern of Leadership in Panchayati Raj Set-up in Mysore State", Jacob, George (ed.), *op. cit.*, pp. 121-44,
36. Karipurath, Paul *The Emerging Pattern of Leadership in Mysore State*, (mimeographed), Administrative Training Institute, Mysore., *n. d.*

gence of a younger, better educated leadership, as well as to the increasing involvement of scheduled castes in successive elections. The hold of upper strata in terms of both caste and class is said to be persisting; however, K.S. Bhat in his study has also pointed out that progessive sections of the rural community are acquiring leadership positions in panchayati raj bodies.[37]

V.M. Sirsikar[38], in his study of the rural elite, brings out some important points. His study is exclusively devoted to the structural bases, functioning and psychological make-up (in relation to value-orientations and political perspectives) of the rural elite. Based on field work in Satara, Aurangabad and Akola districts of Maharashtra, the study points out : "The gap between the 'led' and the 'leader' is, to say the least, quite shocking from the angles of wealth, land holdings and property".[39] Similarly, looking at the role of caste, it is interesting to note that the "social plurality of 40% (that is the strength of Maratha caste) has a multiplier effect when it gets translated into a political majority of over 75%."[40] What further distinguishes the Maharashtra rural elite from those of other parts in India is the phenomenon of coincidence of triple monopoly : "of a class—the rich peasantry, a caste—Maratha, and a party—the Congress."[41] The study also reveals that there is less ideological orientation among the leaders than a discernible power orientation. Yet with a younger and better educated leadership emerging, there are indications that the situation may improve. However, the process has yet to ensure that the

37. *Cf.*, "The emerging pattern of leadership seems to be also an improved pattern as 'the idea of constructive leadership in the public interest' is gradually emerging. Traditionally, the villagers obsessed by caste regulations and social conventions, were apt to look suspiciously towards modern changes—social or economic; they would think twice before accepting any progressive idea. However, the situation has changed considerably; they have been induced to think and act differently." from Jacob, George (ed.) *op. cit.*, p. 144.
38. Sirsikar, V.M. *The Rural Elite in a Developing Society* (Delhi : Orient Longmans Ltd., 1970).
39. *Ibid.*, p. 185.
40. *Ibid.*
41. *Ibid.*

benefits of community projects do not become the exclusive spoils for a dominant section of society.

Summary

The foregoing overview of the more important studies yields some important formulations, the more important of which are listed below :

1. Traditionally, elite and leadership positions have been acquired in rural India by persons belonging to high castes, and as such enjoying social status, having wealth and holding power. Caste, economic status and power thus go together.

2. The changes in the land tenure system have tended to cause a split in the triple bases of elite position, as the landed gentry, often consisting of middle-strata castes in terms of ritual hierarchy, has now acquired hegemony in village affairs.

3. The present-day elite is giving up traditional ways of life in preference to western and/or modern practices. However, its members are not sufficiently cognizant of the need and urgency of social changes aimed at diffusion of modernization.

4. The rural elite is more power-oriented and less development-oriented. This follows from the fact that the acquisition of higher power positions helps in acquiring wealth and thereby a higher social status, whereas development orientation cuts across prospects of a position of influence as it seeks to bridge the gulf between a powerful minority and a vast but poor majority. The vested interest in the *status quo* is at the root of the anti-progressive character and anti-egalitarian outlook of the rural elite.

5. The panchayati raj and community development schemes have only helped powerful groups to make a further improvement in their own position. This has been made possible by the rampant collusion between officials and entrenched power groups.

6. Party affiliations and political linkages are clearly discernible at the panchayat samiti level and upwards. But they are rather vague at the village level.

7. It is only where better educated and comparatively young leadership is emerging that an ideological orientation may be discerned. Since a radical transformation of the rural social

(mainly agrarian) structure is necessary, a certain sense of professionalism, rather than a mere effort to control the distributive mechanism of benefits, has to be generated. This alone will make rural politics purposive.

These are only some of the general trends. There may be differences in terms of degree between two States or within regions of a State. And, as the studies bear out, these differences are proportionate to differences in terms of the depth of land reforms, the extent of agricultural development, the degree of exposure to external impact, and the level of literacy.

2

LOCATING THE RURAL ELITE

A STUDY OF the rural elite is basically an enquiry into the cultural orientation and structural determinants of power processes in society. Thus we are trying to answer here such questions as : who are members of the elite group in rural Rajasthan ? What sections of society do they come from ? What socio-economic traits help them to attain their position in the elite group ? Does the member of an elite group excel the masses in particular respects or in all respects ? Do elite positions tend to depend more on factors of accumulated privileges and influence based on birth, or are they the result of individual efforts ? The focal point of our enquiry thus is whether one enjoys an elite position because of ascribed status or whether one achieves it. If it is due to ascribed status, then it would be a hangover of a traditional lineage system and a reflection of the status-ridden character of society. This would also mean that the sources of recruitment of leadership are limited and pre-ordained, which would place a fetter on competitive politics and its potential for social change. The reverse would be an earnest for modernization. A profile of the socio-economic status of the elite and its comparison with that of the masses should help us in locating the extent of the gap between the two and in identifying the prospects and limits of social mobility. It is against this broad perspective of tradition and modernity that an attempt has been made to study the location of the rural elite in Rajasthan.

Socio-Economic Status

We now turn to delineating a profile of the socio-economic status of these elite in positions against a comparative perspective of a similar profile of citizens with a view to enquiring into the pattern of the location of elite status.

Age

The over all pattern of age distribution of citizens in our sample is as follows : 27.0% of total citizens interviewed belong to the age group of 'below 30'; 49.0% to age group '31-50' and the rest (24%) to age group '51 and above'. But among elite persons, the age group distribution is different. While the representation of age group 'below 30' is only 7.3%, the next age group of 31-50 contains 56.1% of the total number of persons in the elite group, and in the next age group of 51 and above, 36.6% elites are to be found. Thus in the second age group category the increased share of those of the elite in comparison to that of citizens is just 14.3%, while in the next category it shoots up to more than 50%. From this it is obvious that age is an important factor in acquiring elitist position in rural society[1].

Analysing the data by districts, one finds that within the elite group, the younger age group, ('below 30') is slightly better represented in Ganganagar. Though this district has the highest percentage in this bracket among citizens also, the proportion in the elite category is even larger. This may be due to a higher level of education and/or rapid economic growth. But we shall return to this point later. On the other hand, in Nagaur about two-thirds of the elite comes from the '30 to 50' age group, while the rest belong to the 'above 50' category and none belong to the youngest age group. This might be due to the geo-economic condition of Nagaur. The desert and barren terrain there compels a large number of people to leave in search of subsistence. It is quite likely that those who migrate are mostly the hardy and young, leaving the home scene to the elders. In Bharatpur the second and third age-group categories share, more or less equally, the proportion of the elite, though there are indications that the younger age group is coming up, and while in Jhalawar the

1. The analysis falls short of a comparative study in respect of time. Hence it is difficult to say whether the bias in favour of the older age group has an increasing, decreasing or a *status quo* trend. Other studies available, however, suggest a decreasing trend. For example, see the trend identified in, *The Pattern of Rural Development in Rajasthan*, (Jaipur; Government of Rajasthan, Evaluation Organization n.d.,) pp. 1-4.

strength of the younger age group is similar to that in Bharat-pur, it is 6.5% in Bhilwara. Altogether, thus, if we project the data about age-distribution of members of the elite by districts, it becomes obvious that the more developed a district is, the more chances there are for younger people to assume positions in the elite group.

CASTE

For analysing the role of caste as a basis of elite position, we have grouped various castes into three broad groups, *viz.*, upper castes, middle castes and lower castes. Broadly, the criteria have been rooted in the concept of pollution as a basis for social interaction among castes, the nature of occupations pursued (whether clean/dirty) and the rank the caste groups accord to each other[2].

Our study corroborates the finding of other social scientists that higher castes dominate the elite stratum. While among the citizens the strength of the upper castes is 16.0% within the elite group the figure is 25.0%. The middle castes also enjoy a proportionately greater share in elite positions. The middle castes constitute 51.5% of the citizens, and 64.0% of the elite. The excessive share of upper castes comes to 56.3%, while that of the middle castes is 24.3%. That gives the upper castes a clear excess figure of 32%. While it is true that the bulk of the elite (nearly two-thirds) is from the middle castes, which also have a share favourably disproportionate to their number, the share of upper castes is much more disproportionate to their advantage. In Rajasthan, therefore, though the middle castes are assuming leadership positions, they have not pushed the upper castes in the background—a trend which has been identified in the states of Tamilnadu and Maharashtra[3]. The contribution of the economic factor to this situation will be looked into later. The share of upper and middle castes, far in excess of their numerical strength, naturally diminishes the share of the lower castes. While the actual strength of the

2. Thus, broadly, *Brahmins*, *Mahajans*, and *Rajputs* are placed in upper-caste group, *Kulami*, *Gujar*, *Sikh*, *Jat* and *other* agricultural castes, goldsmith and other artisans in the middle group; and the scheduled castes and tribes along with other service castes of like occupation in the lower group.

3. See Beteille, Andre, *op. cit.* pp.185-225, Sirsikar, V. M. (see chapter 1)

lower castes in the sample population is 32.5%, they hold only 11.0% elite positions. This group, as is well known, has been given the opportunity for its members to be coopted at panchayat and panchayat samiti levels. But for this provision, their actual share might have been smaller. It may be that the obvious economic dependence of the lower caste groups upon other groups, coupled with their socio-economic backwardness, precludes them from acquiring positions in the elite group in large numbers. And as reports of the neglect of Harijans keep pouring from various regions, it is quite likely that in a politico-economic oppressive situation, they happen to be deprived of their legitimate share[4]. Let us look at this issue district by district. In Ganganagar district, Harijans, 27% of the citizenry, have a 12.9% share in the elite positions. This incidence might be due to some development on the economic front as a consequence of higher wages as well as allotment of land to landless Harijans. On the other extreme in this regard is Bharatpur where, with a strength of 25.2% among the citizens, there is but one Harijan (2.9% of the total) in the elite group. The area is Jat dominated, demographically and economically. Hence, the lower caste groups cannot usually expect any concessions from caste-alliances in politics. Jhalawar offers a different picture. There the lower castes, notwithstanding their absolute majority in numbers (50.5%), command only 21% of positions in the elite group. Apparently quantitative superiority did not help the lower groups. Besides their low socio-economic position, what has made matters worse is the rivalry among scheduled castes and tribes. Of the total strength of the low caste group, 50% are members of scheduled castes (*Chamars* and *Meghwals*) and 30% are members of scheduled tribes (*Bhils*). The remaining 20% belong to other backward castes like *Teli* (Oil-presser), *Dhobi* (Washerman) etc. The second and third groups consider themselves superior to the scheduled castes and prefer to ally

4. The research team came across instances of neglect of and discriminations against lower caste people. In every district allotment of land to Harijans has been resisted by other caste groups. Further the latter ensure that the former remain subservient. Harijans continue to be plagued by the atrocious system of debt. In Jhalawar and Ganganagar, the team came across several such pathetic cases.

themselves with the *Kulamis* and *Gujars* of the middle caste group. They thus, lose the support of their counterparts among scheduled castes and, in the bargain, undermine any expectations of assuming leadership of the lower caste group by forging links with them. In the districts of Nagaur and Bhilwara the situation is not satisfactory. It was found that the low caste groups rarely have the strength to ensure election of one of their own representatives to the panchayat. Their weakness here springs from their social and economic backwardness and their sparse population in the given area. Also, other caste groups seldom wish to align with the low caste groups unless it is for their own ends.

An overview of district and caste-wise distribution of elite positions would indicate that Ganganagar and Bharatpur offer a deviant pattern from the aggregate picture. In these districts the middle caste groups have a far greater share of elite positions than the upper caste groups have because the former are in the position of a dominant caste there. The other three districts—Nagaur, Bhilwara and Jhalawar—conform to the aggregate pattern because the areas in our sample in these districts happen to be multi-caste in character. And these two patterns are also in conformity with the levels of economic and general development of these districts. In this regard the districts of Ganganagar and Bharatpur lead at the first and second positions. They also witness the predominance of the middle castes—Sikhs in Ganganagar and Jats in Bharatpur. This means that development, both general and economic, has been more to the advantage of the middle castes than to that of other two caste groups. This trend conforms to the pattern in other states also.

EDUCATION

Table 2.1 shows that among the elite, literacy is high in comparison to the citizenry. In fact, it can be said that a high level of literacy ensures an elite position. Thus of the 16 "above-matric" in our sample all but one are among the elite[5].

5. The solitary citizen who is not in the elite group is from Ganga-nagar and, as our data show, his father occupies an elite position. Since the father is barely literate, it shows that in rural societies it is still age that counts and older age is held as a status symbol. This confirms our earlier conclusion in this regard.

TABLE 2.1

Respondents by Literacy and District

Literacy status		GANGANAGAR		NAGAUR		BHILWARA		JHALAWAR		BHARATPUR		Total	
		Citizen	Elite	Citizen	Elite	Citizen	Elite	Citizen	Elite	Citizen	Elite	Citizen	Elite
Illiterate	N	23	7	28	9	32	10	27	7	22	9	132	42
	%	57.5	22.5	70.0	27.3	80.0	32.3	67.5	20.6	55.0	25.7	66.0	25.6
Literate	N	11	10	11	15	6	10	11	15	17	10	56	60
	%	27.5	32.3	27.5	45.4	15.0	32.3	27.5	44.1	42.5	28.6	28.0	36.6
Upto High School	N	5	10	1	7	2	10	2	11	1	9	11	47
	%	12.5	32.3	2.5	21.2	5.0	32.3	5.0	32.4	2.5	25.7	5.5	28.7
Above Matric	N	1	4	—	2	—	1	—	1	—	7	1	15
	%	2.5	12.9	—	6.1	—	3.2	—	2.9	—	20.0	0.5	9.1
Total	N	40	31	40	33	40	31	40	34	40	35	200	164
	%	100.0	100.0	100.0	100.0	100.0	100.0	100.0	100.0	100.0	100.0	100.0	100.0

But the fact that the illiterate also share a position in the elite group, though in reduced proportion (25.6% as against 66.0% of citizens in our sample), indicates that education is not the sole determinant. It works in conjunction with other factors such as caste, occupational status and the like. It is to be noted in this context that only 6.0% of the citizens and 37.8% of the elite have had a definite and substantial period of schooling—that is, from completion of primary education to upper levels (up to high school and 'above matric' combined). This has got to be viewed in the context of the overall low literacy standards in the State[6].

District-wise, the picture is rather disturbing, as it is replete with glaring contrasts. In Bharatpur 20.0% of the elite are 'above matric'. In Ganganagar the percentage is 12.9, in Nagaur 6.1 and in the highland districts of Bhilwara and Jhalawar, it is almost negligible. Analysing the data by the period of schooling, that is, 'upto high school' and 'above matric' combined, the districts of Bharatpur and Ganganagar again stand at the top (45.7% & 45.2%, respectively) followed by Bhilwara, Jhalawar and Nagaur a pattern which, more or less, corresponds to the general economic level of these districts. Among the illiterate, the pattern is identical in all the districts except in Bhilwara, where 32% of the members of the elite group are literate. This only reflects a general pattern, since Bhilwara has one of the lowest percentages of literate people.

EDUCATION AND CASTE

Let us explicate for a while the *conjunctional role* of education in relation to the elite status. The study shows that high literacy is associated with upper caste membership. Among citizens, 34.% of the members of upper castes, 64.1% of the persons in middle castes and 84.6% of lower caste people are illiterate. Within the elite, the corresponding figures are 4.9% 26.7% and 66.7%. Moreover, the upper caste people are much more privileged in terms of high as well as middle order lite-

---

6. Fifteen percent of the population in aggregate terms in the areas studied, was literate. Even according to 1971 Census reports, the situation has not altered radically, it is now as follows: Ganganagar-20.3%, Nagaur—14.8%, Bharatpur-18.9% Jhalawar-17.1% and Bhilwara-14.9%.

racy. The gap between upper and middle caste groups is quite substantial (26.6% in the last two categories combined). Of importance is the fact that among the lower castes only one citizen (1.6%) and one member of the elite group (5.6%) have had some schooling. Comparing citizens and members of the elite group, the earlier trend is confirmed in that the latter have a higher literacy rate than the former. This holds true for all the caste categories. Thus the members of the elite group are superior not only to the masses in general but also to their own caste-fellows. The data reveal that the inequalities in terms of literacy are greater among upper castes than among the lower caste groups. The members of the elite group and citizens of lower castes are alike in terms of low literacy. While upper caste membership ensures a higher ascribed status, education helps them further in achieving an elite position. Our data thus support more the idea that elites are composed of *dominant individuals* as propounded by S. C. Dube rather than the concept of *dominant caste* as suggested by M.N. Srinivas[7].

ECONOMIC POSITION

Many studies, as seen in the survey of literature, have pointed to the role of money in according higher position to a person or a group, and thereby ensuring influential status in society. Two major indices of economic status are occupation and income. Yet neither of the two explains fully the relative economic position of persons in our sample. Taking agriculture, for example, it is a well established practice that irrespective of the size of land-holding (whether one acre or several) every one calls oneself an agriculturist. Besides size, the fertility of land varies from place to place. This further complicates the task of researchers. This is true in case of other occupations as well, *e.g.*, trade (whether wholesale or retail), artisan (with varying turnouts) and so on.

To overcome this ambiguity, we have taken economic status as a variable in place of occupation and income. This, with its sub-categories of 'rich', 'middle' and 'poor', has been evolved out of assessment of returns of annual income in the

7. *Supra*, n. 21 and n. 22 in Chapter 1.

light of business transactions (including agriculture) and size of the family. Thus one earning enough to save (irrespective of the amount of the saving) after having ensured minimum standards of comfortable life in the rural area has been placed in the 'rich' category, one earning enough to live a comfortable life by rural standards without any saving has been taken as belonging to the 'middle' category and one managing just a meagre subsistence living, has been classified as 'poor'. After personal observations and enquiries, it was also decided to take into consideration the per capita land owned by agriculturist-respondents for classification into rich, middle and poor groups. Per capita land was computed by converting the actual holdings into standard holdings[8] and dividing by the total number of family members directly dependent upon that particular holding. Thus a respondent having a per capita holding equivalent to '5 standard acres and above' was classified as 'rich'; one having equivalent to '2.5 to 5 standard acres' into 'middle' and one having '2.5 and below' standard acres was placed into the 'poor' category. For maintaining as fair a classification as possible, subsidiary occupations, if any, were also taken into consideration. For other occupational categories, the criterion of income was adopted. One having per capita annual income of 'Rs. 1200 and above' was categorized as 'rich', one with 'Rs. 500 to 1200' as 'middle', and one having 'Rs. 500 and below' as 'poor'.

An overview of the economic status of respondents can be had from table 2.2. In the aggregate, 'poor' citizens form 46% of the population, citizens in the 'middle' 47%, and the rich only 7%. But if we take the data by districts, the variations are of an extreme order. The figure for 'poor' is 27.5% in Ganganagar, while the coresponding figure for Bhilwara is 72.5%. In the other three districts, the figures vary from 40% to 47%. Among the 'middle', in all the districts, they vary between 47% to 57% except in Bhilwara where they come down to

8. For conversion of actual holding size into standard acres we have used the table prepared by Dool Singh basing on the Rajasthan Gazette Extraordinary, dated 11 December, 1963, pp. 115-117. (See, Singh, Dool, *A Study of Land Reforms in Rajasthan*, (New Delhi, Government of India, Research Programme Commitee, Planning Commission, 1964.) pp. 214-15.

TABLE 2.2

Economic Status of the Respondents by District

District		RICH		MIDDLE		POOR		Total	
		Citizen	Elite	Citizen	Elite	Citizen	Elite	Citizen	Elite
Garganagar	N	6	17	23	12	11	2	40	31
	%	15.0	54.8	57.5	38.7	27.5	6.5	100.0	100.0
Nagaur	N	2	14	22	18	16	1	40	33
	%	5.0	42.4	55.0	54.6	40.0	3.0	100.0	100.0
Bhilwara	N	1	13	10	12	29	6	40	31
	%	2.5	41.9	25.0	38.7	72.5	19.4	100.0	100.0
Jhalawar	N	4	19	19	11	17	4	40	34
	%	10.0	55.8	47.5	32.4	42.5	11.8	100.0	100.0
Bharatpur	N	1	12	20	21	19	2	40	35
	%	2.5	34.3	50.0	60.0	47.5	5.7	100.0	100.0
Total	N	14	75	94	74	92	15	200	164
	%	7.0	45.7	47.0	45.1	46.0	9.2	100.0	100.0

25%. Similarly, among the 'rich', the figure for Ganganagar is 15%, followed by Jhalawar with 10%. In the rest of the districts, the figures vary from 2.5% to 5%. The pattern that emerges shows that Ganganagar is comparatively the most affluent district, whereas Bhilwara is the poorest. In between are placed Jhalawar, Nagaur and Bharatpur, in that order. Though Bharatpur in terms of the level of development holds second place after Ganganagar, it occupies fourth place as far as the category of the rich is concerned. This is so because the area is the most densely populated of all the districts and therefore the land-man ratio is quite low. In Ganganagar, however, which in terms of geographical and climatic conditions is not as favourably endowed as Bharatpur, the people are comparatively well off because of canal complexes and a high land-man ratio. The incidence of the highest number of the 'rich' occupying an elite position in Ganganagar district on the one hand and those of the 'poor' in Bhilwara district, broadly, conform to the pattern of the levels of development of these areas. As already seen, Ganganagar is the most developed and Bhilwara the least developed among the five districts in our sample.

The position of the elite in all the areas is uniform : they come from the strata of rich people, supplemented by a substantial number from the middle group. The poor segment has a very low percentage share of elite positions. Thus it could be inferred that the major stratum which produces members of the elite is that of the rich.

This conclusion is further confirmed by an analysis of respondents by economic status and caste and economic status and education.

Economic Position and Caste

The enquiry reveals that among the upper castes, whereas only 9.4% of the total number of citizens are rich, 75.6% of the members of the elite group are rich. Correspondingly, 68.7% of the citizens and 22.0% of the elite are in the 'middle' group of economic status, and 2.4% of the upper caste elite are 'poor', while 21.9% of upper caste citizens are in the 'poor' category. In the middle caste group rich citizens are only 10.7%, while in the elite stratum the figure is 41.0%. In this caste group, 54.4% of the citizens and 54.2% of members of the elite are in the middle economic groups, and 34.9% of the citizens but only 4.8% of the elite membership are to be found in the 'poor' category. This trend is significant insofar as it shows that while middle caste people with 'middle' economic status can still reach elite positions, upper caste people in this category of economic status cannot hope to make it. The prevailing disparities among various caste groups (among elites of different caste groups as well as between the elite and citizens) indicates the extent to which upper economic status determines an elite position in society. Further, the wide gap between the citizens and the elite, especially of the upper caste and to some extent of the middle caste group, makes it clear that caste membership alone is not always the decisive factor. It is only when caste membership gets synchronized with upper economic status that one may acquire an elite position in society. This gives credence to our earlier observation that dominant individuals are more significant than dominant castes in the rural power structure. And the fortunate few are those who enjoy upper economic status along with (though not always) upper caste status.

While discussing caste and economic status as bases of an elite position, one may also analyse the emerging trends in the context of the transforming character of caste organisations. It has been pointed out in some studies that caste organisations are adopting new secularising roles, that is, they are assuming the responsibility of furthering the socio-economic interests of their members. This new role further consolidates a caste in the form of a caste association and also explains the phenomenon of casteism in politics. This trend is only partially borne out by our study. This is evident from the fact that, while upper castes have a share in the elite structure which is disproportionately large to their members, it is just the reverse in the case of lower castes. In the context of Rajasthan, it may be said that caste-consciousness in terms of newly acquired roles, is not of a high order. But more than that, it is also a fact that multiple loyalties to locality, employer, moneylender, (and consequential multiple-pressures); and intra-caste factionalism and the like are also important since they cut through caste solidarity. These inner contradictions may only be expected to grow with economic advancement. Thus it is difficult to accept caste as the sole base of elite position, though it may always play a conjunctional role together with economic status.[9] In this context, it is worth noting that the middle caste group, which has a 51.5% share of the sample population, has thrown up 64.0% of the elite, which is disproportionate to their numerical strength. But this disproportion is there to a far greater extent in the case of upper castes (56.3%) than in the case of middle castes (24.4%). Secondly, among the upper caste elite, 75.6% belong to the category of the rich, while among middle caste group, the 'middle' category of economic status contributes the highest percentage, 54.2%. It is relevant that since the upper castes are in a minority, it is their economic status which helps them acquire a position in the elite stratum, while in the case of the middle caste group, the numbers seem to be of some consequence. Thus it would seem that numbers and economic status are likely to be decisive factors in the acquisition of an elite position.[10] In this context, the aspirations of those belonging to the lower socio-economic group are not likely to be fulfilled, as a general rule; whereas this group forms almost one-third of the sample population, its share of the elite positions is only 11%. It would perhaps have been even less but for the provision of co-optation.

Our analysis leads to the conclusion that affluence and higher literacy are correlated. The richer sections in rural areas are comparatively better educated. Our data also show that slightly more than 25% of the members of the elite group

9. This is illustrated in a number of recently conducted studies; See especially, Rudolph, Lloyd I. Rudolph, and Susanne H., *The Modernity of Tradition : Political Development in India* (Chicago : University of Chicago, 1967), and Kothari, Rajni (ed.) *Caste in Indian Politics* (Delhi: Orient Longmans Ltd., 1970); see particularly Kothari's introduction pp. 3-25.

10. That the people in rural areas are quite articulate in this regard was in evidence during meetings with respondents. In Bhilwara, comparatively a backward region, several agriculturists had acquired effective say in matters of decision-making owing to reasons already identified.

are illiterate, while among citzens illiteracy is as high as 66%.[11] This confirms that literacy has a positive role in getting a position in the elite stratum in rural areas, though as we have seen, affluence, together with caste and literacy, present an effective synchronization of determinants of an elite position.

FATHER'S POSITION

Looking at the data on father's education, one finds a significant difference between the elite and the citizens. The gap has widened. While the families of the elite have forged ahead in education, the families of the citizens have lagged behind. Thus a tradition of education in the family in conjunction with other factors has not merely helped in obtaining elite status but also in perpetuating elite positions in the family. This may well have also contributed to the widening of the communication gap between the elite and the masses in rural society.

The degree of father's involvement in community activities also seems to have played some role in encouraging tradition of membership of elite group in the family. This is clearly borne out if we group the categories of 'highly involved' and 'largely involved' in Table 2.3. Note that 86 of 143, or about 65%, (excluding the N.R.s from the total) of fathers of members of the elite group were significantly involved in community activities in villages. They might not have held positions of institutional importance in the village, yet they were certainly 'leaders' in the broad sense of the term. And this leads us to the inference that members of the elite stratum also owe their present status in some measure to their father's involvement in community activities.

VILLAGE NOTABLES

We have seen how socio-economic factors have served as bases of elite position in rural society; the correlation is positive. Thus the rural elite in our study is, in fact, a socio-

11. The 1971 census shows that the rural literacy percentage among males in Rajasthan is estimated at 28.42%, while in our sample it is 34 percent. This difference is due to the fact that in our sample of 5 districts, 2 positively have a higher literacy percentage than the average of Rajasthan. Another reason may be that in the replacement in the sample, the literates may have replaced the illiterates.

TABLE 2.3

Degree of Involvement of the Fathers of Members of the Elite Group in Community Activities

Degree of Involvement	GANGANAGAR	NAGAUR	BHILWARA	JHALAWAR	BHARATPUR	Total
Highly involved	9	9	7	14	13	52
Largely involved	8	7	8	4	7	34
Averagely involved	5	5	8	2	1	21
Less involved	-	1	1	2	4	8
Not at all involved	7	6	5	6	4	28
N. R.	2	5	2	6	6	21
Total	31	33	31	34	35	164

economic elite. A good number of persons in the elite category owe their position to the strength of their own caste or
kinship group. Persons of lower strata are understandably
handicapped in this regard except where they are helped by
statutory provisions like co-optation.

But apparently, and some studies also point this out, institutional position is one thing and capability to exercise influence
is quite another. In this regard it is pointed out that institutional position does not automatically enable a person to become influential. Thus a positional elite is to be differentiated
from a reputational elite. We also attempted to find out whether this proposition is also relevant in the context of our study,
and so a specific question was addressed, to both members of the
elite group and citizens. They were asked to identify persons
who were usually looked up to for consultation and guidance.
Further, with a view to having a comparative picture, we also
asked about the persons who used to be approached in the past
for consultation and guidance. By 'past' we meant the
pre-1953 period when panchayats were formally introduced all
over Rajasthan. This latter question was addressed to elite respondents only as it was assumed that citizens would not
easily recall events of the past.

Before undertaking an analysis of the questions it may be
emphasised that these responses are just opinions. Secondly, we
are not using the much more familiar term 'reputational' elite for
the persons recognized as exercising substantial influence. This
is so because we are using the term 'reputational' elite for a
distinct category of elite who hold no formal position and yet
have been interviewed by us on the basis of the ranking method
specified in Chapter 1. Thus in the context of our study a
reputational elite is a non-institutional elite, though technically
the term covers an institutional elite also if they are defined
that way. To cover both categories we have used the term
'village notables' or 'influential elite' members.

FORMER INFLUENTIAL ELITE PERSONS

First let us look at members of the elite group who exercised influence before the formal introduction of panchayats
in 1953. From the data it is evident that there is a consensus
over very few names who have been recognized as influential

members of the elite group. Nearly 75% of the total names enumerated on this count in all the districts have come from 15% or fewer of the respondents. It is only in Bharatpur that three names figure as influential in the replies of 30% to 50% of the respondents. One may suggest by way of an explanation that the panchayat sampled in Bharatpur district has had Jats as a dominant caste. Caste solidarity would make it possible for a few persons to enjoy popularity in a wide circle. Ganganagar, in which also the phenomenon of single caste dominance is prevalent, may be treated an exception akin to multi-caste areas since it is a new locality yet to be solidified in terms of kinship relations.

Consider Table 2.4[12]. It is evident that all three former influential members of the elite group who stand 'high' in overall popularity also stand 'high' in terms of popularity within their own caste. But even a good number of those who enjoy 'medium' and 'low' degrees of overall popularity stand 'high' in the popularity scale within their own caste also. Analysis of district-wise data (the presentation of which we are avoiding for reasons of space) also confirms the same trend. However, the role of caste as a factor in influence should not be surprising as, in a relatively less mobile society, caste provides a major forum for social interaction.

PRESENTLY INFLUENTIAL ELITE PERSONS

To have a study in contrast an attempt has also been made to ascertain names of presently influential elite persons. Since

12. The table presents the data in regard to only those former elite persons who have been identified as influential by at least 15% of the respondents. The index evolved to prepare the high—medium—low degree scale is as follows :

For overall popularity :   High — 50% and above,
                              Medium— 25% to 50%,
                              Low — 20% and less.

For popularity Within One's 'Own Caste' :
                              High — 67% and above
                              Medium— 33% to 66%
                              Low — 33% and less.

The score for the latter category of popularity has been somewhat arbitrarily fixed at higher magnitude. This has been done on the assumption that it is easier to enjoy popularity within one's own caste than in over-all village context.

TABLE 2.4

Degree of Popularity of former Influential Members of Elite group within their own Caste in the Village

Level of overall popularity	Level of popularity of majority caste elite persons within their own caste				Level of popularity of minority but largest caste elite persons			
	H	M	L	T	H	M	L	T
High	3 100.0	–	–	3 100.0	–	–	–	–
Medium	5 83.3	1 16.7	–	6 100.0	1 33.3	1 33.3	1 33.3	3 100.0
Low	4 50.0	4 50.0	–	8 100.0	4 80.0	1 20.0	–	5 100.0
Total	12 70.6	5 29.4	–	17 100.0	5 62.5	2 25.0	1 12.5	8 100·0

TABLE 2.4 (*contd.*)

Level of overall popularity	Level of popularity of other minority caste elite persons within their own caste				Total levels of popularity within one's own caste			
	H	M	L	T	H	M	L	T
High	–	–	–	–	3 100.0	–	–	3 100.0
Medium	2 28.6	2 28.6	3 42.8	7 100.0	8 50.0	4 25.0	4 25.0	16 100.0
Low	4 18.2	2 9.1	16 72.7	22 100.0	12 34.3	7 19.9	16 45.8	35 100.0
Total	6 20.7	4 13.8	19 65.5	29 100.0	23 42.6	11 20.4	20 37.0	54 100.0

Note : H=High;   M=Medium;   L=Low ; and T=Total.

it concerns the present, the citizens were also asked to indicate names in this regard. The data show that 112 names have been commonly mentioned as influential both by elite and the citizen respondents. This is quite a good percentage by any standard. Considering the data district by district, Nagaur only appears to be an exception to this general trend. It is quite possible that the panchayat selected in Nagaur, being faction-ridden, has made the members of the elite group and citizens think in diverse ways. Another interesting trend is also brought out. In a village panchayat normally there are 10 to 15 institutional elite persons, including those in the co-operative sector. It is surprising that of them the highest numbers have been identified as influential in panchayats of Ganganagar and Bhilwara districts, which stand at opposite ends in respect of levels of development. But the criteria for considering the institutional elite persons to be influential do not differ very much. The personal integrity of the members of the elite group has been the key to their influence. We are not analysing the data here, though the extent of other factors can be seen in Table. 2.5.

It will also not be out of place to add here that institutional elite persons are treated, generally speaking, as very influential. We have categorized the influential elite persons into three categories — one of *present institutional members* of the elite group, another of *traditional institutional elite persons* called Lambardar/Patel etc. and still another of *non-institutional elite persons*. This is done with a view to ascertaining which of elite is considered to be most influential. There is an overwhelming response in favour of the institutional elite both on the part of elite respondents and the citizenry, though the category of preferred elite changes from district to district. This variation can be explained in terms of situational exigencies and personality factors. Thus, both in Ganganagar and Nagaur members of the elite group based in cooperatives are considered most influential. Besides catering to credit needs, they are matriculates and hail from families of former lambardars. In Bhilwara the sarpanch being a man in his seventies is almost a functional non-entity and as such the upsarpanch is considered to be more influential. Such examples can be multiplied.

TABLE 2.5

Reasons behind the Influence of present-day Elite Persons

Degree of factors accounting for Influence	Personal merit		Socio-economic Status		Political-institutional Status	
	Elite	Citizens	Elite	Citizens	Elite	Citizens
High	23	32	–	2	2	2
Medium	22	12	12	5	8	6
Low	7	8	40	45	42	46
Total	52	52	52	52	52	52

Note : High indicates 67% and more responses.
Medium indicates 34% to 66% responses.
Low indicates 0 % to 33% responses.

Another interesting point to note is that in the case of the institutional elite, there is consensus among elite and citizen respondents, which is missing in the case of the residual category of the non-institutional elite. This underlines the difficulty in judging a person as influential, if he holds no institutional position.

SOCIO-ECONOMIC STATUS

Table 2.6 deals with the caste status of former and present influential elite persons. In aggregate terms, it appears that at the expense of both upper and lower castes the middle caste elite persons have tended to acquire influential positions. However, the shift is quite modest. In the agriculturally more developed districts of Ganganagar, Jhalawar and Bharatpur, the middle castes hold complete sway in village affairs. In contrast, the upper castes have substantially added to their influence in Bhilwara as the middle castes have lagged behind in the developmental process there. Finally, the lower castes, for the very reason of their economic backwardness, have not produced elite persons with substantial influence. Similarly, the trends on literacy of present as well as former influential members of the elite group also follow an expected pattern. An increase in the literacy of present-day elite persons may naturally be expected. Bharatpur alone presents a slightly different picture as the increase in literacy standards there is not so marked as in other districts. This may be due to the fact, as the detailed data at our disposal bear out, that the replacement of traditional leadership has been least in the Bharatpur area. Consequently, members of the present-day elite group fall largely in an age group of 50 and above. Thus an increase in literacy of presently influential elite persons may not be expected in the Bharatpur district.

Summary

The study of locational factors indicates that the members of the rural elite group are those few who are born with certain traits that differentiate them from, and put them above, the citizens. They belong to relatively mature, educated and prosperous sections of society. In this respect they are ahead of, not only all the citizens in general, but also of their own caste brethren.   Further, caste and education play a conjunctional role in elevating rural people to elite positions. It is in this context that the concept of the dominant individual, rather than the dominant caste, has been validated by our analysis.

Apart from these general observations, regional variations were reflected in the presentation of data.   Thus Ganganagar, being the most advanced district in our study, has produced a more prosperous and middle caste elite than any other district. There are also more young members of the elite than in other districts. On the other extreme is the least developed Bhilwara district, where the middle caste elite has come up to share but not displace the upper castes from elite positions. In Nagaur there is a bitter clash between the Brahmin-led upper castes and Jat-led middle castes for acquiring hegemony in village affairs. The difference in the situation of Bhilwara and Nagaur also relates to the political traditions and cultures of two peasant castes—Jats in Nagaur and Gujars in Bhilwara.   Both have shared the common legacy of a feudal past, and yet Jats have come out of isolation, became educated and acquired certain political skills which are helpful in doing battle with the upper castes.   Gujars on the contrary appear to be baffled by their exposure to the outer world.   They have been sluggish in coming forward to acquire education and have been content with sharing power with upper caste elites.

But the most deprived of the positions in the elite group are the lower castes.   They are handicapped on all counts, *e.g.*, educational level and socio-economic status.   Consequently but for the statutory provisions of cooptation, their share of elite positions would have been nil.   In this respect even their numbers has not been helpful to them. As the experience of Jhalawar area in our sample suggests, the inner contradictions of these castes have been exploited by the middle and upper caste elite persons in elections.   Even then, here also the imprint of democratic politics is evident.   As the analysis of responses to questions about substantially influential elite persons would suggest, the present member of elite group, whether of majority or of minority castes, have to care more for the support of their own caste people than former counterparts did.

TABLE 2.6

Caste Status of formerly and presently influential Elite Persons

District	Caste status of presently influential elite persons								
	UPPER		MIDDLE		LOWER		TOTAL	
	No.	%	No.	%	No.	%	No.	%
Ganganagar	1	5.6	15	83.3	2	11.1	18	100.0
Nagaur	2	40.0	3	60.0	–	–	5	100.0
Bhilwara	4	44.4	5	55.6	–	–	9	100.0
Jhalawar	1	11.1	7	77.8	1	11.1	9	100.0
Bharatpur	–	–	11	100.0	–	–	11	100.0
Total	8	15.4	41	78.8	3	5.8	52	100.0

TABLE 2.6 (Contd.)

Caste Status of formerly influential elite persons

Districts	UPPER		MIDDLE		LOWER		Total	
	No.	%	No.	%	No.	%	No.	%
Ganganagar	–	–	12	100.0	–	–	12	100.0
Nagaur	6	37.5	7	43.7	3	18.8	16	100.0
Bhilwara	2	20.0	7	70.0	1	10.0	10	100.0
Jhalawar	1	14.3	6	85.7	–	–	7	100.0
Bharatpur	–	–	9	100.0	–	–	9	100.0
Total	9	16.7	41	75.9	4	7.4	54	100.0

Coming to regional variations, the case of Nagaur suggests that in situations of intense factionalism, members of the elite group are handicapped in the exercise of influence. Our data also suggest that in such a situation the displacement of the elite is greater and easier.

3

POLITICAL CAREER : RECRUITMENT, MOTIVATIONS AND CIRCULATION

IT HAS BEEN shown in the preceding chapter that the elite structure in rural Rajasthan does not reflect proportionately the various segments of society. In fact, the balance is tilted in favour of that segment which has privileges—social or economic, and often both. This was found to be more relevant in the case of members of the elite group of the "substantially influential" category. Another notable trend is that the institutional elites dominate this particular category of elite persons.

In this chapter we propose to study the political career of members of the elite group, examining the positions they hold; positions[1] for which they aspire; and the span and extent of their political life. The analysis will take into account different facets of recruitment, motivation and circulation. The assessment of motivations will bring out the considerations—abstract and idealistic as also pragmatic and environmental—which have made elite persons assume leadership roles. In addition, it will be useful to find out what groups and individuals

---

1. In the framework of panchayati raj, which isthe context of the present study, these positions are knit into a three-tier system, *viz.*, panchyat, panchayat samiti & zila parishad. The panchayat is mainly an executive body which is presided over by the sarpanch and includes 10 to 15 panchas. Panchayat samitis are centrally placed, as far as deliberative and executive powers are concerned. It consists of a Chairman, called pradhan and ex-officio members, the sarpanchas. Zila parishads have mainly a supervisory and coordinating role. They are presided over by the zila pramukks and include pradhans as ex-officio members. Besides, there are provisions for cooptation and association of certain categories of persons at all the three levels. (For details, see *Report of the Study Team on Panchayati Raj* 'Jaipur' Government of Rajasthan, Panchayat and Development Deparment, 1964). pp. 9-18.

actually succeed in attaining positions of power. That would explain the pattern of recruitment and induction of particular individuals to particular roles[2], thereby providing some insight into the links between the social strata and seats of power. But the recruitment processes are not merely a test of the degree to which various social groups and individuals assert themselves to acquire seats of power but, as Apter has pointed out, the "limit between social stratification, party and government itself are in part determined by the method of recruitment to and the definition of the role of government[3]." Hence the context of a particular electoral system is also relevant to the analysis of recruitment patterns.

It is in the logic of a transitional society and a competitive democratic polity like that of India that the persons controlling one or a group of posts get replaced by others. Pareto has called the process of change or replacement of persons, the 'circulation of elites', and we will be using the term, broadly, in the same sense, to supplement the understanding of recruitment patterns. It should explain the rise and fall of social groups from positions of viable control over decision-making organs. However, often scholars think of the circulation process as involving change from one group (in terms of social stratification) to another[4]. But in a developing society like

2. *Cf.* Almond, Gabriel A. and Coleman, James S. (ed.) '*The Politics of the Developing Areas*, (Princeton University Press, 1970), p. 32. Almond refers to the "recruitment function" as consisting of "the special political role socializations which occur in a society 'on top of' the general political socializations. They include orientation to the special role and the political system of which it is a part, and to political inputs and outputs."

3. Apter, David E. *Some Conceptual Approches to the Study of Modernisation* (New Jersey, Prentice-Hall, 1968), p. 31. Apart from theoreticians, politicians have also shown awareness of this limitation. The legislators on the floor of Rajasthan Legislative Assembly, for example, have discussed time and again, since the early fifties, what sort of persons would be returned by a particular election system, open or secret ballot, restricted or universal franchise and so on. See, for example, discussion on Rajasthan Panchayat Bill 1953, *Rajasthan Vidhan Sabha Ki Karya Vidhi Ka Vritant*, 3, (8, 9, 11 & 12), 19, 20, 24 and 25 February, 1953 respectively.

4. For example, Apter holds ". . . change means the degree of alteration in the basic characteristics of the stratification system itself,

that of Rajasthan, which is rooted in feudal traditions and a less differentiated social system[5] and yet gradually shedding its immobilism, one cannot always identify clear-cut group loyalities and stratum considerations. Thus a change of institutional position from one person or faction to another, even if belonging to the same stratum is to be taken as part and parcel of the concept of circulation, all the more because it may mean a change in the style of functioning of a particular institution.[6] Further, a change of power-holders even within the same stratum would indicate the degree of competition obtaining within a system, while continuance of the same persons in political offices for a long time would mean absence or near-absence of a competitive situation. We have, therefore, used the concept of circulation of elites to indicate a change in power holders, irrespective of whether or not it involves a change in the social stratum from which they hail.

Career Patterns

As already stated, 164 elite respondents in all were interviewed in the five districts. District-wise distribution of their positions in Table 3.1 shows that elite persons in our survey in different categories are not uniformly distributed. An explanation of the discrepancy in the number of elite respondents will not be out of place here. First, at times the elite respondents belonging to a particular group were not available for interviews, in spite of all our efforts to see them. Second, in some districts certain posts have continued to be vacant. This applies mostly to posts filled by co-optation. For instance, in Nagaur district, some standing committees of the

reflecting alteration in the concrete groupings of the unit under observations" (p. 28). Lasswell has also broadly taken the same position. (See Lasswell, Harold D. *The Policy Orientation of Political Science* (Agra : Lakshmi Narain Agarwal, 1971), especially chapter 6 entitled "Studying Leader-Follower Relations" pp. 68-78.

5. The term 'differentiated' has been used here in relation to social roles.

6. Thus there have been situations where in case of a contest between two persons belonging to the same stratum or even same family, one would be over-whelmingly preferred. In such cases the choices may be guided by personal behaviour, nature of alliance with local groups and/or in value-commitments and personality of the candidates.

TABLE 3.1

Present Position of the Elite by Districts

Present Position	Ganganagar		Nagaur		Bhilwara		Jhalawar		Bharatpur		Total	
	No.	%	No.	%	No.	%	No.	%	No.	%	No.	%
1	2	3	4	5	6	7	8	9	10	11	12	13
Panch	7	22.6	9	27.3	11	35.5	8	23.5	7	20.0	42	25.6
Sarpanch	5	16.1	3	9.1	5	16.1	9	26.5	8	22.9	30	18.3
Pradhan	3	9.7	4	12.1	4	12.9	4	11.7	5	14.3	20	12.2
Zila Pramukh	1	3.2	1	3.0	–	–	–	–	–	–	2	1.2
M.L.A.	–	–	–	–	–	–	2	5.9	2	5.7	4	2.4
Cooperative elites	2	6.5	2	6.1	1	3.2	–	–	3	8.6	8	4.9
Coopted	4	12.9	8	24.2	6	19.4	2	5.9	1	2.9	21	12.8
Reputational	7	22.6	4	12.1	4	12.9	7	20.6	7	20.0	29	17.7
Progressive farmer	2	6.5	2	6.1	–	–	2	5.9	2	5.7	8	4.9
Total	31	100.0	33	100.0	31	100.0	34	100.0	35	100.0	164	100.0

panchayat samiti had no chairman even though the former incumbent had retired. Third, at times, one person has held more than one post. Thus in Jhalawar, both the president and the secretary of the cooperative society of the panchayat under study happen to be members of the panchayat also. Since the latter post has a more representative character, they were included in that category. Fourth, as in Nagaur and Bhilwara, the number of reputational elite persons was rather small; there were few nominations in Nagaur, and reputational and institutional elites coincided in Bhilwara.[7] And, finally, in the district of Bhilwara, we did not come across a progressive farmer in the village under study.

In the discussion of political career of members of the elite group, it is worthwhile to look into the positions they held immediately preceding their present one. That should explain the stability pattern and maturity of experience on the one hand, and mobility and circulation of elite persons on the other. The data in this regard have been presented in Table 3.2.

It is clear from the table that to a large extent a sense of professionalism is developing in the career pattern of the members of the political elite group. This is evident from the fact that, while among the panchas and coopted members nearly two-thirds (62.0% to 66.7%) have been recruited from the reputational elite respondents, this is not in regard to other higher level categories (as of pradhans with the exception of one pradhan). In contrast, 45% of present pradhans, 50% of present pramukhs and 50% of present MLAs have held the same position in the previous term as well. The rest of them, more or less, had occupied a position placed immediately below the present one. The trend is much more obvious in the case of sarpanchas, 56.7% of whom occupied the same post previously. While 10% of the sarpanchas were demoted from the pradhanship, 16.6% had previously belonged to 'reputational' and 10.0% to 'panch' categories. The same is true of the office-bearers of a co-operative society.

The gradual elevation of elite persons from a lower to a higher category and non-institutional (reputational) elite persons starting their career from positions at the lowest level and

7. See for details in this regard section III of chapter 2.

TABLE 3.2

A Comparative Statement of Positions held Presently and Immediately Before

Present Position	POSITIONS HELD IMMEDIATELY BEFORE													
	Panch		Sarpanch		Pradhan		Zila Pramukh		M.L.A.		Cooperative		Coopted	
	No.	%	No.	%	No.	%	No.	%	No.	%	No.	%	No.	%
Panch	13	31.0	...	...	...	...	...	...	...	...	...	...	...	...
Sarpanch	3	10.0	17	56.7	3	10.0	...	...	...	...	...	...	...	...
Pradhan	...	...	7	35.0	9	45.0	...	...	...	...	1	5.0	...	...
Zila Pramukh	...	...	...	...	1	50.0	1	50.0	...	...	...	...	...	...
M.L.A.	...	...	...	...	1	25.0	...	...	2	50.0	...	...	...	...
Cooperative elite	1	12.5	1	12.5	...	...	...	...	...	...	4	50.0	...	...
Coopted	2	9.5	...	...	...	...	...	...	...	...	...	...	1	4.8
Reputational	6	20.7	...	...	...	...	...	...	...	...	...	...	...	...
Progressive farmer	1	12.5	...	...	...	...	...	...	...	...	...	...	...	...
Total	26	15.9	25	15.2	14	8.5	1	0.6	2	1.2	5	3.1	1	0.6

TABLE 3.2 (contd.)

A Comparative Statement of Positions held Presently and Immediately Before

Present Position	Positions held immediately before		Position held in distant past		Total	
	Reputational and Progressive farmer					
	No.	%	No.	%	No.	%
Panch	26	61.9	3	7.1	42	100.0
Sarpanch	5	16.6	2	6.7	30	100.0
Pradhan	1	5.0	2	10.0	20	100.0
Zila Pramukh	...	...	...	...	2	100.0
M.L.A.	...	...	1	25.0	4	100.0
Cooperative elite	2	25.0	...	...	8	100.0
Coopted	14	66.7	4	19.0	21	100.0
Reputational	20	69.0	3	10.3	29	100.0
Progressive farmer	6	75.0	1	12.5	8	100.0
Total	74	45.1	16	9.8	164	100.0

going up the ladder, further testifies to the emerging phenomenon of professionalism among persons in the category of the rural elite. It will not be out of place to mention here that the consideration of the same data by districts also confirms the trend identified here.

A large number of political careers begins at the level of panchas. However, some variations are also apparent. All but one of the panchas and sarpanchas among the respondents in Ganganagar district has held no elective post in panchayati raj institutions. On the other hand, in Nagaur and Jhalawar districts a majority of panchas and sarprnchas has held the same post previously also. Though not contradicting the earlier trend, it shows that fresh recruitment is speedier in Ganganagar and slower, or perhaps slowest, in Nagaur and Jhalawar. In between are placed, in descending order, the districts of Bhilwara and Bharatpur. It may be noted that in terms of economic and educational advancement Gangangar is ahead of any other district under study. Thus, it is not a mere coincidence that the highest degree of replacement, or circulation of elites, is also to be found there. However, ascribing the situation to economic factors alone would be an over-simplification, for the simple reason that Bhilwara, the least developed area in our sample, would otherwise have been relegated to the lowest position. Socio-economic factors together seem to account for this trend. For instance, comparatively speaking, in Bharatpur and Bhilwara districts (especially the panchayat circle and panchayat samiti in our study), with pronounced social homogeneity, one finds evidence of a larger replacement of persons than one finds in the districts of Jhalawar and Nagaur—districts of less social homogeneity.

Thus far, the elite respondents in our sample have been l assified in nine categories on the basis of the positions they hold. In order to streamline the classification, a re-grouping has been attempted by identifying the particular areas of operation of these elite groups, whether at village, samiti or district level, in keeping with the three-tier system. Where a particular elite respondent operates at more than one level, due weight has been given to the intensity of operational involvement.[8]

Thusre-grouped, the following categories emerge :

1. *'Panchas etc.'* This category includes both elected and coopted panchas.

2. *'Sarpanchas etc.'* This category includes, besides the sarpanchas, the member respondents coopted at panchayat samiti level and the cooperative elite persons.

3. *'Pradhans etc.'* This category includes, besides the pradhans the zila pramukhs and the MLAs for the same reason.

4. *'Reputational elite etc.'* This category includes, besides the members of the reputational elite group, progressive farmers as well. Though functionally the two are different, often they conjoin to the extent that in rural areas a resourceful person comes to wield influence and also manages resources for better modes of cultivation.

Bases of Recruitment

It has already been seen that fresh recruitment begins at a lower level, as panch and, in some cases, as sarpanch. Those who move up from this level man positions at samiti and district levels in good measure. This also implies that a good number of elite persons would not be able to go beyond this level because opportunities at upper levels are not uniformly guaranteed. It is, therefore, useful to look into the data on socio-economic variables, pertinent to the identification of elite-evolution. Specifically, these variables relate to age-group, literacy, caste and economic background.

Table 3.2 shows the generational background of elite persons (especially age-groups) of various positional categories. The middle age group, that is 30-50 years, is predominant, collectively as well as individually, in all the positional categories

8. Thus one may think of panchas and coopted panchas operating primarily at the panchayat level. In contrast, pradhans, zila pramukhs and M.L.As also operate beyond their own levels and, more often than not, have mutually reinforcing linkages.

TABLE 3.3

Present Position of members of the Elite group by Age

Position	Below 30		30 to 50		Above 50		Total	
	No.	%	No.	%	No.	%	No.	%
Panch	4	33.3 / 8.7	24	26.1 / 52.2	18	30.0 / 39.1	46	28.0 / 100.0
Sarpanch etc.	5	41.7 / 9.1	38	41.3 / 69.1	12	20.0 / 21.8	55	33.5 / 100.0
Pradhan etc.	...	... / ...	19	20.7 / 73.1	7	11.7 / 26.9	26	15.9 / 100.0
Reputational elite persons	3	25.0 / 8.1	11	12.0 / 29.7	23	38.3 / 62.2	37	22.6 / 100.0
Total	12	100.0 / 7.3	92	100.0 / 56.1	60	100.0 / 36.6	164	100.0 / 100.0

except that of reputational elite persons. In the category of reputational elite persons, the older generation dominates to the tune of 62.2%. The traditional respect given to age seems to survive, by and large, dissent and protest notwithstanding; village folks habitually give respect to the older generation, at least on the personal level. Also, the older generation apparently has tended to be cautious with respect to innovations brought about by panchayati raj institutions and processes. Hence old people do not appear to be very enthusiastic about filling various panchayati raj posts. And, yet, they have managed to keep a substantial share of participation at all levels, more so at the panch level. The 'below 30 years' generation has no representation in the category of pradhans. Thus, even if someone from this generation wishes to begin his political career at the second tier of panchayati raj and above, he might be unacceptable. The implication is that age does tend to be an important factor for recruitment to various positions of power.

Barring minor variations, the district-wise pattern is not much different. In all the districts the 'middle-age' group is in a dominating position. Some minor variations are noteworthy. In Ganganagar, for instance, the younger generation has a share of 12.9%, which is higher than that in any other district. In itself, the percentage may not be impressive; but the important aspect here is that half of the elite respondents in the younger age group belong to the category of 'reputational elite persons', which is dominated everywhere else by the older age group. We gathered that these younger members of the reputational elite category are post-graduates and are rich. The situation is understandable because this is the most advanced district in our study. This yields a hypothesis for future study that the coincidence of high economic status and higher education helps in breaking through the hegemony of age.

Nagaur district presents quite a different picture. There the contribution of the younger age group to all the categories is nil. The middle-age group is more predominant. If the panchayat circle included in our study sample is representative of the district as a whole, two trends are noticeable : first, in this area a greater number of younger people ventures to seek their fortunes outside because of limited opportunities; second, the area abounds in traditional Jat-Rajput factionalism. The younger generation, obviously, does not have adequate experience of political processes and as a consequence, prefers not to take over from the older generation.

As regards the literacy level of elite respondents, one finds that illiteracy is confined mostly to the panchas and reputational elite persons to the tune of 95.3%. The respondents in the reputational elite category are slightly better placed than the panchas. While 50.0% panchas are illiterate, the figure for reputational elite respondents is 45.9%. Sarpanchas have a better literacy background; 92.7% belong to 'matric and below' category. It is interesting that two sarpanchas are also illiterate. By Statute, they are expected to be able to read and write. Be that as it may, for our purposes, absence of formal schooling was considered equivalent to illiteracy. The elite respondents of the pradhan category are well educated and they belong over-whelmingly to the 'above matric' group.

The district-wise pattern emerging from Table 3.4 might appear to be somewhat intriguing at the outset. The elite respondents in Ganganagar district appear to be less educated than those of Bharatpur and Nagaur. To repeat, Ganganagar district is far ahead of other districts, included in this study, both economically and educationally. The detailed data at our disposal show that in Ganganagar district all four pradhans belong to middle-level castes, and are agriculturists. On the other hand, two pradhans in Nagaur are lawyers. This trend can be seen in the category of panchas also. In Ganganagar district, peasants (whether peasant-cultivators or peasant-proprietors) have come to wield greater influence than that in any other district. Apparently, the difference in class character has caused this deviation from the normal pattern. Secondly, in Ganganagar district alone some of the reputational elite respondents (22.2%) are highly educated ('matric and above' category). This does not mean, however, that in other districts education plays no significant role in enhancing influence. We gathered that educated persons tend to enjoy considerable influence in rural areas.

More than half (58.1%) of the illiterate belong to the age

TABLE 3.4

Present Position of the Elite Respondents by Education and District

Present position	Ganganagar				Nagaur				Bhilwara			
	Illiterate	Matric & below	Above matric	Total	Illiterate	Matric & below	Above matric	Total	Illiterate	Matric & below	Above matric	Total
1	2	3	4	5	6	7	8	9	10	11	12	13
Panch etc.	5 62.5	3 37.5	–	8 100.0	6 54.5	5 45.5	–	11 100.0	6 50.0	6 50.0	–	12 100.0
Sarpanch etc.	–	9 90.0	1 10.0	10 100.0	–	11 100.0	–	11 100.0	1 9.1	10 90.9	–	11 100.0
Pradhan etc.	–	4 100.0	–	4 100.0	–	3 60.0	2 40.0	5 100.0	–	3 75.0	1 25.0	4 100.0
Reputational elite persons	2 22.2	5 55.6	2 22.2	9 100.0	4 66.7	2 33.3	–	6 100.0	2 50.0	2 50.0	–	4 100.0
Total	7 22.6	21 67.7	3 9.7	31 100.0	10 30.3	21 63.6	2 6.1	33 100.0	9 29.1	21 67.7	1 3.2	31 100.0

TABLE 3.4 (*contd.*)

Present Position of the Elite Respondents by Education and District

Present position	JHALAWAR				BHARATPUR			
	Illiterate	Matric & below	Above matric	Total	Illiterate	Matric & below	Above matric	Total
	14	15	16	17	18	19	20	21
Panch etc.	3 33.3	6 66.7	—	9 100.0	3 50.0	2 33.3	1 16.7	6 100.0
Sarpanch etc.	—	9 90.0	1 10.0	10 100.0	1 7.7	12 92.3	—	13 100.0
Pradhan etc.	—	5 83.4	1 16.6	6 100.0	—	1 14.3	6 85.7	7 100.0
Reputational elite persons	4 44.4	5 55.6	—	9 100.0	5 55.6	4 44.4	—	9 100.0
Total	7 20.6	25 73.5	2 5.9	34 100.0	9 25.7	19 54.3	7 20.0	35 100.0

group 'above 50'. As literacy increases, the percentage share of this age group decreases, and comes to naught in the 'above matric' category. The percentage share of the age group in the 'below 30' category goes up with the increase in literacy. However, since the number of respondents in this age group is quite limited, their percentage share, though over-proportionate, also registers a low ebb. Naturally as such there is an obvious pre-eminence of the age groups of 30 to 50 years in both the 'matric and below', and 'above matric' categories of literacy. An analysis of the same data by position of the elite-respondents brings out that those belonging to both 'below 30' and 'above 50' age groups are mainly in positions at the lower tier, while elite respondents of the age group '30 to 50' years dominate the middle and upper tiers. Moreover, the elite persons of this age group in the 'above matric' category are in the sole occupation of upper tier posts, while the elite persons of the 'below 30' years age group—though falling in the 'above matric' category—have had to rest content with lower level posts. Thus, age appears to add to one's extent of influence if one is also placed higher in other respects, such as literacy.

An examination of the distribution of respondents by caste-status corroborates our observation that the higher the position in the hierarchy the greater the percentage share of the upper strata of society. The share of upper castes is less than 11% among the panchas and members of the reputational elite, while among the category of sarpanchas and pradhans it rises to 32.7% and 53.8%, respectively. In our sample, 16.0% of the citizen-respondents are upper caste. If this is indicative of a trend, it might be observed that whereas at the lower level this segment remains under-represented,[9] at the upper level it is over-represented. The middle caste group is slightly over-represented barring the category of pradhans, where its share cannot be considered flattering. The lower castes are the prime losers. Even at the lowest rung of the ladder their

9. This under-representation may be due to several factors : there may not be too many aspirants among the upper castes for the lowest posts ; and the wards which the panchas represent are generally concentrations of middle and lower level castes. Naturally, caste-sentiments play a vital role and those returned bear this out.

share is minimal. Lower caste panchas, including those coopted, are 23.9% of the total number of panchas, and this share
is reduced to 3.6% in the category of sarpanchas. In the next
category there is no representation at all. Evidently, the
lower castes continue to suffer from social discrimination, with
the result that they have insignificant opportunities of holding
positions of influence in local affairs. It was also found that
lower castes generally, and to some extent the middle peasant
castes (especially in Bhilwara and Jhalawar districts), remain
insulated against exposure to external contacts and impacts
and, consequently, their present plight is not being eased.
Similarly, their continuing low economic status is a vital
constraint on their prospects of upward political mobility.

The district-wise pattern in this regard presents three
distinct patterns. In Ganganagar and Nagaur districts, the
middle level castes are well entrenched, comparatively more so
in the former district. In the districts of Bharatpur and
Jhalawar, at the level of sarpanchas, the middle castes are in
control of an overwhelming majority of seats. But at the
pradhan level, their share is lower than that of the upper
castes. In Bhilwara district, at both the levels — sarpanchas
and pradhans — members of the upper caste are in a dominant
position.

The extent of the dominance of middle level castes follows
the level of development (especially agricultural) of a district.
At one end stands the district of Ganganagar and at the other
that of Bhilwara. In terms of degree of modernization of agriculture also, Ganganagar stands ahead of all the other districts,
while Bhilwara brings up the rear. The main aim of the
panchayati raj set-up is the creation of developmental opportunities, especially in the field of agriculture. More than anything else, panchayati raj is also a mechanism for the identification and distribution of developmental resources. It is, therefore, natural that the more articulate peasant classes should
strive for the control of such agencies. Where the developmental
orientation is weak, as in Bhilwara, these sections might
continue to lag behind, thereby precluding themselves from
obtaining the benefits of economic viability. Comparatively
speaking, as already stated, Bhilwara region is more poverty-
ridden than others. It was also found that agriculturists were

less assertive in this region than elsewhere. However, Nagaur district, with little to commend itself by way of agricultural progress compared to the district of Bhilwara, seems to be an exception. One obvious reason is that political awakening came early in Nagaur,[10] and since then several State-level leaders have emerged from the rural regions of this district.[11]

Table 3.5 which presents the positional distribution of members of the elite group by economic status, is self-explanatory. It will be observed that, while persons of middle status hold a majority of the posts at the *panch* level, those of the 'rich' category hold an appreciable number of the higher level posts of pradhan and zila pramukh. For members in the reputational elite category economic status does not appear to count much, as more than 70.3% belong to 'middle' status group. Perhaps our respondents nominated members of the reputational elite group more out of traditional reverence than out of power considerations. This elite group does not exercise appreciable control over affairs. Most of its members belong to the older age-group and only a few of them have held a post previously. Those in the category of 'poor economic status' seem to be confined to the level of the *panch*. It is significant that the district-wise analysis shows an almost uniform pattern. At the higher levels (pradhan etc.) the 'rich' dominate the scene ; at the sar-panch level the middle status people keenly compete with the rich. At the panch level, however, the decisive factor seems to be the intensity of economic development of the district concerned. For instance, in Ganganagar district, the 'rich' have a much larger share since, comparatively speaking, it is a more prosperous region. In Bhilwara district, comparatively a backward region, the share of the poor is extensive.

10. Saxena, K.S., *Political Movement and Awakening in Rajasthan* (Delhi : S. Chand 1973) p. 196 and Shrader, Lawrence, 'Rajasthan' in Weiner, Myron, ed., *State Politics in India*, (Princeton, New Jersey : Princeton University Press, 1967), pp. 320-96.

11. Among these leaders mention may particularly be made of Ram Niwas Mirdha, Nathu Ram Mirdha and Moti Lal Choudhary. For a lucid discussion of the emergence of peasant castes in Nagaur see : Richard Sisson, "Caste and Political Factions in Rajasthan" in Kothari, Rajni ed., *Caste in Indian Politics* (Delhi : Orient Longman, 1970) pp. 175-227.

TABLE 3.5

Present Position of the Elite Respondents by Economic Status

Present position	Rich		Middle		Poor		Total	
	No.	%	No.	%	No.	%	No.	%
Panch etc.	12 26.1	16.0	24 52.2	32.4	10 21.7	66.7	46 100.0	28.0
Sarpanch etc.	31 56.4	41.3	22 40.0	29.7	2 3.6	13.3	55 100.0	33.5
Pradhan etc.	24 92.3	32.0	2 7.7	2.7	— —	—	26 100.0	15.9
Reputational Elite persons etc.	8 21.6	10.7	26 70.3	35.2	3 8.1	20.0	37 100.0	22.6
Total	75 45.7	100.0	74 45.1	100.0	15 9.2	100.0	164 100.0	100.0

A very high percentage (from 72% to 86%) of upper caste persons manning various posts in panchayati raj institutions are 'rich'. On the other hand, elite persons of middle economic status in the middle caste category hold 63.3% of the posts at the panch level. At the sarpanch level, the posts are equally shared by the 'rich' and 'middle' status groups of middle castes. However, at the pradhan level, only the 'rich' among middle castes control various posts. Of the lower caste elite respondents, none holds an elective post, except at the panch level.[12] Of this group 50.0% are 'poor' and are confined to strata of lower levels of power.

It is clear that the share of upper caste elite persons is greater at the 'Pradhan, etc.' level, because they are 'rich'. The midddle status elite persons of upper castes are handicapped in getting returned to various posts as they can have neither numerical strength as a caste nor wealth to buttress their position. This explains to some extent the low share of this sub-group in the quota of various panchayati raj posts. The concentration of 'middle' status elite persons of 'middle' castes at lower levels is also significant. This also explains why only the 'rich' among them can aspire for higher posts. One can see that the lower caste groups depend largely on the two higher social groups.[13]

To sum up : while at the lower level of panchayati raj the middle status groups (both socially and economically), with minimal literacy, are the recruiting bases of elites, at the upper levels, leaders emerge from the upper sections of society (both socially and/or economically).

Period of Recruitment

Of equal significance is an enquiry into the processes of initiation into rural politics that enabled the different sections of society to be effectively involved. Three major

12. The three elite persons in the category of 'Sarpanch etc.' are the co-opted members at the panchayat samiti level.
13. In Rajasthan, most of the village panchayats have the middle castes in majority, or at least in the largest number. Both the upper and lower caste groups are in a minority. Further, the inter-caste practices are such that the middle caste groups succeed in securing full or partial support of upper and/or lower castes. Thus, whenever the 'numbers' are allowed to play their role, the most likely beneficiaries are the middle castes.

TABLE 3.6

Period from which the Elite Respondents Date their Involvement in Community Activities by Position

Position	Pre-independence days	1947-52	1953-59	1960 and after	Total
Panch etc.	3	9	26	28	46
	6.5	19.6	13.0	60.9	100.0
	9.7	23.1	17.1	47.5	28.0
Sarpanch etc.	8	15	16	16	55
	14.6	27.3	29.1	29.1	100.0
	25.8	38.5	45.7	27.1	33.5
Pradhan etc.	12	9	4	1	26
	46.2	34.6	15.4	3.8	100.0
	38.7	23.1	11.4	1.7	15.9
Reputational Elite persons, etc.	8	6	9	14	37
	21.6	16.2	24.3	37.9	100.0
	25.8	15.4	25.8	23.7	22.6
Total	31	39	35	59	164
	18.9	23.8	21.3	36.0	100.0
	100.0	100.0	100.0	100.0	100.0

milestones can be identified: The first, beginning with the dawn of independence and culminating in 1949, was the process of the integration of various princely states ; the second was the creation of statutory panchayats in 1953 ; and the third was the launching of the scheme of democratic decentralization in 1959, following the report of Balwant Ray Mehta Committee.

An attempt was also made to ascertain the period during which the members of the persent-day elite strata took to a political career against this background. It was considered worthwhile to enquire into the incidence of recruitment of particular social groups during specific periods and also to identify the extent of circulation of elites in terms of generational change. For this an open-ended question was addressed to all the elite respondents. It ran : "Since when did you start taking interest in community activities ?" We chose the word *community* instead of *political* after careful consideration, since in village India epithets like 'political', 'politics', etc., carry a derogatory connotation. The reactions of the respondents to this question are collected in Table 3.6.

It is noteworthy that the largest number (36.0%) of the elite respondents started taking an interest in politics after the introduction of democratic decentralization, while 21.4% began doing so during 1953-1959 and 23.8% did so in the period 1947 to 1952. Thus it is clear that, while only 18.9% of present-day elite persons have had some standing in public life dating back to pre-independence days, two major events (independence in 1947 and the introduction of democratic decentralization in 1959) proved conducive to added elite recruitment. A survey by positions held shows that on an average the shortest career is that of the panchas and longest is that of the 'Pradhans etc.' The career of 60.9% panchas dates back to the post-1960 period ; that of 46.2% 'Pradhans etc.' to pre-independence days ; and that of 34.6% 'Pradhans etc.' to the next period, *i.e.*, 1947-52. With regard to present-day sarpanchas, it is to be noted that 85.4% of the respondents in this category started their public life in the post-independence period ; 27.2% during 1947-52 ; 29.1% during 1953-59 ; and 29.1% during 1960 and later. On the other hand, 53.8% of the respondents of the 'Pradhan etc.' category started their public life during the post-independence period and the rest, 46.2%, did so before independence. Obviously, a larger proportion of the sarpanchas have been late starters in public life.

The district-wise pattern shows only marginal variance. While in Jhalawar and Ganganagar districts a greater number of members of the elite group started taking part in public life during pre-independence days, in the districts of Bhilwara and Bharatpur a much greater number of elite respondents did so in the post-1960 period.

Analysing the correlation between the recruitment of elite persons with age and position, we find that age has not been an important factor in a person's involvement in community activities. During the pre-independence period, 31 respondents who adopted this career came from two age-groups, namely, '30 to 50' and 'above 50'. The two age-groups are equally represented. However, during the other periods, the contribution of the middle age-group recruits is greater. The younger age-group, with a strength of 12, entered public life during the post-1960 period. Thus the fact that a good number of middle age-group members have been initiated into public life either during pre-independence days or during the period '1947-52', indicates that in the regions under study, people were not averse to the assumption of leadership by younger people. However, field survey reports confirmed that most of these people came from families of village *nambardars* or caste leaders. They were also better educated and thus could make use of the opportunities to enter public life.

Further, the correlation of age and positions also yields interesting results. For instance, elite respondents who started their career early (*i.e.*, before 1952) hold more of the position of pancha than those from the older age-group. In the case of sarpanchas the number is slightly tilted in favour of the middle age-group. The same holds true much more for those holding the office of pradhan.

We now turn to the picture emerging from the correlation of literacy and position held, as presented in Table 3.7. It is noteworthy that the number of the illiterate was the highest in the period 1960 and after. This might be attributed to the impact of the democratic processes generated by panchayati raj in 1959. Illiteracy could not have precluded the aspirants from taking to public life. This is further corroborated by the fact that one of the two illiterate elite respondents who competed for sarpanchship was recruited during '1952-59' and the other during '1960 and after'. However, for pradhanships and other such posts, highly educated persons have been attracted more in the latter periods. Another significant trend is that the literate form a greater number of members of the reputational elite category who were recruited in the last two phases. Thus, in the last period, while the illiterate began to enter the competitive arena in larger numbers, though at a lower rung of the ladder, better educated persons sought higher level positions.

An analysis of the data, when viewed from the standpoint of caste shows that the democratic processes have gradually drawn in an increasing number of people of lower and middle castes into the vortex of public life. The share of middle and lower castes in a total number of 31 recruits in the pre-independence days amounts to 58.1% and 6.4% respectively. The share of the same groups, with some ups and downs in intervening periods, was increased to 67.8% and 15.2% respectively in a total of 59 recruits in post-1960 period. This increase is coupled with the gradual and steady decline of the percentage share of the upper castes from 35.5% of total recruits in the first period to 17.0% in the last period. But it is interesting to note that the share of lower castes increased solely at the panchas level, and that of the middle castes more at the sarpanchas level. On the other hand, the upper castes have slightly increased their share at the level of pradhans. At the panchas level this caste-group supplied new members of the elite strata only during the last period. However, the share of this caste group goes down progressively at the sarpanch level. Among members of the reputational elite group an overwhelming number of recruits came from the middle level castes during all the periods.

One can thus see that at the lower level the middle castes have been steadily consolidating their position. Similarly, the lower castes have also seen their share increase. It is a matter

TABLE 3.7

Participation in Public Life by Period, Position and Literacy

Position	Pre-independence				1947-52			
	Illiterate	Below matric	Above matric	Total	Illiterate	Below matric	Above matric	Total
1	2	3	4	5	6	7	8	9
Panch etc.	1 25.0	2 8.3	–	3 9.7	3 33.3	6 24.0	–	9 23.1
Sarpanch etc.	–	7 29.2	1 33.3	8 25.8	–	15 60.0	–	15 38.5
Pradhan etc.	–	10 41.7	2 66.7	12 38.7	–	4 16.0	5 100.0	9 23.1
Reputational Elite persons	3 75.0	5 20.8	–	8 25.8	6 66.7	–	–	6 15.4
Total	4 100.0 12.9	24 100.0 77.4	3 100.0 9.7	31 100.0 100.0	9 100.0 23.0	25 100.0 64.2	5 100.0 12.8	39 100.0 100.0

TABLE 3.7 (contd)

Position	1952-59				1960 and after			
	Illiterate	Below matric	Above matric	Total	Illiterate	Below matric	Above matric	Total
	10	11	12	13	14	15	16	17
Panch etc.	5 50.0	1 4.8	–	6 17.1	14 73.7	13 35.1	1 33.3	28 47.5
Sarpanch etc.	1 10.0	14 66.7	1 25.0	16 45.7	1 5.2	15 40.5	–	16 27.1
Pradhan etc.	–	1 4.8	3 75.0	4 11.4	–	1 2.7	–	1 1.7
Reputational Elite persons	4 40.0	5 23.8	–	9 25.8	4 21.1	8 21.6	2 66.7	14 23.7
Total	10 100.0 28.6	21 100.0 60.0	4 100.0 11.4	35 100.0 100.0	19 100.0 32.2	37 100.0 62.7	3 100.0 5.1	59 100.0 100.0

for intensive investigation whether this quantitative shift also ensures a competitive capacity for them, or whether it is just an outcome of statutory necessity. The latter, on the face of it, appears to be a reasonable assumption because of the provision of co-optation. It is also clear that, though the middle caste groups have been sharing power at the higher level, the share of upper castes has not been threatened. Perhaps one surmise may be that at the higher level the role of financial resources is a determinant of consequence in view of the widespread nature of the electorate.[14]

Motivations

Apart from ascertaining the areas of recruitment, it was also our endeavour to study the factors motivating persons of the elite group to take part in political life. This facet of our study should provide meaningful insights into the processes of political recruitment of the elite. We asked two questions of the respondents to elicit information on this score. The first question was specifically addressed to the elite respondents and sought to enquire into their own motivations in opting for political life. It read : "What were the reasons that led to your interest in community life ?" The second question was about the motivations of elite persons in general. It was addressed to both elite and the citizen respondents. It reads : "How do you account for the keen interest and active participation of certain persons into public life ?" The questions taken together aimed at eliciting what the members of the elite group think about themselves and what the people think about the elite persons in general. The responses would presumably reflect the effectiveness of communication between the elite and the citizens in the transmission of its self-image by the former to the latter.

14. There are lot of suggestions in this regard in the speeches of MLAs on the floor of the Rajasthan Legislative Assembly, particularly on vote of thanks, budgetary proposals, demands of Panchayat Ministry and so on during 1956-57, 1960-61, and 1964-65. By way of a representative sample one may refer to the speeches of Lakshman Singh, a leader of the opposition and P.C. Vishnoi, representative of Treasury Benches. For the former, see *Rajasthan Vidhan Sabha Ki Karyavahi Ka Vritant*, 7(2) February 25, 1965 and for the latter *Ibid.*, 7 (3 and 4) February 26 and 27, 1965.

The data obtained from responses to the first question have been presented in Table 3.8. The highest number (57.3%) of elite respondents said that they were initiated into public life by the considerations of 'local development and social service'. Another notable response was 'popular pressure', registered by 11.6% of the elite respondents. Some others noted 'independence movement' and 'party programmes' as motivational factors. With some significant difference in the case of Jhalawar district, this trend holds good for all the districts. In the case of Jhalawar it appears that the ideological factor (spirit of independence movement-*cum*-populistic pressure) carries a much greater weight than other factors. It may be because of the fact, as discussed earlier also, that the old leadership, dating back to pre-independence days continues to be in effective control.

It is understandable that those who took to political life in the post-independence period had in mind predominantly developmental considerations. To those who entered political life before independence, two factors, *viz.*, 'spirit of independence movement' and 'village service and development', were decisive. Thus 10 of the 11 respondents who started their political career before independence were motivated by the national movement itself. On the other hand, 37.2% of the 94 respondents who were motivated by developmental considerations, began their career only during the post-1960 period, when developmental functions were entrusted to panchayati raj institutions. Similarly, most of those who entered political life under the influence of 'family traditions' began in early periods, while those who did so under 'popular pressure', started their career after independence, and there also mostly (57.9%) in the post-1960 period.

Table 3.9 regroups the motivational factors into three categories :[15] ideological, local-developmental, and group and

15. It may be argued that developmental considerations are constituents of ideology. But they are distinct from the latter insofar as they pertain to the 'local' context, while ideological considerations have a universal connotation. The impact of the independence movement and party programmes etc. are put under 'ideological'; local-developmental considerations form a second head ; kinship and other personal factors have been collated under the third category of group and family considerations and the rest constitutes the residual category of 'others'.

TABLE 3.8

Motivational Resource for Participation in Community Life by District

District	Independence movement		Party programme		Social service and village development		Family tradition		Popular pressure	
	No.	%	No.	%	No.	%	No.	%	No.	%
1	2	3	4	5	6	7	8	9	10	11
Ganganagar	2 / 6.5	18.2	1 / 3.2	25.0	20 / 64.5	21.3	1 / 3.2	9.1	2 / 6.5	10.5
Nagaur	1 / 3.0	9.1	2 / 6.1	50.0	17 / 51.5	18.1	3 / 9.1	27.3	1 / 3.0	5.3
Bhilwara	1 / 3.2	9.1	1 / 3.2	25.0	22 / 71.0	23.4	1 / 3.2	9.1	2 / 6.5	10.5
Jhalawar	6 / 17.7	54.5	–	–	13 / 38.2	13.8	3 / 8.8	27.3	9 / 26.6	47.4
Bharatpur	1 / 2.9	9.1	–	–	22 / 62.8	23.4	3 / 8.6	27.3	5 / 14.3	26.3
Total	11 / 6.7	100.0	4 / 2.4	100.0	94 / 57.3	100.0	11 / 6.7	100.0	19 / 11.6	100.0

TABLE 3.8 (*Contd.*)

District	Caste consideration		Others		N. R.		Total	
	No.	%	No.	%	No.	%	No.	%
	12	13	14	15	16	17	18	19
Ganganagar	1 3.2	33.3	3 9.7	20.0	1 3.2	14.3	31 100.0	18.9
Nagaur	1 3.0	33.3	6 18.2	40.0	2 6.1	28.6	33 100.0	20.1
Bhilwara	1 3.2	33.3	2 6.5	13.3	1 3.2	14.3	31 100.0	18.9
Jhalawar	–	–	1 2.9	6.7	2 5.9	28.6	34 100.0	20.7
Bharatpur	–	–	3 8.6	20.0	1 2.9	14.3	35 100.0	21.3
Total	3 1.8	100.0	15 9.2	100.0	7 4.3	100.0	164 100.0	100.0

TABLE 3.9

Motivational Factors in taking to Community Life District-wise (Elite Respondents)

District	Ideological	Local developmental	Group family considerations	Others	Total*
Ganganagar	3	20	4	3	31
	9.7	64.5	12.9	9.7	100.0
Nagaur	3	17	5	6	33
	9.1	64.5	15.9	18.2	100.0
Bhilwara	2	22	4	2	31
	6.5	71.0	12.9	6.5	100.0
Jhalawar	6	13	12	1	34
	17.7	38.2	35.3	2.9	100.0
Bharatpur	1	22	8	3	35
	2.9	62.8	22.9	8.6	100.0
Total	15	94	33	15	164
	9.1	57.3	20.1	9.1	100.0

*Total includes the responses 'N.R.s' mentioned in Table 5.1 which have not been given separately in the table.

family considerations. One can see that 'local-developmental' motivation holds the prime place, with a total of 57.3% falling in this category, followed by 20.1% who are swayed by group and family considerations. The two factors together total 77.4%. Jhalawar district presents a different picture. Though the two factors—local development and group and family considerations—together add up to 73.5%, ideological considerations have a 17.7% share, which is the highest of all the districts. This may be due to the fact that the erstwhile Praja Mandal leaders are still holding the sway in the area.

In the final analysis, it is a fact of considerable significance that 57.3% of the elite respondents were motivated by considerations of local development. With the crystallization of the positive impact of the processes of panchayati raj, this was to be expected. A large number of elite respondents also feel the same way. The replies to another question accounting for increase included increase in political consciousness (40%), 'personal interest' (34.3%) and 'factional considerations' (10%). That, however, is not to belittle the tilt in this context. District-wise, Nagaur and Bhilwara show predominance of 'political awakening' as a determinant with 60.0% and 53.9% responses, respectively. In the case of Jhalawar and Bharatpur, 'personal interest' played a greater role with 48.2% and 48.4% responses respectively.

For further corroborative evidence of the motivations of members of the elite group taking to public life, as identified by elite respondents, the particulars in Table 3.10 are important. We are analysing here the responses to the second question mentioned in the beginning of the section. When these are seen along with the particulars of Table 3.8, some interesting trends emerge. In both the cases, the respondents showed an overwhelming preference for village social service and considerations of development—62.8% in Table 3.8 and 57.3% in Table 3.9. Factors such as selfish ends (12.8%), popularity (12.8%) and popular pressure (11.6%) speak for themselves. It should be noted that the role of political parties has been relegated to a shockingly insignificant level. Political parties cannot absolve themselves of this clear verdict against their operational and participatory aspects.

A similar question was addressed to citizen respondents.

TABLE 3.10

Elite Respondents' view of Factors Motivating People to Take Part in Political Life

District	Selfish ends		Popularity		Village service & development		Political party etc.		Others		N. R.		Total	
	No.	%	No.	%	No.	%	No.	%	No.	%	No.	%	No.	%
Ganganagar	4	19.0	7	33.3	17	18.1	–	–	2	15.4	1	7.1	31	18.9
	12.9		22.6		54.8		–		6.5		3.2		100.0	
Nagaur	6	28.6	5	23.8	14	14.9	–	–	2	15.4	6	42.9	33	20.1
	18.2		15.1		42.4		–		6.1		18.2		100.0	
Bhilwara	2	9.5	2	9.5	24	25.5	–	–	3	23.1	–	–	31	18.9
	6.5		6.5		77.4		–		9.6		–		100.0	
Jhalawar	5	23.8	1	4.8	21	22.4	1	100.0	1	7.7	5	35.7	34	20.7
	14.7		2.9		61.8		2.9		2.9		14.7		100.0	
Bharatpur	4	19.0	6	28.6	18	19.1	–	–	5	38.5	2	14.3	35	21.3
	11.5		17.1		51.4		–		14.3		5.7		100.0	
Total	21	100.0	21	100.0	94	100.0	1	100.0	13	100.0	14	100.0	164	100.0
	12.8		12.8		57.3		0.6		7.9		8.6		100.0	

The replies received point out that the image of the elite that emerges from citizen responses cannot be called very flattering. 49.5% of the respondents held the view that the members of the elite group were moved by selfish considerations when they chose to enter public life, and 21.0% treated considerations of village service and development as determining factors. Other factors mentioned were 'popularity' (10.5%) and political parties (6.5%) which, once again, appear to be relegated to the background.

The district-wise break-up of the reasons given by citizens for participation by members of the elite group in public life was also collated. They gave predominance to 'selfish ends' as a vital factor in Bharatpur (60%), Ganganagar (57.5%) and Nagaur (55%). The response from Jhalawar (42.5%) and Bhilwara (32.5%) is also substantial in favour of this factor. The next factor, in order of preference, is 'village service and development' and here Bhilwara (35.0% of the responses) and Jhalawar (32.5%) lead, followed by Ganganagar (22.5%). Nagaur and Bharatpur lag behind with 7.5% of the responses each. The role of political parties, once again, is given little importance, with Nagaur leading (15.0% of the responses), followed by Bhilwara (7.5%) and Ganganagar and Bharatpur (5%) each. In Jhalawar, citizens just ignored this factor.

Circulation

With the introduction of processes of democratic decentralization, whereas the erstwhile overall monopoly and hegemony of the socially and economically predominant groups have been seriously challenged, a competitive alternative to the former leadership has been made available to the middle and lower groups. This holds true much more for panch and sarpanch level positions. At the pradhan level, though significant inroads have been made by the middle caste elite, only those persons with financial resources have succeeded. The paucity of financial resources has hampered general and effective mobility and circulation of elites, exceptions at all levels notwithstanding. Since upper level positions are more important, both politically and administratively, the rural rich will continue in their efforts to hold on to these positions.

In the social milieu that exists in Rajasthan, the style of panchayati raj institutions is likely to be influenced not only by the replacement of one social group by another but also by that of one person by another. Investigations to assess the extent to which the circulation of elites has implied and brought about the circulation of personalities reveal that panchas have contested elections with a diminished frequency while pradhans have stayed in the fray much longer. This seems to corroborate the inference that there is growing careerism in politics. At the lower level, there is more fresh recruitment, which is almost negligible at the upper-most level. In between is the sarpanch level elite. A natural corollary of this trend is that at the upper level, the replacement of elites seems more difficult or, at best, is confined to a few individuals active at that level. This is evident from the fact that only 5 (3.7%) of 137 elite persons were defeated two or more times. It is further borne out by the data that these defeats were confined to the early years of the career of most of the elite members.

Aspirational Profile

In order to supplement the analysis of circulation of elites, identification of levels of aspiration of persons of the elite was also sought. A direct question was put to elite respondents which ran : "Do you think, on the basis of your past experience that you will contest any of the panchayati raj posts or assembly seat or Lok Sabha seat ?" The response is collated in Table 3.10. A majority of elite respondents (50.6%) do not intend to contest elections while 6.1% of the repondents are 'uncertain' about their intentions, and only 43.3% of the respondents have answered in the affirmative. In the aggregate, this figure of 'non-intenders' would appear rather substantial. But it should be noted that this 'no' cannot be considered decisive in the context of respondents' expression of 'ifs' and 'buts', when informally probed. The usual feeling was that, if circumstances warranted, or if unavoidable pressure was exerted, they might reconsider their decision and would not hesitate to contest.

A position-wise analysis of these reluctant elite respondents shows that 57 of 83 (68.6%) of the total are panchas and members of the reputational elite group. In other categories, the number of reluctant elite respondents is not so high. It seems that members of the elite group confined to village-level politics are more reluctant to contest in the future than those at higher levels. The reasons advanced seem to indicate that at least in the near future they anticipate no prospects for upward political mobility. It is all the more surprising that these elite persons at the lower level do not feel the urge to ascend to higher levels where they would have a greater say in processes of decision-making. On the other hand, of the higher level elite persons M.L.As. and zila pramukhs seem committed to contest higher posts, though, 25% of the pradhans showed uncertainty and another 20% of the pradhans replied in the negative when asked if they intended to contest elections at the next opportunity. It would seem that among the present-day pradhans there is a discernible lack of enthusiasm to continue in politics compared to zila pramukhs, sarpanchas and M.L.As. It might be added that basically the office of pradhan is a coveted one in view of the influence and powers of patronage it carries. And, yet, it is surprising that the present incumbents seemed reluctant to continue as pradhans; what is more, they expressed a wish to quit and seek no elected posts. However, only time will prove the credibility of such responses. One can only surmise why the pradhans gave this reluctant response : perhaps they are aware of the uncertainties of electoral politics, of the tensions and pressures of the prevalent party system and the growing quest for prize posts.

An attempt was also made to ascertain the generational and socio-educational background of those respondents who expressed categorically their wish to contest the elections. The results show that the most enthusiastic and categorical in their intentions are those who belong to the lower age group (below 30), are upper caste and are 'above matric' in education. While in generational terms this may not be surprising, the data on education and caste is quite astonishing. If this is the trend for the future, it may reverse the trend identified earlier that with the introduction of democratic decentralization, more illiterate and middle and lower caste group people had started taking to political life. This may be due to uncertainties among the middle and lower category people about either the worth of such an attempt or their own capacity to compete for these posts. Perhaps both reasons are correct, as the negative responses on intentions to contest were made mostly by those at the low end of the ladder, whose posts do not carry much power. Thus, as one can see in table 3.10, 71.4% of the panchas and 73.0% of reputational elite members expressed the intention of declining to contest the next elections.

An attempt was also made to ascertain the positional levels aspired to as against the present positional levels. There is a discernible trend towards upward aspiration. Except the panchas, a majority or near majority of elite respondents in all the other categories aspire for higher-level posts. The remaining ones intend to stand for the post they presently occupy. Another trend is that nearly two-thirds of the pradhans and 20% of the sarpanchas aspire for higher or intend to contest for assembly seats. This may be taken as an aspiration for entrance into state politics. If this is so, panchayati raj can be taken as a spring-board for going upto state level roles. The position of the sarpanch is also a coveted one. Not only do a substantial number of elite respondents of equal or lower ranking categories intend to stand for that post, but there is also a pradhan who wishes to become a sarpanch. The pradhan, who is from Bhilwara district, explained his desire thus: "For old age I cannot discharge public roles fruitfully. Still I think I should serve at least my village. And, therefore, I intend to contest for the post of sarpanch."

Lastly, we turn to the factors that make members of the elite group reluctant to contest. A good number (28%) of elite respondents are unable to advance any specific reason in this regard. Some might not be too confident of their record in office and would like to play around, weighing pros and cons. The fact that 26.7% of these elite persons in the non-response category are pradhans is significant. A substantial number of panchas (26.7%) and members in the reputational elite group (30.4%) also fall in this category.

The reasons specified by the various elite respondents for their dropping out may be said to be of two broad types. In

TABLE 3.10

Whether various Elite Persons intend to Contest Various Posts

Present Position	Yes		No		Uncertain		Total	
	No.	%	No.	%	No.	%	No.	%
Panchas	11	15.5	30	36.1	1	10.0	42	25.6
	26.2		71.4		2.4		100.0	
Coopted members (Panchayat level)	—		3	3.6	1	10.0	4	2.4
			75.0		25.0		100.0	
Sarpanchas	19	26.8	10	12.1	1	10.0	30	18.3
	63.3		33.3		3.4		100.0	
Co-opted members (Panchayat Samiti level)	11	15.5	4	4.8	2	20.0	17	10.4
	64.7		23.5		11.8		100.0	
Pradhans	11	15.5	4	4.8	5	50.0	20	12.2
	55.0		20.0		25.0		100.0	
Zila Pramukhs	2	2.8	—		—		2	1.2
	100.0						100.0	
M.L.As.	3	4.2	1	1.2	—		4	2.5
	75.0		25.0				100.0	
Cooperative Elite	4	5.6	4	4.8	—		8	4.9
	50.0		50.0				100.0	
Reputational Elite persons	10	14.1	27	32.5	—		37	22.6
	27.0		73.0				100.0	
Total	71	100.0	83	100.0	10	100.0	164	100.0
	43.3		50.6		6.1		100.0	

the first category, are two reasons, *viz.*, 'to keep out of dirty politics' and 'being indifferent', meaning thereby that 'politics' is distasteful to them for ethical reasons. The second type includes responses which indicate constraints of resources and means.

Summary

The power-structure in rural areas has been only slightly broadened. A commonly held view so far has been that in a traditional rural society like that of Rajasthan, power, status, and wealth have tended to reside in a complex of upper caste groups, that is, in a Rajput-Brahmin-Baniya combine in which, especially in *jagirdari* areas, Rajputs have been slightly better placed. The domination of the combine has been the product of cumulative inequalities, the exploitation of which enables them to exercise influence in rural areas. Our survey, however, shows that middle castes have come to share power with the upper caste groups. While they enjoy a dominant position in controlling the lower level offices of panchas and sarpanchas, they also command a substantial share with upper castes in controlling higher level posts. In contrast, the share of lower castes in controlling middle and higher level posts is almost nil. The access of middle level castes to higher level panchayati raj posts and the state of deprivation of lower level castes in this regard may be largely attributed to economic factors. While with the modernisation of agriculture, middle castes, generally living on agriculture, have improved their economic position, the lower caste people have not.

This trend is further substantiated by the pattern of circulation of elites. With the introduction of the democratic decentralization scheme in 1959, a large number of elite respondents have vouched for the intensification of political competition at the village level and entry of people, relatively backward in terms of literacy and caste, into public life during 1960 and after. Although there has been a trend towards a broadening of the rural power structure, the weak aspirational level of some elite persons may serve as a damper on that trend. It may be recalled here that 20.0% of the illiterate, and 44% of the lower caste elite respondents, aspire to contest the next elections. The major reasons advanced by those who are reluctant to contest the elections are the paucity of resources and the growing exertions of public life. If this holds true, the political area may again become the monopoly of upper caste and/or rich people. As certain studies have shown, this elite group is interested in manipulating power processes under panchayati raj institutions, the control of which means leverage in terms of developmental benefits, patronage, linkage with higher level political elites, and, cumulatively, strengthening of their power base.

It is in this context that the delineation of a motivational profile of the elite becomes imporant. If we are to accept what the elite respondents have said, we find that more than half (57.3%) treat local developmental considerations as an important motivating factor. About 9% also mention ideological considerations. The citizens, however, think differently. Nearly half of the citizens in our sample feel that it is the self-seeking and self-fulfilling impulse which is the key motivating factor. Even if the element of exaggeration is duly discounted, it cannot be denied that there is a wide gap between the perceptions of the two in regard to motivational factors.

Area-wise, an interesting trend which emerges is that the largest number of younger people to be recruited to various posts is found in Ganganagar, which is, economically speaking, an advanced district. On the other hand, in Jhalawar and Nagaur, an older leadership is continuing. Again, while in Ganganagar, the middle level agricultural castes have complete sway over various high level posts, in other districts persons with a different background man higher level panchayati raj posts. These variations will become all the more meaningful when we discuss in the next chapter the factors that help in acquiring elite status.

4

THE NEXUS OF INFLUENCE : ELITE PERCEPTIONS ABOUT POWER INSTRUMENTALITIES

A STUDY OF the rural elite in the context of panchayati raj is essentially a study of the mechanism and instrumentalities of attaining influence. The means and techniques adopted by elite persons in this context would have to be seen in the light of their mass appeal without which they could not have attained their position of influence. A study of this kind leads us to trait *versus* situational theories of leadership, which have for long been a matter of controversy between social psychologists and sociologists. While the former hold that owing to their peculiar traits certain persons come to assume public roles, the latter argue that it is the social situation that determines which persons are allowed to play public roles.[1] It would be a reasonable starting point to assume that both theories carry some truth. However, we are only concerned with the reactions of the respondents in this regard ; we are not undertaking a detailed examination of these theories here.

We divide the discussion of perceptions of 'means' employed to gain influence into two parts : first, those of instrumentalities for acquiring 'public roles in general' ; and, second, of means employed to acquire specific positions under panchayati raj.

Necessary Traits : The Man of Character

To begin with, we shall identify the general traits which are considered essential for one aspiring for an effective public role. The open-ended question put to respondents in this regard ran : "In your opinion, what should the qualities of an

1. For a brief but lucid discussion of the point, see Kessel, John H., Cole, George F. and Sedding, Robert G. (ed.), *Micropolitics : Individual and Group Level Concept* (New York : Holt., Rinehart and Winston Inc·, 1970), pt. I, pp. 17-25.

effective public worker at the village level be ?" This was followed by questions seeking information pertaining to specific
group support in the specific context of political parties and
caste. All these questions were addressed to elite respondents
only.

Responses to the first question are recorded in Table 4.1.
While processing the data, we have concentrated on the first
three traits listed by the respondents. It will be noted in the
table that out of 492 (164 × 3) expected total responses, 38.4%
are non-responses. though a large number of non-responses are
related to second and third replies (30.5% and 77.4%, respectively). A first reply has come from all but 12 (7.3%) of the
elite respondents. Among the positive responses received, the
largest number (28.9%) point to 'character' of aspirants as the
prime requirement. 'Development orientation' is the next
preferential trait (11.4%). The difference of response-level
between these two is considerable. It is significant that 25%
of the respondents, in the second answer, considered 'Development-orientation' as a vital trait. Surprisingly, education
figures as a requirement for successful public figures only in
4.3% of the responses. Similarly, other requirements such as
'mass mobilizer' and 'non-factional character' elicited 3% and
4.5% of the responses.

Taking an overall view, it would appear that personal
qualities[2] are considered most important for elite persons who
have to take up effective public roles. It is implied that those
that have succeeded in creating such a public image have had
greater chances of success than others. But it is to be noted
that this quality cannot be effective in isolation and ought to
be supplemented by other qualities such as education, inclination, involvement, and capacity to undertake developmental
activities and the like, *i.e.*, traits from no. 2 to no. 5. Comparatively, responses for the trait pertaining to developmental
activities in the first preference aggregate to just 18.2% and
those in the second preference to 42.2%. That, however, does
not mean that all these traits are actually in evidence : they are
only considered vital. The hiatus between expectation

2. In the present context, this includes traits such as honesty, judicious
   mindedness, selflessness, peace-loving nature, arbitrational skill, etc.

TABLE 4.1

Qualities Considered Essential for a Successful Village Level Public Figure: (Elite Response)

Preference about qualities of a public figure	Man of Character		Educated		Development-oriented		Mass-mobilizer	
	No.	%	No.	%	No.	%	No.	%
1	2	3	4	5	6	7	8	9
First	115 70.2	81.0	10 6.1	47.6	10 6.1	17.9	4 2.4	26.7
Second	20 12.2	14.1	9 5.5	42.9	41 25.0	73.2	8 4.9	53.3
Third	7 4.3	4.9	2 1.2	9.5	5 3.1	8.9	3 1.8	20.0
Total	142 28.9	100.0	21 4.3	100.0	56 11.4	100.0	15 3.0	100.0

TABLE 4.1 (*contd.*)

Preference about quali-ties of a public figure	Non-factional character		Others		N.R./D.K.		Total	
	No.	%	No.	%	No.	%	No.	%
	10	11	12	13	14	15	16	17
First	6 3.7	27.3	7 4.2	14.9	12 7.3	6.3	164 100.0	33.3
Second	11 6.7	50.0	25 15.2	53.2	50 30.5	26.5	164 100.0	33.3
Third	5 3.0	22.7	15 9.2	31.9	127 77.4	67.2	164 100.0	33.3
Total	22 4.5	100.0	47 9.5	100.0	189 38.4	100.0	492 100.0	100.0

response and expectation fruition should make all the difference, as the analysis clearly bears out.

An analysis of first preference responses in Table 4.1 shows that out of a total of 164 elite respondents, 70.2% hold 'man of character' as the most vital pre-requisite, followed by 'education' and 'development-orientation' (6.1% each), 'non-factional character' (3.6%) and 'mass-mobilizer' (2.4%). About 4.2% of the responses point to 'other traits' and 7.3% are non-responses. Of the second preferences, 'development-orientation' is at the top with 25% of the responses, followed by 'man of character' (12.2%), 'non-factional character' (6.7%), 'education' (5.5) and 'mass mobilizer' (4.9%). Other traits total 15.2% of the responses and non-responses are 30.5%. Of the the third preferences, as seen earlier, 77.4% are non-responses. 'Other traits' lead with 9.2% responses followed by 'man of character' (4.3%) 'development-orientation' (3.1%), 'non-factional character' (3.0%), 'mass mobilizer' (1.8%) and 'education' (1.2%).

It might be presumed with reasonable assurance that whereas it is a healthy sign that the qualities of head and heart continue to be recognized as the most vital, priorities of socio-economic change are also recognized. The egalitarian philosophy, however, is yet to take roots.

The district-wise pattern of the responses in this regard is also interesting. Excluding non-responses from the total number and summing up all the three preferences, we found the 'man of character' response leading with 46.9% followed by 'development-orientation' (13.5%), 'non-factional character' (7.3%), 'education' (6.9%) and 'mass-mobilizer' (5.0%). Also, 15.4% of the responses were in the 'other reasons' category. In all five districts, 'man of character' is the trait considered most effective. In Bhilwara, that category held 55.9% of the responses; in Bharatpur the figure was 50.0%, in Jhalawar 47.7%, in Nagaur 42.9%, and in Ganganagar 39.1%.

The second trait in order of preference shows a slightly different pattern, if we ignore the responses in the category of 'other traits'. Thus 'development orientation' is considered effective in Ganganagar (26.5%), Nagaur (19.0%), Bhilwara (18.6%) and Jhalawar (18.5), whereas Bharatpur respondents chose 'non-factional character' (11.5%) of responses as the second trait followed by 'development orientation' (7.7%).

There is little to say about the first preference trait except that all the turmoil and twists of politics notwithstanding, the faith in men of character has not eroded. And when respondents in four districts (barring Bharatpur) preferred 'development orientation', an emphasis on the priorities of pervasive communitarian transformation is obvious. That Bharatpur respondents opted for 'non-factional character', only reflects the state of affairs in public life in that district, which is all too well known. It is a matter of some consolation that the respondents are not only conscious of a faction-ridden public life but also feel inclined to believe that non-factional public figures alone could deliver the goods.

The presence for a 'man of character' is found in all age groups. The below-30 group gives 59.1% preference, followed by the 30-50 age-group (47.1%) and above-50 age-group (44.0%). Similarly, persons in all three age groups preferred 'development orientation' as the next trait : for the below-30 age-group the figure was 18.2%, in the 30-50 age-group it was 18.6%, and the above-50 age-group it was 18.3%. Education has been treated as a prime requirement by 9.1% of respondents in the age group of below 30 years, 9.3% of those of the middle age-group, and 2.8% of those of the old age-group. Non-factional character is prized by 4.5%, 8.7% and 5.5% of young, middle and old age groups, respectively. Lastly, the image of 'mass mobilizer' as a pre-requisite has been put forward by 4.0% and 7.3% of middle and old age groups, respectively. Thus it would appear that the young age-group preferes qualities of head and heart even more than two higher age groups, while some among the latter also underline such traits as mass mobilizer, non-factional character etc.

It is significant that the caste-wise response, in this context, also does not show any basic variations. On the whole, the 'man of character' trait gets first preference (46.9% of responses) followed by 'development orientation' (18.5%). The lower-caste group leads in giving top priority to the trait 'man of character' (48.5% of responses), followed by the middle-caste group (47.4%) and the upper-caste group (45.0%). The upper-caste group seems to be more conscious of the trait of 'development orientation' (22.5% of responses), followed by the lower-caste group (18.2%) and the middle-caste group (16.8%). It may be that the lower-caste group has known the pinch of unscrupulous elements and perhaps, therefore, they gave top priority to the 'man of character' trait. It was expected that the middle-caste group, predominantly agriculture-oriented, would give top priority to the trait of 'development orientation'. However, the upper-caste group leads in this respect, perhaps owing to the fact that more and more people from that group have been taking to agriculture and have been more consciously aware of the impact of development than middle caste elite members.

Party Links

We now turn to the role of factors such as political parties and caste as bases for acquiring influence. The first question in this regard read : "Do you think that a public man at the village level to be effective should be associated with a political party ?" With relevant alteration, the question was repeated with regard to caste leadership as a factor of influence.

Of the positive[3] responses, 32.9% emphasised party membership as an essential factor for a public figure at the village level : 20.7% of the respondents called it 'necessary' and 12.2% of the respondents thought it 'very necessary'. On the other hand, 25.6% of the respondents held the view that the factor of party membership made 'no difference'. Considering the negative responses, 26.8% indicated that party membership was not needed ; 14.6% indicated that it was not very necessary, and 12.2% were of the view that it was not at all necessary. This response, on the whole, is surprising because rural politics cannot be said to be completely devoid of influence of political parties. The district-wise pattern of response is also interesting. Nagaur respondents favour party membership with an aggregate of 51.5% of the responses (18.2% say it "very necessary" and 33.3% say it "necessary") followed by Bharatpur respondents with

---

3. Positive responses are those which treat party membership as an instrument for acquiring elite status.

34.3% (28.6% "very necessary" and 5.7% "necessary") Jhalawar respondents with 32.4% (8.8% "very necessary" and 23.6% "necessary") ; while Ganganagar and Bhilwara respondents registered identical views with 22.6% of the responses favouring party membership. In case of Ganganagar, it might be noted, all the responses were in the category of "necessary" and none read "very necessary", whereas in Bhilwara the emphasis was on "necessary" (19.4%) and "very necessary" (3.2%). It might be recalled that in Nagaur district, the protracted Jat-Rajput rivalry has been reflected in political alignments. The Jats have been identified with the Congress and the Rajputs with the Ram Rajya Parishad (RRP), to begin with, and later with the Swatantra party. During the land reform movement, the Jats were backed by the Congress in their struggle against the entrenched hegemony of Rajput landlords. The latter, naturally, turned towards the RRP and the Swatantra. The elites of these caste-groups, consequently, came to be identified with the respective political parties. The *Bhumihar* agitation[4] further confirmed these political alignments. The emphasis on the affiliation of elite persons with political parties in Bharatpur might also be ascribed to the faction-ridden state of affairs there. Moreover, this district has been a stronghold of the S.S.P., a leftist party, which has been, off and on, organizing agitations and mobilizing people on different issues. At other places also, by and large, this argument holds good. However, in the case of Bhilwara, not a very developed district, it was gathered that the low response in favour of party affiliation is not so much a reflection of the futility of party linkages as of the frustration resulting from continued neglect of the region despite the assurances of political parties. The story in the case of Ganganagar is different. Despite considerable development in the district, respondents did not consider political parties to be the decisive factor ; the view was that, if one had resources enough to satisfy the corruptible administrative hierarchy, anything be got done[5]. Surprising

4. This was a movement launched by the freeholders of land in the mid-fifties to get higher amount of compensation in lieu of their land (*Jagirs*) by the State Government. Generally speaking, the Bhumihars enjoyed an inferior status to that of jagirdars.

5. Informal discussions by our field staff have yielded several such responses which have been frank and revealing.

though such reflections might sound, they ought to be carefully considered. One may even ask if the responses of those in Bhilwara and Ganganagar are not sufficiently revealing ?

It turns out that those who put a premium on the issue of party affiliation are themselves members of one political party or the other. Our analysis shows that 65.0% (45% Congress; 20% non-Congress) of the respondents who think party membership to be "very necessary" and, 73.5% (58.8% Congress; 14.7% non-Congress) of the respondents who regard party membership as "necessary", are affiliated with one party or the other. On the other hand, 58.5% of the total respondents who are not associated with any party show their indifference; 25.7% hold that "it makes no difference"; 17.1% hold that it is "not much necessary"; and 15.7% categorically assert that "it is not at all necessary". About 18.6% of non-affiliate respondents have expressed no opinion. That means that 22.9% of elite respondents who treat party membership as very necessary or necessary are not at the moment affiliated with any political party.

Looking at the issue from the angle of party preferences, we find that the Congress respondents lead in considering membership of a political party as "necessary" (58.8%) and "very necessary" (45%). This response can also be seen in the light of the fact that the Congress has been the ruling party in Rajasthan since Independence and after the integration of States. The concomitant availability of lovers of power-patronage and resources is appreciated by those in that political party and hence the emphasis on membership of a political party to ensure greater influence as an elite.

The main consideration for the largest number of elite respondents who think party membership as essential is that party membership makes available to the local people guidance and other aid from above which is helpful in carrying out various assignments that add to the prestige of public figures. This view is held by 60.0% and 44.1% of the respondents who think party membership as "very necessary" and "necessary", respectively. The other significant consideration with a good number of elite persons is that party membership helps in disciplined organization of public work. But a larger number of members of the elite group think quite the reverse. To them party membership is not conducive to disciplined organization of work. Hence they regard party membership as not necessary. Further, nearly 40% (18 of 44) of those who think party membership as not very necessary or not at all necessary, are more specific and contend that party membership breeds factionalism in the village. Consequently, a substantial number of persons get alienated, and they withdraw support to developmental works. Lastly, those who are indifferent to the issue of party membership and contend that "it makes no difference", mainly advance the reason that the organization of various works depends on the personal merits of public figures and, therefore, the issue of party membership is immaterial. In the wider context of a participating democracy, the very fact that there is evidence of awareness of the primacy of 'politics' and the role of parties in this regard is a welcome development. Nevertheless, the emphasis on the 'qualities of publicmen' also shows that politics in India has not yet come to be treated entirely as a manipulative art in the public psyche.

Caste Leadership

The question on the extent to which caste leadership is a vital factor in ensuring a more effective climate for the activities of elite persons was a delicate one. While 21.4% of all the respondents gave positive answers (of varying emphasis), 70.1% of the respondents gave categorically negative answers, and 8.5% of the respondents preferred to remain uncommitted either way. District-wise, there is a uniformity of emphasis on the 'negative' response that caste leadership does not materially affect the influence of the elites, with Bhilwara leading at 77.4% and Bharatpur at the rear at 60%. Of 'positive' responses that caste leadership does affect the influence of the elite, Ganganagar leads with 25.8% and Bhilwara brings up the rear with 16.2%. Whatever opinions are to the contrary, elite perception is that caste does not have a decisive impact in rural politics. A generally held notion, however, is that the factor of caste is of great help in the assumption of village leadership, especially when one considers entrenched castes. Since the question we asked happened to be of a general nature, the respondents should not have been hesitant in telling us so, if they were conscious of, and felt that, a caste base was essential for an effective public leader. It is thus important to note that 70.1% of elite respondents categorically deny the role of caste as a basis of leadership, as against only 26.8% elite respondents who categorically denied the necessity of party membership. Thus, irrespective of the fact whether or not casteism has some role to play in village politics, members of the elite group do not perceive its need—perhaps genuinely or perhaps just because of a guilty conscience.

A comparison of the responses which held both party and caste leadership to be essential or the reverse brings out some interesting points : 80% of those who hold that party membership is not 'much' necessary or not 'at all' necessary also hold that caste leadership is not 'much' necessary or not 'at all' necessary. In contrast, 35% of those who think that party membership is 'very necessary' and 17.4% of those who think it to be 'necessary', hold caste leadership also to be 'necessary' or 'very necessary'. Thus, even here a greater percentage of those who think party membership is essential, does not think that caste leadership is essential. Hence there is greater consistency among those who regard neither type of organizational support (party or caste) as essential for effective village level leadership.

The reasons advanced for the need or denial of the need of a caste basis were also analysed. The two positive reasons preferred are : 'sound character' (28.6%) and 'community support' (21.9%), relegating responses favouring caste-based support to 20.2% (affinities 4.3%+caste-support 15.9%). This is quite interesting because caste leadership is deemed to be dependent on qualitative traits other than the mere membership in a particular caste group.

Vote Getting Image

The respondents were also asked with the help of a structured question to specify factors on the basis of which people were to decide. The assumption here is that it is one thing that people, by and large, are impressed and influenced by a particular candidate and quite another that they prefer a specific person when it comes to their individual choice. The responses reveal that in all, 75.6% of the respondents preferred 'personal

merit of candidate' as the decisive factor though with difference of emphasis (58.5% 'much' and 17.1% 'a little' responses).
Other factors are : 'support of relations/caste leaders' (63.4%),
'political factors' (61.6%), 'support of the rich' (22.5%) and
'manipulative tactics' (6.1%). It is also significant that 59.8%
of the respondents hold the view that support of rich sections
is an inconsequential factor. The primacy of 'personal merit'
as a consideration in voting is self-explanatory. In India where
institutionalization of the secondary association is yet to take
place, this pattern of responses is not unexpected.

It would not be out of place to mention here the qualified
statements that the respondents made on detailed probing.
Thus they pointed out that it is in local elections that caste
considerations play a considerable role. Similarly, party of the
candidate and issues raised are included among political
factors. Other things being equal, most people would prefer
the candidate of the ruling · party. The term 'issues raised'
meant that rural electors, overwhelmingly belonging to
peasant sections, would vote for a candidate promising to serve
their developmental interests.[6] Surprisingly, people do not
attribute any significant role to the economic strata of candidates. Nearly 60% of the respondents said that electors do
not care whether one hails from, or is backed by, rich sections.
Note the contrast to the trend shown earlier (in the previous
chapter) that a good number of members in the institutional
elite category come from the upper economic strata. It might
be that the people generally do not get swayed by candidates'
economic strata but the fact cannot be denied that only the
affluent can afford to contest elections under the present
circumstances.

The district-wise analysis shows that the factor of 'personal
merit' has been rated under the category of 'much' by 27.1%
of the respondents in Jhalawar—the highest among all the

6. A subtle example of this was offered by the respondents belonging to
   Banera Assembly constituency (Bhilwara district). They said that
   in the 1967 elections they rejected an SSP MLA, who was seeking re-
   election from the same constituency, because he held that all the
   pastoral and other fallow land be distributed among landless Harijans.
   The people said that otherwise the legislator was held high in
   popular esteem but that particular view proved to be his undoing.

districts. Bharatpur, with 26.0% of the responses in this category, is next. The corresponding figures for other districts are : Bhilwara 18.8%, Nagaur 14.6% and Ganganagar 13.5%. On the other hand, Bhilwara and Ganganagar share between themselves more than half (53.0%) of total respondents who have attributed 'a little' role to 'personal merit' as a factor in the elections. However, since responses favouring the category of 'much' consideration would carry greater weight in the final analysis, it can be held that 'personal merit' as a factor plays greater role in Jhalawar and Bharatpur districts than in others. Similarly, it can be held that social factors like caste and relations play the maximum role in Nagaur, closely followed by Ganganagar. Political factors play the greatest role, again, in Nagaur. It can be held that in Nagaur, political activities are quite intense as much as they date back to a much earlier period in comparison to other districts. It may also be restated here that in Nagaur district, political competition also coincides with Jat-Rajput rivalry and, therefore, it is likely that both the factors may be said to be playing a role in conjunction with each other.

The above analysis can be further elaborated by considering the conjunctional role of various factors in determining voters' choice. Considered from this angle, two clear patterns emerge. One is that the conjunctional role of various factors is much more apparent in Ganganagar, Nagaur, and Bharatpur, than in Bhilwara and Jhalawar. In the former category, as already mentioned elsewhere, Ganganagar and Bharatpur regions have Sikh and Jat as predominant castes, respectively. In Nagaur, Jat *versus* Rajput-Brahman rivalry is in evidence. It could, therefore, be said that the existing complexities in these regions resulted in the emergence, and subsequent recognition, of more than a single factor in influencing the voters' choice. In the districts of Bhilwara and Jhalawar (the former a backward area), on the other hand, conditions are different and hence, there is an inconsequential conjunctional role of factors determining the voters' choice. Secondly, this difference is sharply brought out where the inter-play of socio-political factors is in evidence as in Nagaur, Ganganagar and Bharatpur. Economic factors also play vital conjunctional roles along with socio-political factors. However, 'personal merit' obviously plays a more vital independent role.

Conjunctional role analysis by position of the respondents does not reveal significant differences. Still one finds some variations which can be identified here. About 26.5% of panchas who have responded to the query have identified the role of personal factors along with that of support of rich sections. The corresponding figures for sarpanchas etc. and for persons in the reputational elite category are 19.7% and 20.7%, respectively. Thus panchas place more weight on personal merit in elections, along with the support of the rich. In a similar fashion, to put it briefly, it can be said that in comparison to other categories of the elite, fewer reputational elite persons think of the conjunctional role of personal merit and political factors and more of them think of the conjunctional role of social and political factors. To elaborate further, elite respondents in this category think that the nature of party support, issues raised etc., together with caste and community support, play a significant role in influencing the voters' choice. Considering the situation that reputational elite respondents are those who could not by will or by design get into the panchayati raj set-up, the essence of the thought processes of the reputational elite also becomes clear. These persons may be nourishing a grudge, consciously or unconsciously, and may be explaining away their failure in terms of being handicapped by social factors.

A more intensive enquiry on the extent to which the pronounced trait theory of leadership played a decisive role in a developing society might well be considered. This could be conducted by looking at the contrary view, *i.e.*, what precisely is the syndrome impact of situational factors which present a conducive climate for personality traits.

The above analysis seeks to show the variety of factors that tend to influence the voters' choice. It would seem that, broadly speaking, 'personal merits' or 'sound character' of the prospective candidates are significant traits. In addition, the role of party or factional affiliation is also recognized by elite respondents. But the role of 'caste and relations' has been differently interpreted. Recall that responding to the vital question of whether one's own caste leadership is essential for an influential public figure at the village level, a large majority of elite respondents replied in the negative. But when it came to identifying the role of the same factor in determining voters' choice, a majority of replies have been positive. One possible explanation of this variation might be the different context and different settings of questions put to the respondents. Responses in the former category were related to a question about the role of caste in isolation ; in the second category the role of caste was sought to be identified in the context of the larger syndrome of factors. It might, therefore, be inferred that caste does play a role which is not decisive in isolation but becomes important if viewed in a conjunctional context.

Support Bases

We now turn to an analysis of the forces that help one in getting elected to a particular post. First, we will look into the replies received from various panchayati raj functionaries in response to a question about the type of support they made use of when they contested for a post, and the consequent results. We have taken into account only the most significant response. In the second place, we will look into the various decisive considerations that influenced the extension of personal support by functionaries. For our purpose, the posts considered here are : sarpanch, assembly, and parliamentary representative (for which direct elections are held). Thus, while the first analysis will be in the nature of a self-evaluation, the second will be an exercise in inferring the general nature of personal support.

Table 4.2 deals with responses from elite respondents (who contested at least once for any of the posts mentioned earlier), about the nature of support available to them. The frequency of contest of elite respondents is also mentioned. Thus the total would give the number of contests entered into and not the number of people contesting. This, however, excludes the time factor which is likely to vary from one election to another though it is doubtful if it would decisively affect the emerging trends.

Coming to the table itself, it is interesting to see that 63.5% of the respondents reported "all sectors' support" for their victories. The maximum response in this category came from panchas (74.7%), followed by sarpanchas (61.8%), pradhan

TABLE 4.2

Support Bases of Elite Respondents in terms of Aggregate Electoral Performance

Position for which contested	All sectors' support		Support of Caste/castes		Higher level support		Party support		Others		N.R.		Total	
	Won	Lost	Won	Lost	Won	Lost	Won	Lost	Won	Lost	Won	Lost	Won	Lost
Panch	71 74.7	1 25.0	11 11.6	1 25.0	–	–	6 6.3	1 25.0	3 3.1	–	4 4.2	1 25.0	95 100.0	4 100.0
Sarapanch	42 61.8	5 33.3	10 14.7	3 20.0	2 2.9	–	11 16.2	3 20.0	1 1.5	1 6.7	2 2.9	3 20.0	68 100.0	15 100.0
Pradhan/Zila Pramukh	17 54.8	1 11.1	3 9.7	1 11.1	–	–	7 22.6	2 22.2	3 9.7	–	1 3.2	5 55.6	31 100.0	9 100.0
M.L.A./M.P.	4 44.5	2 50.0	–	–	–	–	2 22.2	1 25.0	1 11.1	1 25.0	2 22.2	–	9 100.0	4 100.0
Cooption	14 46.7	–	–	–	1 3.3	–	6 20.0	–	3 10.0	–	6 20.0	1 100.0	30 100.0	1 100.0
Total	148 63.6	9 27.3	24 10.3	5 15.1	3 1.3	–	32 13.7	7 21.2	11 4.7	2 6.1	15 6.4	10 30.3	233 100.0	33 100.0

zila pramukh (54.8%), co-opted members (46.7%) and MLAs/MPs (44.5%). It may be worthwhile to observe here that respondents at the primary level of the rural unit are unable to make a neat differentiation in terms of the nature of various support bases and, consequently, believe that their aggregate electoral performance has been materially affected by *all* the support bases. This is true at the village level or, if not of the entire village when it is a big one, at least at the level of the wards into which it is delimited, all of which tend to be identified with a caste. This caste support is at times not differentiated and taken as the support of all sections. However, as we go upwards, the response in this context gets comparatively speaking, milder.

The support base next given is that of political parties (13.7%). Note that responses giving this support base increase as one goes upwards : beginning with panchas (6.3%), sarpanchas (16.2%), co-opted members (20%), pradhan/zila pramukh (22.6%) and MLAs/MPs (22.2%). District-wise, predominant support from political parties came from Congress in Bhilwara, Bhartiya Kranti Dal (BKD) or Janata Party (in 1967) in Jhalawar, and SSP and Congress in Bharatpur. In the other districts, the role of the Congress is, of course, predominant. This variance is in conformity with the regional and situational determinants. Despite this, it is significant that political party support is believed to be relevant at all levels, though the intensity varies. Respondents held that caste support was irrelevant at the MLA/MP level, while 14.7% felt that it affected the level of sarpanchas ; 11.6% felt that it affected the level of panchas and 9.7% felt that it affected the pradhan/zila pramukh level. It is significant that caste considerations are progressively more intense as one goes nearer the rural units and recede in intensity as one goes higher up.

As we turn to the cases of the losers among our respondents (33 in all), we find that it is difficult to ascertain why, despite recognised support-bases, candidates lose elections. That is, it is not possible to pin-point any particular reason for adverse verdicts at the polls. Among those who lost the elections, 27.3% claimed "all sectors' support" followed by party support (21.2%) and caste support (15.1%). It might also be noted that 30.3% of the losers did not give any response and 6.1% losers gave other factors as support-bases. A reasonable surmise might be that the losers who failed to identify support-bases in their favour, failed to muster any support. So once they have lost, all they manage to do is to avoid any specific response out of sheer despondency.

It would also be seen that there is more reliance on caste support at the lower levels owing, obviously, to the fact that localized caste support can easily sway election results either way at that level. However, as the area of electoral contest widens, exclusive reliance on caste support loses its effectivity.

To take up the main thread of our analysis again, it may be re-stated that elite as well as citizen respondents were asked specifically to identify considerations that made the voters opt for this or that candidate and our enquiry concentrated upon three major posts for which direct elections are held : sarpanchship, MLAship, and MPship. 'Personal merit' of the contestant is held in highest regard both by citizens (42%) and the elite (23.8%). Factional/party alignments has been rated next in order of preference : citizens (6%) and elite (26.8%). Citizens mentioned 'village consensus' (9.5%) as another important factor. Contrast this with the elite respondents' emphasis on factional/party alignments. Another interesting reaction is the low-key response for caste affiliation by both citizens (3%) and the elite (0.6%). Perhaps, as was gathered during informal discussions with the respondents, citizens implied its role in their response for 'village consensus' and the elite respondents did likewise in their response for 'party/factional alignments'.[7]

Before we turn to a district-wise analysis, two prefatory notes will not be out of place here. First, in Ganganagar district, in the panchayat included in our study, no contest for sarpanchship was held. Hence all the citizens and the overwhelming number of elite respondents is placed in the category

---

7. It may be noted here that in the last election for sarpanchship, the broad caste-based alignment of factions has broadly followed the following pattern : in Nagaur Brahmin-Swami-Rajput *versus* Jat-Gujar-Harijans; in Bhilwara Brahmin *versus* Gujars; and in Jhalawar the factions were locality based.

TABLE 4.3

Considerations held by Elite Respondents in Intending Support to Contestants for MLAship and MPship

District	Personal merit		Caste fellow/relation		Candidate of ruling party		Own Party candidate		Princely House candidate	
	MLA	MP	MLA	MP	MLA	MP	MLA	MP	MLA	MP
1	2	3	4	5	6	7	8	9	10	11
Ganganagar	3 9.7	3 9.7	1 3.2	1 3.2	8 25.8	8 25.8	4 12.9	2 6.5	–	–
Nagaur	5 15.2	3 9.1	1 3.0	1 3.0	8 24.2	11 33.3	4 12.1	5 15.2	–	–
Bhilwara	4 12.9	3 9.7	1 3.2	–	11 35.8	11 35.8	6 19.4	5 16.1	–	–
Jhalawar	1 2.9	2 5.9	2 5.9	–	5 14.7	4 11.8	4 11.8	4 11.8	–	1 2.9
Bharatpur	5 14.3	6 17.1	1 2.9	–	3 8.6	6 17.1	2 5.7	3 8.6	4 11.4	3 8.6
Total	18 11.0	17 10.4	6 3.7	2 1.2	35 21.5	40 24.4	20 12.2	19 11.6	4 2.4	4 2.4

TABLE 4.3 (Contd.)

District	Local Candidate		Village consensus		Protest vote		Others		Total*	
	MLA	MP	MLA	MP	MLA	MP	MLA	MP	MLA	MP
1	12	13	14	15	16	17	18	19	20	21
Ganganagar	—	—	2 / 6.5	—	4 / 12.9	1 / 3.2	5 / 16.1	5 / 16.1	31 / 100.3	31 / 100.0
Nagaur	—	—	7 / 21.2	3 / 9.1	2 / 6.1	2 / 6.1	2 / 6.1	4 / 12.1	33 / 100.0	33 / 100.0
Bhilwara	—	—	—	—	2 / 6.5	—	2 / 6.5	2 / 6.5	31 / 100.0	31 / 100.0
Jhalawar	—	—	1 / 2.9	—	3 / 8.8	3 / 8.8	5 / 14.7	6 / 17.6	34 / 100.0	34 / 100.0
Bharatpur	4 / 11.4	1 / 2.9	—	—	—	2 / 5.7	5 / 14.3	1 / 2.9	35 / 100.0	35 / 100.0
Total	4 / 2.4	1 / 0.6	10 / 6.1	3 / 1.8	11 / 6.7	8 / 4.9	19 / 11.6	18 / 11.0	164 / 100.0	164 / 100.0

*Total includes N. Rs and N. As in each district.

of 'not-applicable' responses. The response of elite persons is from those not belonging to this panchayat. Secondly, we have more responses in the category of 'party/factional alignments' from elite persons of Bharatpur than of any other district. In Nagaur, factional-alignments have been a strong consideration, but respondents preferred more 'safe' rational replies as 'personal merit' than others, which, at times would reflect what Morris-Jones has called the "saintly idiom" of Indian politics.

Table 4.3 summarises the response to two separate questions, which elicited the respondents' considerations for extending support to the contestants for Vidhan Sabha and Lok Sabha seats. This question, however, was confined to elite respondents considering the need of clarity of perspective in this regard. The emphasis on considerations for support given to contestants is almost reflective of *real politik*. To some extent it may also explain the significance of MLAs' support to aspiring contestants for Parliament. It also shows that members of the elite gave maximum consideration to the 'candidate of the ruling party'. The reasons are not far to seek as the potential resources of the ruling party, ups and downs notwithstanding, have been universally recognized. Another allied factor eliciting sizable response is 'own party candidate'. Other factors advanced have been relegated to the position of minor responses. Despite Rajasthan's feudal antecedents, the response for 'princely house candidates' is inconsequential and might be taken to mean a significant erosion of such impact.

The district-wise pattern is also interesting. In Ganganagar, Jhalawar and Nagaur districts, which were among the most affected by the Congress split in the 1967 elections, some elite respondents seem to have been influenced by their loyalty to the 'leader' rather than to the party. It might be called a sort of 'protest-vote'. Secondly, the consideration of a candidate being sponsored by the ruling party prevailed most obviously in the case of the elite of Bhilwara district. This only reflects the strong hold of the Congress party in the Mewar region. Thirdly, in Bharatpur district, where the former ruler himself was a contestant for the Lok Sabha, the factor 'princely house candidate' received the maximum response.

In sum, the support of a political party along with the popularity or (personal merit) of a candidate weighs heavily with the elite. Because of the large area covered by a constituency, 'caste considerations' cannot be relied upon. When one adds to the considerations of a political nature, the overwhelming potentiality of the ruling party, one gets a far clearer insight into the responses in the preceding analysis.

Summary

Summing up, it can be said that situational factors play an effective role in the acquisition of positions of influence. This does not minimize the 'attribute' theory, but only explains that, though factors like honesty, judiciousness, impartiality, and capacity for developmental work are factors that matter, these cannot be relied upon in isolation from the socio-political forces of competitive politics. Take, for instance, the district of Nagaur, where Jats, a middle class peasant group have revolted against traditional domination of higher caste groups led by the Brahmin-Rajput combine.

The role of economic factors in this regard is not so clearly evident from the respondents' reactions. And yet, as we have seen in Chapters 2 and 3, the elites belong to well-placed groups. As we move up from lower to higher level positions in the panchayati raj set-up, persons of upper strata, by and large, man various posts. Our informal contacts show that economic factors do tend to play an indirect role, especially in the sense that only members of the elite group belonging to well-placed groups are usually drawn into the vortex of competitive politics. Perhaps in the consciousness of the electors, this factor has not been well-articulated or they just take it for granted and, therefore, do not feel like mentioning it.

Finally, it has also been found that as we move up from lower to higher level positions, the role of social factors diminishes and that of political factors, such as political parties and factions, increases. The affiliation with the ruling party naturally tends to possess the psyche both of elite persons and citizens in their decision to support a candidate in the electoral contest.

5

THE RURAL ELITE AND PANCHAYATI RAJ : ROLE EXPECTATIONS, PERFORMANCE AND CONSTRAINTS

THE DISCUSSION HAS so far centered round the locational factors and instrumentalities of access to power positions in the panchayati raj system. In the present chapter we intend to delineate a profile of role-expectations, performance, and constraints in the specific context of panchayati raj, on the basis of the perceptions of the rural elite.

It will not be out of place to mention at the outset that, not entirely unexpectedly,[1] the performance of panchayati raj institutions has largely been equated with the role-performance of the rural elite. There is a close relationship between the two, though, we have not treated the two as synonymous. Our assumption is that the rural elite is just one of the significant factors in the performance of panchayati raj institutions and as such the two cannot be taken as interchangeable. Again, we have preferred the expression 'role' to 'function'. Functions emanate from the very character of the relationship of elites with society.[2]

1. *Cf* : Suzanne Keller, who has aptly argued that "societies regulate themselves and institutions act only in a metaphorical sense. Even in small and relatively small and homogeneous societies men must assume responsibility for the varied activities and operations of the system". *Beyond the Ruling Class* ; *Strategic Elites in Modern Society* (New York : Random House, 1963), p. 95.
2. According to Talcott Parsons, functions are the observable consequence, a dynamic aspect of structures which caters to certain systemic needs. To quote him "the significance of the concept of function. implies the conception of the empirical system as a 'going concern'. Its structure is that system of determinate patterns which, as empirical observation shows, within certain limits, 'tend to be maintained' or on a somewhat more dynamic version, tend to develop "according to an empirical constant pattern." *Essays in Sociological Theory* (London : Collier Macmillan Ltd., Paperback, 1964), p. 217.

Thus, being a superior group, or 'reference group' in society an elite can be expected to perform educative, communicative and other functions. On the other hand, 'role' assumes a specific context of office or status. "A role", explains Lynton, one of the early exponents of role theory, "represents the dynamic aspect of a status...When (an individual) puts the rights and duties which constitute the status into effect, he is performing a role."[3] Since the activities termed role(s) emanate from the office or status a person holds, and with every office certain norms have to be prescribed, roles have a normative context also.[4] The incumbents are expected to be guided in their behaviour by these norms. And, yet, behaviour of no incumbent can be thought to match in entirety the expectations set or norms of an office. The personality and perspective of the person holding an office set limits to his performance and cause it to fall short of, or overshoot, or even deviate from expectations. Thus no study of the role is complete with just a study of role expectations. It has also to focus its attention upon the performance or role-behaviour of incumbents. Besides, a role player is constrained by various other factors, such as resources, attitudes, and cooperation extended by other institutions, such as the bureaucracy, more so because a role is performed in a given social situation. Thus, a study of role has to be inclusive of role expectations, role-behaviour and role constraints.[5]

3. Lynton, Ralph, *The Study of Man* (New York : D. Appleton : Century Co., 1936), p. 114. Talcott Parsons, concurring with the basic postulates of the concept as described by Lynton, further clarifies it by observing that, "...in most relationships, the actor does not participate as a total entity, but only by virtue of a given differentiated "sector". Such a sector, which is the unit of a system of social relationships, has come predominantly to be called a "role", (*Essays in Sociological Theory*, p. 230).

4. John C. Wahlke, explaining the normative character of roles, states that the concept of role "relates to social rather than individual psychology. It is a normative concept also in the sense that it refers to expected and preferred actions, to imperatives of behaviour, as well as to description of observed statistical regularities". "American Legislatores' Roles", in Kessel, John H., Cole, George F. and Sedding Robert G. (ed.), *Micropolitics : Individual and Group Level Concepts* (New York : Holt, Rinehart and Winston, Inc., 1970), p. 111.

5. For an explanation of these terms, see editors' Introduction in *Ibid.*, pp. 103—109.

The questions we put to citizen and elite respondents did not directly probe the role of the rural elite *vis-a-vis* panchayati raj institutions.[6] Our intention was to avoid chances of hostile or acutely biased reactions. An indirect reference and subsequent follow-up questions in depth served our purpose more effectively.[7]

Another obvious limitation of this study is that we could not observe the rural elite at work to the extent we wanted. We could not verify what respondents said, much as we wished to do so. Often, meetings of panchayati raj institutions were not convened, notwithstanding legal provisions. Many a time, meetings did not have the requisite quorum. We have, however, included in our analysis some observations based on some of the meetings held during our stay in the field and they give some idea of the role dynamics of the elite under study. It might be noted that the way in which panchayati raj institutions have been working and the frequency of their meeting are significantly related. It should also be noted that the mechanism of panchayati raj institutions has not been a device natural to the social system and behaviour pattern of the rural folk. The accepted pattern has been for village and caste elders to dictate and direct the people ; this reflected a relationship which was not in keeping with democratic norms and practices as envisaged under panchayati raj. Living a new role, as envisioned in the concept of community development

6. Thus we avoided a direct-reference question like the following : "What has been the contribution of the sarpanch (or the panchas etc.) to the success or failure of the panchayats ? In what fields have they contributed and to what extent ?" and so on. Our question read : "What, in your opinion, has been the performance of your village panchayat : excellent, average or token ?" Then in the next question we have probed into the role of functionaries in support of the answer given by the respondent to the preceding question. Similar questions were also asked about the performance of panchayati raj institutions in general.

7. Among the rural folk, who are exposed effectively to modern communication net work, it is difficult to explain the difference between an academic enquiry and official enquiry. We wished to avoid such confusion. However, on several occasions it was found we were given a mistaken (and not at all flattering) identity. as if we were on a fault-finding mission.

through the people's own representatives,[8] would naturally take its own time,[9] though this observation should in no case be taken to minimize the strides that have already been achieved in this direction.

Profile of Role Expectations

Despite all the codified normative prescriptions, or conventions associated with a role, it is the perception of the nature of a role that goes a long way in determining the fashion in which that role will be performed. This is natural also as whatever the degree of codification, it will still leave some room for the actor to determine priorities, both in terms of ends and means, according to his preference. Hence the present study concentrates upon the perception of 'role expectations'.

THE PERCEPTION OF THE ELITE

We began with a simple question to elite respondents which read : "How was panchayati raj received by the people of your area on the eve of its introduction ? Was it welcomed by all or did it meet significant opposition also ?" In this regard we made a further probe and sought the names and social background of those who consciously welcomed it or opposed it. The response, however, was not entirely adequate. We are, therefore, examining only the first part of the question.

An analysis of our data shows that in Ganganagar 87.1% of elite respondents recalled a favourable reaction to panchayati raj institutions, and in Bharatpur, 85.7% recalled a similar reaction. The figures for Bhilwara and Nagaur elite repondents were 80.6% and 69.7%, respectively. It is only in Jhalawar that the response went down to 58.8%. Though it is not easy to offer any plausible explanation for this low response, it is

8. See in this regard, the *Report of Balwant Rai Mehta Committee on Community Development and National Extension Services* (New Delhi : Planning Commission, 1957), and Iqbal Narain, "The Concept of Panchayati Raj and its Institutional Implications in India", *Asian Survey*, 5 (9) September, 1955, pp. 456-66.

9. Myron Weiner, in a recent study of party building activities of Congress in India, tells of a similar situation and analyses the role of the socio-cultural legacies in party building efforts. See chapters 22 and 23, *Party Building in a New Nation* (Chicago : University of Chicago Press, 1967, pp. 459-496.

not unlikely that after the passage of time the people's verdict might have been coloured by the actual role performance of these institutions. In Jhalawar district, with the exit from the Congress and subsequent death of Raja Harish Chandra in 1967, the area seemed to have withdrawn its support to the Congress ; consequently, developmental activities slackened, leaving the people in an anguished mood. Perhaps that explains the response in Jhalawar. The overall response (76.2%.) is, however, not discouraging.

In response to another part of our query—whether the introduction of panchayati raj had met with some significant opposition in their area—only 15.9% of the respondents answered in the affirmative. Region-wise, 38.5% affirmative responses from the Nagaur district, indicated the maximum extent of perception of the opposition. The overall figure of 15.9% respondents identifying opposition to introduction of panchayati raj institutions is self-explanatory. The reasons for the higher incidence of opposition in Nagaur district will be discussed in detail later, and here it suffices to recall that this district has been a hotbed of intense Jat-Rajput rivalry. The reaction of respondents has, therefore, been conditioned by the faction with which they are aligned and with their assessment of the nature and extent of benefits likely to accrue from possible control of these institutions.[10]

We now turn to the reasons assigned by respondents for a favourable or unfavourable response to the introduction of panchayati raj. These imply expectations of roles envisaged in the context of panchayati raj institutions as well as the respondents' reaction to them. The largest group of respondents (39.2%) was of those who felt that with the introduction of panchayati raj, the pace of developmental activities would be quickened. When this figure is added to the response of 23.8% to the effect

10. Such a reaction has been echoed on the floor of the Rajasthan Legislative Assembly also. Many Rajput M.L.As., especially those belonging to esrtwhile Jodhpur and Jaipur states, opposed even moves like the use of secret ballot in parchayat elections and open door meetings of panchayats, fearing loss of influence in such situations. See the debate over first and second reading of Rajasthan Panchayat Bill, 1953 in *Rajasthan Vidhan Sabha Ki Karyawahi Ka Vritant* (particularly the debate on 19 and 20 February, 1953).

that as a consequence of panchayati raj local people would be put incharge of planning, the total figure becomes 63.0%. Thus there is a significant perception of the developmental role. Among other expectations were 'providing better and cheaper justice' (12.3%) and 'relief from feudal grip' (14.6%).

Region-wise, the analysis shows that Ganganagar district respondents put the most emphasis on developmental expectations. The emphasis is natural as the district is the most developed area and people in general there are far more development-conscious. On the other hand, respondents of Bhilwara, comparatively a less developed district, accorded a 13.7% response in this category. Similarly, in the districts of Nagaur, and Bhilwara, which have undergone the rigours of *jagirdari* system, 31.6% and 47.4% of respondents, respectively emphasised the expectation that panchayati raj institutions would bring about relief from the feudal grip.

In sum, it can be said that, while an over-riding expectation from panchayati raj has been that it would perform developmental roles, this as well as other expectations have been somewhat influenced by local environmental factors and the level of consciousness of the people. It also follows that in no district have the elite respondents put forward the other expectations usually associated with panchayati raj, like inculcation of community conciousness, spread of social education, accent on socio-economic justice, and the like.[11]

To continue this analysis, Table 5.1 sets out the affirmative responses accorded to the introduction of panchayati raj institutions by position of the elite respondents.[12] Note that

11. See *n.* 8. This leaves quite open or even places under doubt a question raised by Beers and Ensminger on the eve of introduction of the democratic decentralization scheme. They had asked whether the developmental blocks would emerge as a social system in terms of common norms, ends, beliefs and sentiments. Perhaps we have a negative answer to offer. For details see Beers, Howard W. and Douglas Ensminger, "The Block Development as a Social System" *Indian Journal of Public Administration*, V, 2 (April-June, 1959)

12. The four positional categories referred to elsewhere have been compressed into three for purposes of cumulative analysis. Thus the co-opted and the Nyaya Panchyat members are included among the panchas etc. category. Similarly, the sarpanchas, pradhans, zila pramukhs and elite persons belonging to the cooperatives, are included in the sarpanchas etc. category.

TABLE 5.1

Reasons for Welcome to Panchayati Raj by Official Position

Position	Quicker development expected		Local people held in charge of planning		Better and cheaper justice		Relief from feudal grip		Others		Total*	
	No.	%	No.	%	No.	%	No.	%	No.	%	No.	%
Panch etc.	16	31.4	16	51.6	6	37.5	4	21.1	2	50.0	44	36.4
		36.4		36.4		13.6		9.1		4.5		100.0
Sarpanch etc.	22	43.1	11	35.5	6	37.5	11	57.8	2	50.0	52	43.0
		42.3		21.2		11.5		21.2		3.8		100.0
Reputational Elite etc.	13	25.5	4	12.9	4	25.0	4	21.1	–		25	20.6
		52.0		16.0		16.0		16.0				100.0
Total	51	100.0	31	100.0	16	100.0	19	100.0	4	100.0	121	100.0
		42.1		25.6		13.2		15.7		3.3		100.0

*Total excludes N. Rs. in all the categories.

the elite supports the expectation of 'quicker development', in large numbers, especially the higher level elite ('sarpanch etc.') with 42.3%, and the reputational elite (53.0%). The lower level elite ('panchas etc.'), on the other hand, gives greater consideration to the role of 'local people held incharge of planning'. It might seem paradoxical that the elite at lower level prefers a more sophisticated 'role expectation' (in which they may be less involved) than the elite at higher levels. However, if we take into account the situational factor, the paradox may be resolved. It may be recalled here that before the introduction of the three-tier panchayati raj system, the people's representatives were not directly responsible for local development, and yet, the upper level elite as M.L.As, sarpanchas of tehsil panchayats, and chairmen of district boards, influenced the implementation of developmental programmes through their association with advisory bodies at the block level. But the lower level elite was deprived of such a role. It is, therefore, natural that the lower level elite gives primacy to local planning in their profile of role expectations from panchayati raj.

There is significant difference in regard to other role expectations : 'relief from feudal grip' has received the highest response (57.8%) from the elite of the 'sarpanchas etc.' category. It might be recalled that under the feudal system, while village level posts, such as that of *numberdar*, were held by members of the local elite group, upper level posts were more or less inaccessible to them. In this context, it is understandable that aspirants for upper level posts in panchayati raj institutions have perhaps interpreted the new political opportunities in terms of relief from the feudal grip. This brings into focus 'power' considerations as well as the motives of the elite respondents who regard panchayati raj as a device for access to seats of power. This is further substantiated by the fact that responses of this type have come mainly from two districts—Bhilwara and Nagaur, where access to higher level positions has been quite restricted to non-feudel sections.

Perception of role expectations is said to be determined by the social backgound of respondents. In this connection, let us examine the role of education and caste. The study from this

angle reveals that the higher the level of education of respondents, the greater the number pointing to the role of the local
people in the planning process. Thus, while 20% of the total of
'illiterate' respondents gave that reason, the respective responses
for 'below matric' and 'above matric' are 25.3% and 41.7%. The
respondents in the 'above matric' category are not very concerned with issues of 'administration of better justice' and 'relief
from feudal grip'. Though the number of respondents with 'above
matric' education is too small to show any definite trend, it can
be surmised that higher level of education is functional to a more
precise role perception. This could also be interpreted differently
—that is, with an increase in education, persons become more
conscious of immediate problems and future perspectives, while
lack of education, perhaps, tends to confine reactions to an
adulation of the past.

Analysing the data by caste, we find that while 32.1% of
upper caste and 20.2% of middle caste respondents mention
association with local planning, the response of lower caste respondents is as high as 55·6%. Similarly, more than other
caste categories, they selected the reason of anticipating the
availability of better justice. It might, therefore, be safe to
assume that elite expectations are directly related to the incidence of deprivations suffered before the inception of panchayati raj. That is, if a particular elite group has hitherto been
deprived of a participatory role in planning at the rural level,
its expectation has been that the fruition of panchayati raj will
ensure that role. Like-wise, those who have been deprived and
exploited hope that better justice would be achieved through
panchayati raj institutions.

THE PERCEPTION OF THE CITIZENRY

It is interesting to compare the nature of role expectations
as stated by elite respondents with that of citizen respondents.
The simple question put to citizens was : "What were the
changes, in your opinion, that panchayati raj was expected to
bring about ?" The highest percentage (30.0) of citizens expected that panchayati raj would ensure speedier implementation of developmental plans. The next highest percentage
expected better 'administration of justice' (21.5%). Also, 17.0%
expected panchayati raj to serve as a device of local self-govern-

ment. Though only 3.5% said so, a new dimension to role expectations was provided by respondents who expected pan-chayati raj to ameliorate the condition of the poor. District-wise, we come across a pattern similar to that of elite responses. Non-responses are highest in Jhalawar district (45.2%). The same reason given in the case of the elite persons may hold good here : that in the post-1967 phase, when developmental activities came to a standstill, people became indifferent to panchayati raj. The perception of panchayati raj as a mecha-nism both for development programmes and local self-gover-nance is at a maximum in Nagaur district. And, this is not unnatural also, as it was in this dstrict that the fiercest battle was fought against the feudal system withholding popular participation in local governance.[13] On the other hand more people belonging to panchayats of Bhilwara district, which lies in the remote interior, have preferred the sound adjudicative role of the panchayati raj institutions to any other reason. This is not precisely the role assigned to three-tiered panchayati raj structure except in its wider connotation.[14] This might also be a legacy of the past when adjudication or arbitration was usually considered the primary function of local structures, formal or informal. Thus, in Bhilwara the expectations are still much more rooted in tradition as against the developmental requirements usually associated with structures of a moderni-zing society.

   The comparison of elite and citizen responses also brings out that the difference is not so much of kind as of degree. Thus fewer citizens (in percentage terms) expect the performance of deve-lopmental and self-governance roles. On the other hand, 'better justice' is expected by a higher percentage of citizens—percen-tages of citizen and elite respondents selecting this category being 21.5 and 12.3, respectively. And as the citizens are less

---

13. This is true at least, in the districts of our sample. Interviews with the pradhan of Ladnun panchayat samiti and zila pramukh, Nagaur Zila Parishad, also confirm this observation.
14. It may be pointed out, however, that the concept of 'justice' held by the rural folk, is somewhat wider than the legal concept. To rural people 'justice' stands both for a just share in benefits accruing to a community as much as for legalistic connotation implying settlement of disputes.

exposed to the outer world, it is not unnatural that their role expectations centre on legacies of the past.

Turning to the citizens' role expectations in the light of their social background, it was found that the correlation with educational background does not provide us with any significant difference except in terms of degree. Thus, while almost an equal number (24.8% of the total of illiterate and 26.7% of the total of literate citizens) expected panchayati raj to ensure 'better administration of justice', the emphasis on expectation of developmental plans varies somewhat. Thus, more illiterate citizens (40.4%) than literate ones (36.7%) opt for this expectation. On the other hand, more literate citizens (23.3%) than illiterate ones (18.3%) think of panchayati raj as a local self-government device. But this difference is not very significant, since a still higher percentage (36.7%) of the literate group selects the developmental role. Contrary to the role expectations of the elite, it is observed here that education does not play a very significant role in shaping the expectations of the citizens. Two qualifying observations need be made in regard to this finding. First, the educational achievements of citizens are comparatively lower than those of the elite. Second, it has also been observed in the villages that the mobility of the citizens is not correlated with educational achievements. And mobility imparts some political education as well as helps in shaping modern attitudes.

Analysing the responses caste-wise, no appreciable variation in terms of role perception is visible. The developmental role and its speedy fulfilment is an expectation held by a greater number of middle and lower caste citizens than by higher caste citizens. The highest percentage of responses favouring panchayati raj as a 'local self-government device', are contributed by the lower caste group. This only means that, as this group was deprived of participation in local affairs in the traditional order, they would emphasize this role in the hope that they would now get opportunities to participate in these institutions on a basis of equality. Again, the role in regard to 'help to poor' is selected by citizens of both middle and lower social strata, which may be reflecting their comparatively poor economic condition.

NEGATIVE REACTIONS

Together with the question (already analysed) whether "panchayati raj was welcomed by the people of your area", another question was addressed to elite respondents enquiring whether "any significant opposition was offered in certain quarters to panchayati raj on the eve of its introduction and, if so, how do you account for it ?" The highest percentage of respondents recalling the phenomenon of opposition belongs to Nagaur. Now we turn to an analysis of the second part of the question, *i.e.*, reasons advanced by the respondents for opposition. Table 5. 2 presents the data.

It is clear from the table that the most over-riding consideration for opposing panchayati raj, as perceived by elite respondents, was the fear that the innovative device might adversely affect their interests (61.5%). As more than half of these belong to Nagaur district, it can be assumed that such a reaction emanated from either a feudal hold or feudal legacies. It might also be recalled that these interests opposed panchayati raj even on the floor of the Vidhan Sabha from time to time and kept pressurising the government to dilute the scheme. It is understandable why men of the feudal order should come forward to oppose panchayati raj since it provides for participation of the people, without any discrimination, in elections to and working of the institute. The superior status enjoyed by feudal interests was put into direct jeopardy. Other reasons advanced are not so significant. About 15.4% of the respondents said that the opposition was due to the fear that the change in institutional structure would not mean a change in the nature of exercise of influence and the elected elements might also prove equally oppressive. And 11.5% of the respondents held that the opposition was a result of ignorance. However, as the responses in these categories are minimal, one cannot verify the extent of seriousness of these responses. It is also possible that an assessment of performance may have influenced the responses to the query addressed to them a decade after the introduction of panchayati raj.

We now turn to the analysis of the reaction of the elite to the introduction of panchayati raj. The question asked of the elite respondents was : "How did you react to the introduction of panchayati raj ? Did you welcome it or did you not ?" From

TABLE 5.2

Reasons for some People's Opposition to Panchayati Raj

District	Fear of self-interest being hit		New oppressors to replace old		Ignorance of goals		N. R.		Total	
	No.	%	No.	%	No.	%	No.	%	No.	%
Ganganagar	2	100.0	–	–	–	–	–	–	2	100.0
Nagaur	9	90.0	–	–	1	10.0	–	–	10	100.0
Bhilwara	3	60.0	1	20.0	–	–	1	20.0	5	100.0
Jhalawar	1	25.0	2	50.0	1	25.0	–	–	4	100.0
Bharatpur	1	20.0	1	20.0	1	20.0	2	40.0	5	100.0
Total	16	61.5	4	15.4	3	11.5	3	11.5	26	100.0

this question we expected the respondents to specify whether they consciously welcomed panchayati raj and, if so, why ? We had assumed that we would not be told by a respondent that he had opposed the move. We, therefore, put forward a structured question with only two alternatives : 'yes, welcomed' and 'no, did not welcome'. The data show that an explicit response welcoming panchayati raj is higher than in the earlier case. Here, 84.2% of elite respondents speak of having accorded welcome, while earlier only 76.2% had said so. It has already been reported in earlier chapters that with the advent of panchayati raj the nature of the elite structure has largely been changed in favour of agricultural castes. It is, therefore, quite possible that members of the former elite group belonging to upper castes, such as Rajputs, would apprehend a constraint on their influence in the wake of panchayati raj and so would refrain from according it a welcome. On the other hand, the peasant caste elite persons who came to dominate the scene would welcome it not only for the reason of developmental benefits, but also because it could ensure a greater say for them in village affairs owing to their numerical superiority. Since members of peasant caste elite group have gained in terms of participation, a higher percentage of positive response is understandable here.

District-wise, the highest number of positive response (93.9%) comes from Nagaur ; Bharatpur follows with 88.6% positive responses. Ganganagar (80.6%) is in third place, while in the earlier analysis it was at the top. The change might be due to several reasons : first as seen in chapter 2, Ganganagar leads in intensity of participation by the younger generation (below 30). Second, some of the elite respondents happen to be recent migrants from the nearby state of Punjab, who might have given a casual reply. On the other hand, the positive response from Jhalawar has been to the tune of 58.8%. But the present case under the discussion, shows that as many as 84.2% of the elite respondents have given a positive reply. When we analyze the responses 'position-wise' we do not find material difference.

It is natural to ask who these 26 respondents (15.99 of the total) who refrained from welcoming panchayati raj, are and why they did so. A correlation of such replies with age, education and caste variables provides only marginal insight into this question. The data make it clear that poor perception of a new phenomenon (generally associated with the lower age-group, with lower education and with lower caste levels), is not a contributing factor in the indifference shown in certain circles to panchayati raj (except, partially for the age-group 'below 30'). For example, the respondents in the 'above matric' category show similar indifference as do those in other literacy groups.

Table 5.3 presents the data related to reasons advanced by elite respondents for welcoming the introduction of panchayati raj. The picture is not a very different one from that obtained in the case of the reasons for welcoming of panchayati raj by people in general. Here again, (except in Nagaur) an over-whelming percentage of respondents considered panchayati raj as a device for expediting developmental works. Nagaur presents a slightly different picture, as only 32.1% respondents have advanced expeditious execution of 'development pro-grammes' as a reason. This is very low as the second lowest response percentage in this category, from Bhilwara comes to 51.8%. The gap between Nagaur (32.1%) and Bhilwara (51.8%) is much more than the gap between Bhilwara (51.8%) and Ganganagar (66.7%), which records the highest response. But, on the other hand, the responses favouring 'local people held in-charge of planning' and 'relief from feudal grip' are highest in Nagaur (28.5% and 36.8%, respectively). This only substantiates the proposition that the people of Nagaur, who lived for a long time under *Jagirdari* system, had come to look upon the innovation of panchayati raj as an effective alternative and as an opportunity for participation in local affairs. This points to a greater emphasis on the political aspect—that is, participation in the exercise of power rather than cognizance of the potentialities of development. In other districts also this trend is perceptible. Bhilwara comes next. In the districts of Bharatpur and Jhalawar also the responses are substantial. However, from the above analysis one thing is clear. It would be seen that the expectations of members of the elite group tended to favour heavily 'developmental' and 'political roles' whereas other roles, such as the extension of social education and social change, were lost sight of.

TABLE 5.3

Reasons for Elite Respondents' Welcome to Panchayati Raj

District	Quicker developmental activities		Local people held incharge of planning		Better and cheaper justice		Relief from feudal grip		Others		Total	
	No.	%	No.	%	No.	%	No.	%	No.	%	No.	%
Ganganagar	18 66.7	23.7	5 18.5	15.6	3 11.3	33.3	– –	–	1 3.7	50.0	27 100.0	19.6
Nagaur	9 32.1	11.8	9 32.1	28.1	3 10.7	33.3	7 25.0	36.8	– –	–	28 100.0	20.3
Bhilwara	14 51.8	18.4	7 25.9	21.9	1 3.7	11.1	5 18.7	26.3	– –	–	27 100.0	19.6
Jhalawar	16 64.0	21.1	5 20.0	15.6	1 4.0	11.1	3 12.0	15.8	– –	–	25 100.0	18.1
Bharatpur	19 61.3	25.0	6 19.4	18.8	1 3.2	11.1	4 12.9	21.1	1 3.2	50.0	31 100.0	22.4
Total	76 55.1	100.0	32 23.2	100.0	9 6.5	100.0	19 13.8	100.0	2 1.4	100.0	138 100.0	100.0

THE IDEAL PANCHAYAT: SOME IMAGE PROFILES

The next question concerned expectations of an ideal panchayat, which was related to earlier questions about expectations of panchayati raj in general. The question read as follows : "What important activities in your opinion should an ideal panchayat perform ? Please specify in order of priority." This was an open-ended question addressed to both elite respondents and citizens.

For purposes of analysis, however, we have considered only the first two responses. Table 5.4 is self-explanatory. Among elite respondents, the maximum preference (31.1% of responses) was in favour of the traditional role of providing justice, while the first priority of the largest number of citizens (29.5%) is modern, relating to 'provision for civic amenities'. The perception of priorities varies significantly. Citizens appear to be concerned more with their day-to-day needs, such as drinking-water facilities, health and sanitation, street-lighting and so on. The elites treat civic amenities as a second priority because perhaps they already enjoy them and as such do not feel a pressing need of them as much as the citizens do. The other two favoured responses relate to ensuring 'village development' and 'social justice'. It will not be out of place to mention here that the expression 'social justice', as a role expectation, has generally been viewed in the context that the panchayats (institutionally, and through the executive head, the sarpanch) are empowered to allot *abadi* (habitable) plots, recommend cases for allotment of agricultural land, administer the distribution of fertilizers etc.[15]

A district-wise analysis brings out certain interesting trends in this context. In Ganganagar, the maximum emphasis has been

15. Recently some of these powers have been fully, or partially, transferred to the bureaucracy. For instance, in case of land allotment, the sub-divisional officer has been given the final say so much so that he can ignore completely the recommendations of the sarpanch and the pradhan. In the course of informal discussions, several respondents held the view that the sarpanch continued to play an effective role in several ways, for instance in allotment of land, or where a school might be located. It seems this is not entirely baseless, with exceptions, where a sarpanch does not belong to a pradhan's party or group.

TABLE 5.4

Expected Roles of an Ideal Panchayat

Nature of role expectation	Elite Respondents				Citizen Respondents			
	I Preference		II Preference		I Preference		II Preference	
	No.	%	No.	%	No.	%	No.	%
Providing justice honestly	51	31.1	29	17.7	35	17.5	28	14.0
Providing civic amenities	28	17.1	40	24.4	59	29.5	34	17.0
Striving for development of village	32	19.5	29	17.7	38	19.0	37	18.5
Striving for social justice	32	19.5	21	12.8	30	15.0	27	13.5
Striving for village harmony	5	3.0	3	1.8	4	2.0	1	0.5
Others	11	6.7	10	6.1	16	8.0	5	2.5
Total	159	96.9	132	80.5	182	91.0	132	66.0
N. R./D. K.	5	3.1	32	19.5	18	9.0	68	34.0
Grand Total	164	100.0	164	100.0	200	100.0	200	100.0

laid, both by the elite and citizen respondents, on 'ensuring social justice'. It is followed by 'civic amenities' and ensuring 'village development'. On the other hand, 'village development' is expected by 32.0% of citizens in Nagaur and 31.1% of elite respondents in Bhilwara districts. Thus, in a more developed district like Ganganagar, people have started emphasizing the distributive aspect, while in the less-developed districts 'development' is held to be an important priority. It will thus be noted that the process of development sharpens the power of perceptions of various constituents in society as some are better placed to make greater use of opportunities, while others lag behind.[16] Thus in Ganganagar, the greater number of people expect panchayati raj to ensure social justice by dissemination of the gains of development. It remains an open question whether the emphasis on the developmental role of panchayati raj has in any way resulted in the ignoring of the distributive aspect of development and provisions for civic amenities in rural areas—which are universally needed. Also, if more and more emphasis is placed by members of the elite group in Bhilwara and citizens of Nagaur on the developmental aspect they have shown greater articulation on this count than in regard to other important public utilities.

In the districts of Bharatpur and Jhalawar elite respondents have placed nearly equal emphasis upon the traditional and modern roles, the former relating to 'providing of justice'. and the latter concerning 'civic amenities' and 'social justice'. About 20% of the responses belong to each of the two categories in both the districts.

An analysis of the same trend by caste does not bring out differences of much consequence, except that a greater percentage (both of elite persons and citizens) belonging to upper castes have placed emphasis on 'providing justice', than elite and citizen respondents of the other caste groups have done. Still, while the elite of middle and lower caste groups have closely followed their upper caste counterparts in demanding

16. Gunnar, Myrdal has focussed attention very effectively on the aspect of development on the basis of a comparative view of results of certain studies made in this regard. See *Asian Drama : An Enquiry into the Poverty of Nations*, II (Penguin Books, 1968), pp. 849-900.

'justice', the citizens in these two caste categories have put greater emphasis on 'civic amenities' and 'developmental needs'.

ROLE PERFORMANCE

The expectations that are held from a particular institution or office is one thing and performance of roles quite another. Though role expectation, in a normative sense, sets the limits, it is only one of the several factors influencing role behaviour. It is thus necessary to delineate a profile of role performance against the background of role expectations to articulate, at least at the level of our consciousness, the pattern of congruence or gap between the two, as the case may be.

The first question asked in this regard related to the performance of panchayati raj in general. It reads : "Do you think that popular expectations from panchayati raj have been fulfilled ?" It was addressed to elite respondents in structured form and provided alternatives as 'fulfilled', 'partially fulfilled', 'not at all fulfilled' and 'can't say'. It was thought that definite reactions of citizen respondents would be difficult to obtain and hence only elite respondents were asked the question. A much simpler question was put to the citizens.

The replies received from the elite respondents to the above question do not give a bright assessment of the performance of panchayati raj in general. Only 14.0% of the respondents believed that the expectations have been fulfilled. About 40.9% of the respondents saw a partial realization of expectations, while 42.7% saw a complete frustration of popular expectations. Whether in actual operation panchayati raj has or has not achieved perceptible results is quite another matter, it has failed as far as elite and popular perceptions go. A district-wise analysis of responses brings out only minor variations in this respect. Thus, in Bharatpur 28.6% of the respondents say that popular expectations have been fulfilled, while in other districts not even half of the respondents are of this opinion. Bhilwara registers the highest negative response (54.8%). We shall go into specific reasons for the district-wise response pattern later. It can, however, be surmised on the basis of discussions in the field that elite respondents who themselves had been deprived of an effective say in the managment of panchayati raj institutions, have responded negatively. Thus, in Bhilwara where, comparatively speaking, the elite has less to its credit in educational and economic terms, a feeling of deprivation is perceptible, which in turn has perhaps conditioned the response of its members.

A study of reactions position-wise strengthens the contention made above. While more than half of the higher level functionaries (*i.e.*, sarpanch, pradhan, zila pramukh, etc.), speak of 'partial fulfilment', as many as 41.3% of 'panchas etc.' and 67.6% of 'reputational elite' members treat panchayati raj as a completely frustrating experience. This gives credence to the findings made out in certain other studies that panchayati raj has come to serve only those who control important offices or who are allies of these office-holders.

An attempt at a correlation between the degree of popular expectations fulfilled and the specific roles expected of panchayati raj was also made. The inferences that emerge do not bring out any significant pattern, except that one-third of elite respondents expecting better justice from panchayati raj feel fully satisfied with panchayati raj ; of course, this response is more than double than that favouring fulfilment in any other category, but the total response in the category of 'better justice expected' is too meagre (9 or 5.5% of total 164 respondents) to warrant any significant generalization. This also falsifies the claim that panchayati raj has done a shade better in the field of administration of justice.

Taking up the category of 'partial fulfilment', some significant correlation can be established with the responses for the first two categories of role expectations. It is clear that 58% of the respondents who expected 'expeditious developmental programmes' have a sense of partial fufilment, while only 34.4% of the respondents expecting plans to be locally prepared and executed, have a sense of partial fulfilment. Even if we treat the responses received in the category of 'partial fulfilment' of expectations as positive, which in fact, they are not, and group them with the category of 'total fulfilment', the results would not be to any considerable extent altered. It would, however, seem that respondents expecting 'expeditious developmental works' have a greater satisfaction than those who expected panchayati raj to enable local people to prepare and execute plans for themselves. Thus, while some developmental works have been carried out, the objective of letting people prepare and execute plans in the light of their felt needs, has been realised to a much lesser extent. The frustration here may be a result of bureaucratic execution of developmental programmes under panchayati raj.[17] Similarly, very few people feel completely liberated from the feudal grip.

The next question sought to ascertain reasons for the perception of complete or partial realization or frustration of popular expectations. The elite respondents who thought that popular expectations have been fulfilled, argue that 'developmental works' and various social services have been ensured on a larger scale. As far as the analysis of the reasons for frustration goes, it would not affect our analysis if the two responses concerning partial fulfilment of people's expectations or total frustration are grouped together, as done in table 5.5. Thus the largest number of responses (29.9%) fall in the category of 'lack of assistance from government', meaning thereby lack of financial and technical assistance or even expeditious execution of developmental schemes. By inference, the official attitude is taken as hindrance to the realization of people's expectations. A substantial number of elite respondents (43.0%) blame their own counter-parts as being responsible for the frustrating situation: 20.4% allege involvement of

17. Besides, the responses we have analyzed, the field experience and observational reports of certain zila parishad and panchayat samiti meetings also suggest this explanation. For example, in a zila parishad meeting it was found that most of the talking was done by the Collector in his capacity as District Development Officer. The zila pramukh, who presided over the meeting, looked more like an assistant to the Collector who received reports from the vikash adhikaris and instructed them for future course of action.

The pradhan of Jhalrapatan panchayat samiti explained the point very well with the help of an illustration. He said in the course of an interview that "we, the panchayati raj representatives, are like the riders who have been told by the government that you are the masters and can direct the horses to any way, but the reins have been handed over to the person sitting behind us and designated as assistant to us. Now anybody can guess who really rides the horse."

TABLE 5.5

Reasons for Frustration or only Partial Realization of People's Expectations from Panchayati Raj

District	Factional Politics No.	%	Corrupt elected officials No.	%	Lack of assistance by govt. No.	%	Apathy of rural people No.	%	Others No.	%	N. R. No.	%	Total No.	%
Ganganagar	7 24.1	25.0	6 20.7	24.0	3 10.3	7.3	– 	–	3 10.3	21.4	10 34.5	43.5	29 100.0	21.2
Nagaur	11 39.3	39.3	6 21.4	24.0	8 28.6	19.5	1 3.6	16.7	– 	–	2 7.1	8.7	28 100.0	20.4
Bhilwara	1 3.7	3.6	4 14.8	16.0	12 44.4	29.2	2 7.4	33.3	2 7.4	14.3	6 22.2	26.1	27 100.0	19.7
Jhalawar	5 16.7	17.8	4 13.3	16.0	9 30.0	22.0	1 3.3	16.7	6 20.0	42.9	5 16.7	21.7	30 100.0	21.9
Bharatpur	4 17.4	14.3	5 21.7	20.0	9 39.1	22.0	2 8.7	33.3	3 13.0	21.4	– 	–	23 100.0	16.8
Total	28 20.4	100.0	25 18.2	100.0	41 29.9	100.0	6 4.4	100.0	14 10.2	100.0	23 16.8	100.0	137 100.0	100.0

persons of the elite group in factional politics ; 18.2% attribute corrupt tactics to them; and 4.4% allege there is 'apathy of the rural people' owing to which cooperation is not easily forthcoming.

A district-wise analysis brings out the following points : whereas Ganganagar and Nagaur (24.1% and 39.3% of responses respectively) reflect 'factional politics' as a major factor, Bhilwara, Jhalawar and Bharatpur (44.4%, 30.0% and 39.1% of responses respectively) choose 'lack of assistance by the government' as the major factor. We have already discussed factionalism in Ganganagar and Nagaur. In Bhilwara, Jhalawar and Bharatpur, where the pace of development has been halting, and where the elite, comparatively speaking, has acquired less educationally and economically, blaming the government for lack of assistance is not altogether a surprise.

In order to ascertain the assessment of citizen respondents of the performance of panchayati raj, a much simpler and more direct question was addressed to them : "Have you been a beneficiary of panchayati raj in any way ?" An analysis of the responses show that, in all, only 25% citizens feel benefited by panchayati raj. This is a sad reflection on the performance of panchayati raj. The details show that the affirmative response is very low in Bhilwara (10%) and Bharatpur (6%). Even where it is higher—Ganganagar (36%), Jhalawar (26%) and Nagaur (22%)— the % response is not flattering. The negative responses show Bharatpur in the lead (24.7%), followed by Bhilwara (23.3%), Nagaur (19.3%), Jhalawar (18%) and Ganganagar (14.7%). It is significant to recall that in Bharatpur 28.6% of the elite respondents had reported full realization of expectations of panchayati raj. The overall picture seems to be that the elite has failed to extend the benefits to the common man and hence the frustrating responses of the latter.

A look into the replies of citizens identifying the benefits of panchayati raj shows that modernization of agriculture seems to have caught the imagination of the citizens ; 36% of the respondents pointed to that followed by 22.0% who considered extension of education as a major benefit. This may be due, primarily, to the handing over of primary education to panch-

panchayati raj institutions. Fourteen per cent feel benefited on account of better land management. It should be recalled here that panchayati raj functionaries had been assigned a prominent role in matters such as allotment of land and mutations. Significantly, the role of panchayati raj institutions in regard to provision of civic amenities and extension of justice[18] have not impressed the citizens in good measure (the responses are 6% and 8%, respectively).

A district-wise analysis of the data brings out the distribution of emphasis on benefits of modernized agriculture as follows : in Ganganagar (33.3%), Bhilwara (27.8%) and Jhalawar (27.8%), whereas extension of education has been acknowledged in the case of Ganganagar to the tune of 72.7% responses. The literacy percentage is highest in that district, and reports suggest that in this district attendance of children in the primary schools is not a problem, as it is in other districts.[19] In terms of better land management, Jhalawar respondents give the maximum response to the tune of 57.1%.

A correlation of the same data by caste status offered some significant trends. While the upper and middle castes felt most benefited by better facilities for agriculture (44.4% and 41.7% respectively), the lower castes felt benefited by land reforms (29.4%). In regard to educational and drinking water facilities, the middle castes (29.2% and 12.5% of them respectively) felt most benefited. Whereas this pattern reflects an uneven distribution of benefits, it also suggests that, but for the legal provisions, the lower castes would not have got even the very limited benefits that they have received. Altogether the local elite has, by and large, failed in ensuring an even distribution

18. It has been reported from various sources that the withdrawal of judicial function from village panchayats and its being handed over to the nyaya panchayat, has worsened the situation.

19. For a detailed coverage of this aspect, see : Naik, J. P., *The Report of Rajasthan State Primary Education Committee* (Jaipur, Government of Rajasthan, 1965) and Iqbal Narain, Pande, K. C. and Sharma, Mohan Lal : *Panchyati Raj and Educational Administration*, (Jaipur Aalekh Publishers, 1976)

TABLE 5.6

Assessment by Elite Respondents of Performance of One's Own Panchayat

District	Ideal		Average		Poor		Can't say		Total	
	No.	%	No.	%	No.	%	No.	%	No.	%
Gangangar	9	25.7	15	15.8	7	25.9	–	–	31	18.9
Nagaur	2	5.7	16	16.8	14	51.9	1	14.3	33	20.1
Bhilwara	3	8.6	23	24.2	4	14.8	1	14.3	31	18.9
Jhalawar	12	34.3	19	20.0	–	–	3	42.8	34	20.7
Bharatpur	9	25.7	22	23.2	2	7.4	2	28.6	35	21.4
Total	35	100.0	95	100.0	27	100.0	7	100.0	164	100.0
	21.3		57.9		16.5		4.3		100.0	

of benefits among the various strata in society.[20]

We moved from the general to the specific when we asked another question relating to the performance of the respondent's own panchayat. "Considering your expectations of an ideal panchayat, how would you rate the performance of your own panchayat—has it approximated your ideal, or has it been average or poor?" Table 5.6 shows that a majority of respondents (58.0%) consider the performance of their own panchayat to be 'average'; 21.3% consider it to be a case of ideal performance, and 16.5% say that the performance has been 'poor'. A district-wise analysis brings out some variation. While the highest percentage of responses calling the performance 'ideal' comes from Jhalawar (34.3%), the highest response for 'poor' performance has been registered in Nagaur (51.9%). To an extent, the assessment is to be viewed in the light of rising expectations. But it is also relevant that in Jhalawar, officials could ensure that schools, dispensary, electricity, drinking water facilities are provided, thereby satisfying, to some extent, the respondents' expectations. Elite respondents of the area contend that the panchayat has provided all amenities; it is for the people to make use of them. On the other hand, as already reported, Nagaur is faction-ridden ; no meetings of panchayats were held for months and, consequently, developmental projects were ignored. In Bhilwara, nearly half of the respondents speak of 'average' performance and the main contention is that their panchayat might not have done much for development but it has also not been an agency oppressing the common man.

In addition, citizens were asked directly whether they felt satisfied with the performance of their respective panchayats.

20. A few illustrations as given by the respondents, while replying to the question, should make the point clear. In the panchayat selected for study in Jhalawar, the Harijans were denied access to the drinking water wells sunk with the help of panchayat samiti. The pretext advanced was that the Harijans had offered no contribution to the construction of the well, but the fact was that they were not asked to do so. Similarly, in all the districts, it has been observed that the caste Hindus resist very much the allotment of land to lower castes. Even where land is allotted, the latter are not allowed to take possession of it. And the sarpanchas and the pradhans would not listen to petitions of lower sections in this regard.

It was evident from the replies that more than half (52.5%) felt satisfied ; 44% expressed their dissatisfaction, and 1.5% were unconcerned.   District-wise, the comparison showed that more citizens of Bhilwara and Jhalawar were dissatisfied than those of other districts.   What is more surprising is that the elite respondents of Jhalawar had the highest response affirming in ideal performance of their panchayat. This shows a wide gap on thinking of the elite and the citizenry.   Also, this only confirms the earlier conclusion that often the benefits are appropriated by a limited section of society, leaving others with a feeling of deprivation.

A comparison of the patterns of response regarding performance of their panchayats and of panchayati raj in general shows that a greater percentage of citizens feel satisfied with their own panchayat than feel benefited by panchayati raj ; 52.5% of the citizens are satisfied with their panchayat, while only 25.0% feel benefited by panchayati raj in one way or the other.   This wide gap might be ascribed to the fact that in terms of benefits the individual is closest to his own institution while panchayati raj in its totality, is not so near to his perception and reach.   Also, citizen respondents said that they were fearful of adverse reactions of the elite if they made adverse comments about their own panchayat.   All the assurances that their responses would be kept confidential and that the enquiry was exclusively academic could not convince them.   The responses, therefore, have to be assessed against this background.

ROLE CONSTRAINTS

Another important facet of the study of roles relates to an enquiry into the factors that constrain panchayati raj functionaries.   Often, role performance falls short of expectations ; at other times, it deviates from the norms set or evolved.   We have already looked into these shortfalls in the preceding section.   The present section seeks to identify the factors acting as constraints on role performance.   We considered some constraints on an *a-priori* basis and put them to the respondents for their reaction.   Among the more important factors identified in advance were statutory provisions, bureaucratic modes of development administration, and factional and pressure politics.

STATUTORY PROVISIONS

Often the State government is held responsible for starving panchayati raj institutions of powers and resources, as a consequence of which goal realization is hampered. The question in this context read : "Do you think the powers delegated to panchayati raj institutions by the State government are sufficient to enable them to play their role effectively ?" Table 5.7 gives the pattern of responses to this question. One can see that 54.3% of elite respondents consider the present powers to be sufficient, 31.7% consider them to be insufficient, while 14.0% have no comments to offer. Viewed in the light of responses on fulfilment of expectations from panchayati raj (where only 14% of respondents spoke of total fulfilment of expectations), the response from more than half of the respondents that the powers are sufficient means that a large number of respondents absolve the government of the starvation charge and attribute their frustration to other factors.

The district-wise pattern is even more revealing. The feeling that 'powers are sufficient' is most prevalent among the elite of the comparatively developed district of Ganganagar, followed by those of Nagaur and Bharatpur districts. The feeling of insufficiency of powers is held most by the elite of Jhalawar district. Thus the level of development cannot be taken as a variable to explain the pattern of responses received to the question. What appears to be more plausible is that this is due to the phenomenon of political linkages that the local leaders develop, directly or through some intermediaries, with the State level leaders, especially of the ruling party, who are usually considered important in ensuring fulfilment of expectations. Thus Ganganagar district has been represented by four members in the State Council of Ministers. Similarly, Nagaur took pride in three leaders of State stature. On the other hand, Jhalawar district seemed to have lost even a token share among leadership after the death in 1967 of Raja Harishchandra, who was a senior State Congress leader and a minister of standing and renown. The responses of elite respondents of that district, therefore, need to be analyzed against this background.

TABLE 5.7

Sufficiency of Powers Delegated to Panchayati Raj Institutions

District	Powers are sufficient		Powers are not sufficient		Can't say		Total	
	No.	%	No.	%	No.	%	No.	%
Ganganagar	25	28.1	4	7.7	2	8.7	31	18.9
	80.6		12.9		6.5		100.0	
Nagaur	20	22.5	9	17.3	4	17.4	33	20.1
	60.6		27.3		12.1		100.0	
Bhilwara	13	14.6	16	30.8	2	8.7	31	18.9
	41.9		51.6		6.5		100.0	
Jhalawar	12	13.5	13	25.0	9	39.1	34	20.7
	35.3		38.2		26.5		100.0	
Bharatpur	19	21.3	10	19.2	6	26.1	35	21.4
	54.3		28.6		17.1		100.0	
Total	89	100.0	52	100.0	23	100.0	164	100.0
	54.3		31.7		14.0		100.0	

Continuing the analysis, responses by position were also collated. It was found that insufficiency of powers is felt more by those who are directly concerned with the execution of plans and decisions of local bodies. Thus, 50.0% of the 'Sarpanchas etc.' (this category includes pradhans and zila pramukhs as well) find the powers to be insufficient, whereas only 27.0% of 'panchas etc., and 8.1% of elite persons in reputational category (the latter hold no official position) deem the powers vested in panchayati raj institutions to be insufficient. A significant number (29.7%) of reputational elite persons have no comments to offer. Perhaps they withheld their comments because of lack of experience of the working of these bodies. A majority of elite respondents (54.3%), including a substantial number (43.7%) of 'sarpanchas etc.' (who are directly concerned with the exercise of executive powers), think the powers are sufficient, 31.7% feel that powers are insufficient, and 14% have no comments to make.

To seek the reasons for their responses, a straight question was put : "Why do you think so ?" The replies show that, while 43.8% of the respondents believe that no essential work has been left undone, 37.1% respondents have some other reasons to offer : 27.0% contend that these institutions are manned by incapable incumbents.[22] For them, the major trouble with panchayati raj institutions, therefore, is not a dearth of powers but of proper persons getting elected to these institutions. Other answers in this regard assumed these forms : 'work suffers owing to hostile officials' (6.7%), or 'paucity of resources' (3.4%). Thus, to some extent, the bureaucratic structure is also treated as a constraint. District-wise, the bureaucratic constraint has been identified most strongly in Jhalawar district by (50% of the respondents) while the incapacity of elected representatives was the most prominent (with 37.5% of responses) in Ganganagar.

In reviewing this analysis in juxtaposition with that of the role performance of panchayati raj in general and panchayats in particular, a little caution is needed. It would not be safe

---

22. Incapacity of the incumbents, as the respondents interpreted it, means lack of maturity, absence of capacity to lead and guide, and want of articulate involvement.

to assume that since a majority of respondents consider powers to be sufficient, they are also satisfied with the performance of panchayati raj. What the respondents, in fact, want to emphasize is that the trouble lies not so much in the quantum of delegated powers but in their exercise.

Table 5.8 organizes the replies of those elite respondents who think the existing powers are insufficient and have therefore been asked : "What additional powers are needed to enable panchayati raj institutions to play an effective role?" We have considered only the first three replies in our analysis. However, as the table shows, only 28.8% of the respondents supplied three responses to the open-ended question. Summing up all the three replies, as has been done in the table, it should be noted that out of 156 total expected replies, 66.7% are cases where response, varying between 1 to 3 replies, has been available, and the remaining 33.3% forms the 'no reply' category.

The most sought-after alternative relates to added powers of adjudication of civil and criminal cases. It will not be out of place to mention here that the Government of Rajasthan has recently done so. This digression apart, the members of the elite group, in fact, want the panchayats to be empowered to deal with cases involving a sum of more than Rs. 250/-, which is the upper ceiling today, and that they be entitled to deal with even serious criminal cases. Another 9.0% seek merger of *nyay* panchayats with *vikas* panchayats. To them, the separation of the two functions, development and settlement of disputes, has robbed both types of panchayats of effective functioning. If we collate these two replies it will appear that nearly 27.6% seek reorganization and re-strengthening of panchayats by enhancing their powers related to the settlement of disputes. Next in order are responses seeking additional revenue powers. While some respondents (12.8%) would stick to the delegation of revenue collection powers to panchayats, only a few (1.9%) demand that all the revenue functions be handed over to panchayati raj institutions by placing the *patwaries* and *tehsildars* under panchayats and panchayat samitis, respectively. There are 11.5% of the respondents who seek additional financial powers. The category of 'others' includes demands

TABLE 5.8

Nature of Additional Powers Required for Panchayati Raj Institutions

Preference	Additional civil and criminal powers		Nyay Panchayats be merged into Vikas Panchayats		Additional revenue powers		Additional financial powers	
	No.	%	No.	%	No.	%	No.	%
1	2	3	4	5	6	7	8	9
First	12 / 23.1	41.4	10 / 19.2	71.5	15 / 28.8	75.0	8 / 15.4	44.4
Second	14 / 26.9	48.3	3 / 5.8	21.4	4 / 7.7	20.0	7 / 13.5	38.9
Third	3 / 5.8	10.3	1 / 1.9	7.1	1 / 1.9	5.0	3 / 5.8	16.7
Total	29 / 18.6	100.0	14 / 9.0	100.0	20 / 12.8	100.0	18 / 11.5	100.0

TABLE 5.8 (Contd.)

Preference	Local bureaucracy be surbordinated to people's representatives		Others		N. R.		Total	
	No.	%	No.	%	No.	%	No.	%
1	10	11	12	13	14	15	16	17
First	–	–	6 11.5	30.0	1 1.9	1.9	52 100.0	33.3
Second	2 3.8	66.7	8 15.4	40.0	14 26.9	26.9	52 100.0	33.3
Third	1 1.9	33.3	6 11.5	30.0	37 71.2	71.2	52 100.0	33.3
Total	3 1.9	100.0	20 12.8	100.0	52 33.3	100.0	156 100.0	100.0

for empowering panchayati raj institutions to issue gun licences, subordinating local police to panchayats and so on. It is really revealing that the elite does not want any additional powers for the panchayats in the developmental sphere.

A separate question enquired of whether panchayati raj institutions had adequate financial powers. The assumption was that delegation of financial powers constituted the crux of transfer of developmental obligations. It appears that 54.9% of the elite respondents think financial powers are insufficient, while only 31.7% had held earlier that powers of general character were insufficient. The inference is obvious that in the absence of, or with the dilution of, effective financial resources, panchayati raj institutions are starved.

Position-wise, the trends are, more or less, identical with our earlier analysis : with 32.2% of the panchas etc., 58.9% of the sarpanchas etc., and 8.9% of the reputational elite respondents feel that financial powers are inadequate. Respondents in the 'sarpanchas etc.' category feel more strongly that the financial powers are inadequate because they are most intimately concerned with the execution of developmental plans.

When asked to elaborate, elite respondents enumerated two basic issues involved in the phenomenon of limited financial powers. One related to problems of tax-structure and another to those of the tax-collection mechanism. It was also widely felt that the State government had been miserly in delegating financial powers and has granted much less discretion to panchayati raj institutions than expected. As a consequence, the district level staff of revenue, agriculture and animal husbandry continue to perform functions which should have been delegated to panchayati raj institutions. Revenue authorities, by and large, were thought to be non-cooperative and the whole policy structure of grants came in for adverse comments.

THE BUREAUCRATIC SET-UP

Development administration operating under the framework of panchayati raj, is an innovation in rural India. The performance of the bureaucracy has not been considered very flattering[23] and, as a consequence, developmental needs

23. Douglas Ensminger of the Ford Foundation, who played a leading role in community development programme in India, has made a

have usually been neglected or muddled. The role of bureaucracy and its allied functionaries[24] assumes added importance in the context of the emphasis on developmental needs.

The first question addressed to elite respondents in this regard read : "In your opinion, are the officials in charge of different aspects of Community Development Programmes and associated with panchayati raj adequate in numbers and capable of delivering the goods ?"

The responses show that, in all, 59.1% of the respondents felt that there was sufficiency of staff, while 14.6% disagreed; the rest, 26.2% had no comments to offer. District-wise, the maximum support for the view that the staff is sufficient comes from Bharatpur (27.8%), while the most support (24.2% of responses) of the opposite view comes from Nagaur. It was discovered that in districts where staffing was adequate the response was positive. In Nagaur, especially, the negative response is due to under-staffing at the panchayat samiti level.[25] The maximum numbers of elite respondents in Jhalawar district are in the 'no-comments' category, (25.6%) followed by Bhilwara (23.3%). It

significant observation in these words, "the present caste system that operates within the administrative hierarchy is a further major deterrent to the success of the community programmes." V. T. Krishnamachari, former Vice-Chairman of the Planning Commission, has similarly observed : "The greatest obstacle to development in India, in my view, has always been the mental distance between those who are 'educated' and those who are 'not educated'. I have an impression that this mental distance has been increasing in recent years." For both these observations, see Myrdal, Gunnar, *op. cit.*, p. 889.

24. A panchayat samiti has, besides the vikas adhikari as the executive head, one or two agricultural extension officers, two education extension officers, a cooperative extension officer and an animal husbandry extension officer. Two posts of social education organizers and industries officers have been abolished. In some samitis the posts of cooperative extension officer and animal husbandry extension officer have met the same fate.

25. The explanation given is that in Nagaur and other desert areas, agricultural activities are at a low ebb and, therefore, in those areas where a samiti is classified as one for animal husbandry, two A.E.Os. are not required. But one A.E.O. cannot cover a panchayat samiti in its entirety ; and, moreover, Nagaur is not a desert and dry area in the same sense as other districts like Jaisalmer, Barmer, Bikaner and the like are.

was found that in both these districts, contacts between the elite and officials were either spasmodic or exclusively formal.[26]

An analysis of responses concerning the capabilities of officials revealed that in Ganganagar, while 58.1% of respondents reported the number to be adequate as many as 80.6% of the respondents report officials' capabilities to be adequate. This may, again, be reflecting the obvious reality. The situation is the other way round in Bhilwara, where more respondents felt that the officials were adequate in numerical strength but not in capabilities.

The government of Rajasthan introduced a change in the pattern of executive leadership at the panchayat samiti level around 1970. Earlier, a generalist type administrator of the Rajasthan Administrative Service (RAS cadre) used to be the executive head (Vikas Adhikari). Since 1970, the head is a technocrat, who is an agriculture extension officer in panchayat samitis classified as agriculture-oriented, and an animal husbandry extension officer in samitis classified as animal husbandry-oriented. The change was introduced on the plea that panchayat samitis would thus be able to concentrate on area development on the basis of specific requirements. Economy in administration was another factor. The technocrat, therefore, took over from the generalist administrator.

The elite respondents were asked to reflect on this change also. Some 22.6% of the respondents identified no change in the wake of this measure. Another 28.7% gave no comment, leaving just 80 respondents (49.7%) to offer a specific response. 35 of these 80 (43.8%) observed that the change had adversely affected administrative control. For them, a panchayat samiti which has a big staff, needs a person of the generalist type to exercise effective control and supervision. A technocrat, with no knowledge of legalities and other complexities of administration, fails in the task of gearing up the administrative

26. It was reported that officials confine themselves to the headquarters and visit other villages very rarely ; or, that their visits were limited to only the more favoured villages, much to the annoyance of people elsewhere. It was openly said in Jhalawar that officials preferred to visit villages of Kulami caste, which were considered by officials to be more hospitable and cooperative than others.

machinery.[27] Worse still, 7.3% responses indicate that as a consequence of the change, the elected representatives of panchayati
raj have become more irresponsible and over-bearing than before.
However, on the positive side, 7.9% of the total number of respondents (or, 16.2% of positive replies) speak of greater contact
between the people and the vikas adhikari. They hold the
opinion that the new type of incumbent does not believe in
maintaining the distance between himself and the people and
mixes with the people, a prime requirement of a development
official. Similarly, 7.9% of the respondents saw an improvement in the functioning of the system.

Viewed position-wise, positive replies have come from elite
respondents in the category of 'sarpanchas etc.', which is not
unexpected, considering their social background and level of
operation (in one or the other capacity, all are associated with
a panchayat samiti, whose executive head is vikas adhikari),
while members of elite group of the other two categories are, by
and large, not institutionally or functionally involved to the
same extent. This group has, however, pointed in a much
greater number, the adverse impact of the change. Thus 35.9%
of the 'sarpanchas etc.' speak of the slackening of administrative control and 10.9% of 'irresponsible behaviour' of elected
representatives. The respective percentages for 'panchas etc.'
are 4.8 and 11.1 and for the reputational elite, 5.4 and 13.5.
Obviously, the administrative aspect has received more attention
than development priorities, which have not necessarily been
given due consideration.

The extent to which the constraint of the bureaucratic system
is felt may also be assessed on the basis of the prevailing relationship between elected representatives under panchayati raj
and officials in various categories. To the extent that both political and official elites respect the limits set for their respective
roles the nature of the relationship may be cordial. Other-

---

27. Compare an observation by Iqbal Narain and V.P. Grover : "The
    replacement of a generalist B.D.O. may in the Indian context
    militate against the multi-dimensional approach to community
    development and may olso worsen administrative problems without
    necessarily boosting up production." *Economic and Political Weekly*,
    V (51), 19 December, 1970, 2041-2047.

wise tension is bound to erupt. This assumption informed our question regarding the nature of relations among various categories of persons as enumerated in Table 5.9. Our emphasis was on the relations between pradhan and vikas adhikari, the former as the elected head and the latter as the executive head of panchayat samiti. The nature of relationship between the two eventually determines the overall performance of the samitis themselves.

But, as Table 5.9 brings out, no meaningful conclusions can be arrived at in this regard. If we exclude the cases of no-responses and indefinite responses, it would appear that 5.5% of the respondents speak of 'highly cordial' and 50.6% speak of 'cordial' relations among the specified categories of functionaries. On the other hand, 3% of the respondents speak of tense and 1.8% speak of highly tense relations. Those that say relations are cool, are 7.3%. However, these responses have not always been corroborated by field experiences. Quite often when tense and highly tense state of relations have been openly identifiable, the response pattern has just been the other way round.[28]

Altogether it would appear that the rural elites do not treat the bureaucratic mechanism to be a constraining factor to the same extent as they treat the phenomenon of paucity of powers. And, yet, this may not be the whole truth. Informal discussions brought out the fact that development officials generally look down upon the elected representatives, who are considered sub-level functionaries owing to their alleged lack of imagination, partisan attitude and corrupt ways. On the other hand, as the tables given in the preceding section have shown, to some extent, elites also tend to regard the bureaucracy as a stumbling block in the way of development. Our findings based on informal discussions with village people, moreover tend to show estranged relations between

---

28. It was found in the course of field enquiry that where the pradhan belongs to the ruling party, the vikas adhikari would behave tamely and in many cases would lose all initiative. If the pradhan belongs to an opposition party, a vikas adhikari, sympathetic to the ruling party, would be posted there and he would usually tend to ignore the pradhan.

TABLE 5.9

Cordiality of Relations Between Elected Representatives and Various Development Officials

Relations between	Highly cordial		Cordial		Cool		Tense		Highly Tense		Can't say and N.A.*		Total	
	No.	%	No.	%	No.	%	No.	%	No.	%	No.	%	No.	%
Pradhan and Vikas adhikari	25	15.2	79	48.3	14	8.5	11	6.7	1	0.6	34	20.7	164	100.0
Vikas adhikari and other extension officers	17	10.4	70	42.7	23	14.0	10	6.1	-	-	44	26.8	164	100.0
Sarpanch and V.L.W.	8	4.9	86	52.5	25	15.2	5	3.0	1	0.6	39	23.8	164	100.0
Chairmen, Coop. Society and C.E.O.**	12	7.3	67	40.9	19	11.6	4	2.4	-	-	62	37.8	164	100.0
Extension officers and the V.L.W.	9	5.5	83	50.6	12	7.3	5	3.0	3	1.8	52	31.8	164	100.0

*N.A. (Not Applicable) is for a situation where a particular post mainly of an official is lying vacant.
**Cooperative Extension Officer.

political and administrative elites.[29]

FACTIONAL POLITICS

Factional politics has generally been regarded as a hindrance to harmonious life in rural India. Factions are alleged to have robbed panchayati raj of smooth and effective functioning.[30] An attempt is made in the following pages to depict the nature of factions at the village level as perceived by the rural elite, and ways in which they affect the working of panchayati raj. Our concern here is not with factions as such, but primarily with factions that impinge on the functioning of panchayati raj and which are specifically identified as such by the rural elite. The question, addressed to elite respondents in this regard, suggested in advance three types of factions—political, social and economic.[31] Respondents were also asked whether any other type of factions existed which would adversely affect the working of panchayati raj. It is significant that no response was received for this part. The highest number of responses (51) point to the adverse effect of political factions, followed by social factions (30) and economic factions (17). District-wise collation of responses shows that the emphasis is on political (37.3%) and economic (35.3%) factions in the Ganganagar district, and on social factions (33.3%) in the Nagaur district.

29. The statement is brought into bold relief when one comes across the finding in the next chapter that over matters related to panchayats, two-third of the elite respondents in the sample, reportedly, do not hold consultation with the developmental officials. This reflects lack of cordiality, at least in terms of informality of relations between the elected representatives and the developmental officials. This may tend to be a constraining factor in practice.

30. Some of important studies discussing village factions are : Lewis, Oscar, *Village Life in Northern India* (New York : Vintage Books, 1965) ; Miller, D. F., "Factions in Indian Village Politics", *Pacific Affairs* (Spring, 1965), Sharma, Mohan Lal, "Factional Politics in Rural Rajasthan", *RURSA Journal of Research*, 1 (1971).

31. Without attempting a scientific definition of political, social and economic factions, they can broadly be identified as follows : political factions are those which are formed purely out of power considerations to pursue power-positions ; social factions are mainly caste-based factions and are formed to pursue the interests of a caste or sub-caste ; and, economic factions are class-based and represent feuds between the rich and the poor or other economic interests.

In Ganganagar district, quite often the villages are dominated by one caste and hence caste-based factions do not count for much whereas the prevalence of political and economic factions may be a result of imbalanced development and uneven sharing of benefits by various segments of society. We saw earlier that the people in this area expected social justice to be the maximum benefit of panchayati raj, an expectation which was fulfilled to a limited extent. This strengthens the explanation offered by us. In Nagaur district, traditional inter-caste (Jat *vs.* Rajput) rivalries appear to be persisting, and they have come to affect adversely the working of panchayati raj. In Bhilwara, however, the performance of panchayati raj institutions has been thought to be affected adversely by social, economic and political factions by elite respondents to the tune of 6.7%, 5.9% and 15.7% respectively. The limited role of first two types of factions may be due to two factors. First, politics is very much dominated by upper castes there and, unlike other districts, middle castes have not been able to assert themselves. Second, the level of development being low, economic inequalities have not been sharpened.

Turning to the identification of the ways in which political factions affect the working of panchayati raj, it was found that 37.3% of the responses point to the fact that, in-fighting among groups frustrates, developmental programmes. 13.7% of the respondents are inclined to feel that the group in power favours its own men. A district-wise analysis would not be of much consequence as the data available are limited.

The next question related to the considerations that weigh with panchayati raj functionaries in the decision-making process. In this regard, 48.7% of the responses say that decision-making is based on considerations of merit while 36.6% speak of factional considerations as influencing the decision-making process. It seems that those of the elite that find themselves ineffective in making any impact on the decision-making process tend to place the blame on factions. Nagaur leads in the emphasis on factional considerations (33.3%), whereas Bhilwara leads in the emphasis on merit considerations (28.7%). The data being scanty, similar analysis in regard to other districts is not possible.

PRESSURE POLITICS

The operation of pressure politics is another important facet in the study of the decision-making process. At the national level pressure groups seem to be more systematically organized and, therefore, are more clearly identifiable than at the local level. Still, it can well be argued that as every decision is likely to affect certain interests more than others, these interests, in turn, strive to influence decisions to their own advantage. However, not many efforts appear to have been made to study the role of these pressure groups while studying decision-making at local levels in the Indian context. While planning the study, we, therefore, thought of identifying the nature of these pressure groups and the extent to which they influence the decision-making process and, thereby, to find out their role as constraint on the performance and role behaviour of panchayati raj functionaries.

The question we asked was : "Are attempts made to influence decisions over the issues that are brought before the panchayats to the advantage of certain groups ?" If so, what strata of society make these attempts and to what extent?" We also listed 12 types of possible pressures operating in the rural arena. While coding, these 12 alternatives were reduced into 5 broad categories : *viz.,* (1) 'social pressures' (as of relations, friends, etc.) ; (2) pressures from 'caste-leaders'[32] ; (3) economic pressures (of money-lenders etc.; (4) political pressures (of elected representatives or party workers) ; and (5) official pressures (of patwaries, tehsildars, etc.).

Table 5.10 presents the data on the extent to which such pressures are used. If we sum up the responses in two categories of 'very much' and 'somewhat' it is apparent from the table that the largest number of elite respondents (49.4%) feel social pressure to be of paramount importance. Next in order is the allied pressure exerted through caste leaders. Pressures of 'economic sections' is felt 'very much' by 7.9% and 'somewhat' by 27.4% of the respondents. Respective figures affirming

32. Though pressure of caste leaders is also a kind of social pressure, caste is comparatively a more concrete and effective organization, especially in the rural areas. Hence the need of a separate category.

TABLE 5.10

Nature of Pressures Influencing the Decision-making Process of Panchayati Raj Functionaries

Nature of Pressures used	Very much		Somewhat		Not at all		D.K./N.R.		Total	
	No.	%	No.	%	No.	%	No.	%	No.	%
Social pressures	32	19.5	49	29.9	71	43.3	12	7.3	164	100.0
Caste leaders' pressures	20	12.2	45	27.5	86	52.4	13	7.9	164	100.0
Economic pressures	13	7.9	45	27.4	94	57.4	12	7.3	164	100.0
Official pressures	4	2.4	26	15.9	122	74.4	12	7.3	164	100.0
Political pressures	11	6.7	41	25.0	100	61.0	12	7.3	164	100.0

'political pressures' are 6.7% and 25%. Significantly, pressures from civil servants are quite negligible. While nearly 3.4% of the respondents deny the use of pressures by the civil servants only 4 respondents (2.4%) have found as being 'very much' in use.

A district-wise review of the same data was made to bring out variations in the extent of pressures used. It was found that social pressures were exerted most in Nagaur. Jhalawar followed closely the pattern of Nagaur. 'Economic' and 'official' pressures were used most in the Ganganagar district, while political pressures again, were most intense in Nagaur.

If we compare the trends identified here with our findings in the context of factional politics, it would appear that there is a positive correlation between the role of pressure politics and factional politics. The districts of Ganganagar and Nagaur are cases in point. On the other hand, in Bhilwara and Bharatpur, where the pinch of factional politics was felt by fewer elite respondents as a constraining factor, the role of pressure politics as a constraint has also been recognized by fewer members of the elite group. Another trend brought out here is that as the pace of economic development increases, economic pressures build up. Ganganagar illustrates the point.

Summary

In retrospect, it might be said with regard to role expectations that the perception of the elite as well as of the citizens tends to emphasize the developmental role, though some elite persons would qualify it by saying that they expected panchayati raj to help in having plans locally prepared and executed. Hardly any respondent sees panchayati raj as helping to build up community consciousness . or to spread social education. It appears that the backlog of feudal legacies inhibits respondents from having a comprehensive look into the future. Further, economic hardships in rural areas cannot be neglected altogether as a factor in the delineation of profile of role expectations. Third, and of considerable importance, official policies have tended to offer a tilted image of the role-expectations of panchayati raj because of the primacy of production orientation. Because the posts of social education organizer and cooperative extension officer have been fully or partially abolished, all the efforts of development administration have come to be focussed on agriculture.

There, is, therefore, understandable disenchantment with the performance of panchayati raj in terms of developmental expectations. A larger number of elite respondents, and also citizen respondents think of panchayati raj as a totally frustrating experience. The frustrated expectations include on the one hand, planning from below, with emphasis on programmes locally conceived, locally executed, and locally oriented, and, on the other hand, the extension of opportunities of social justice.

While there is a broad consensus that panchayati raj has failed to live upto popular expectations, the elite appears to be divided on the specific factors that have been dysfunctional to role performance. A sizeable number of elite respondents refrained from openly criticizing the limitations of statutory provisions, the bureaucratic structure and officious attitudes, factional politics and pressure politics. Nevertheless, it is obvious, that these are the factors that act as constraints and which, in turn, have cumulatively inhibited the performance of panchayati raj institutions.

6

PATTERNS OF COMMUNICATION

A STUDY OF the patterns of political relationships necessarily involves a study of patterns of communication between the rulers and the ruled, as well as among the rulers themselves. It is only through the flow of information and exchange of ideas which form the content of a communication system that political relationships can be activised, sustained, and put to some use.[1] Every political system, or for that matter any system, maintains a communication network. The advent of science and technology has revolutionised this network. This has not only helped to increase the volume of information flow but has also tremendously increased the pace at which information flow takes place.

1. To Lasswell, the study of communication involves, "Who Says What, in Which Channel, ToWhom and With What Effect", Lasswell, Harold D., "The Structure and Function of Communication in Society" in Bryson, Lyman (ed.), *The Communication of Ideas* (New York : Harper and Row, 1948), p. 37 ; and Lasswell, Harold D. *et al.*, (ed.), *Language of Politics : Studies in Quantitative Semantics* (The M.I.T. Press, 1965), particularly chapters I and II. Thus the channels as well as the contents and effects (as reading meaning out of symbolic expressions) forms an essential ingredient of the communication systems that help maintain power relationships and determine 'Who Gets What, When and How ?' Thus the two appear to be closely linked. Yet a sharp dichotomy is maintained between approaches to politics as a study of power process and of communication process. Exponents of communication theory maintain that politics is talk, though not all talk, that implies communication. They maintain that certain minimum political processes do occur even if the threat of use of force is not there. See in this regard Deutsch, Karl W., *The Nerves of Government* (New York : Free Press and Macmillan, 1966) Roelofs, H. Mark, *The Language of Modern Politics : An Introduction to the Study of Government* (Homewood, Illinois : The Dorsey Press, 1967), especially its first chapter entitled "The Nature of Political Talk", pp. 19-52. For a theoretical background to the concept and scope of political communication see Fagen, Richard R., *Politics and Communication* (Boston : Little, Brown and Company, 1966).

"Mass culture", covering mostly rural areas (which conform to traditional cultural patterns) trails behind in the process of modernization and overall development, as the masses are less privileged in terms of use of various media of communication and, consequently, in getting benefits from the flow of political, economic, and other types of information.[2] This hampers efforts that aim at increasing mass participation in political processes. It was to break into this very insulation of rural societies that the scheme of democratic decentralization was introduced. Community development programmes were meant to extend to the rural folk vital information about technological innovations, especially in the field of agriculture and allied occupations, and thereby to create a self helping rural community.

We propose to report here very briefly the communication pattern obtaining in rural Rajasthan, especially in the context of democratic decentralization, and analyse its nature and role.

Media of Communication

Prominent media of communication, both mass and interpersonal, used in village India are : newspapers, radio, urban contacts, and *chopals*.[3] Questions relating to these media were

2. A number of studies bear out the point in the Indian context. Damle attempts to deal with problems of communication from structural-functional point of view and finds that not only distance but nature of structure also determines the extent of effectivity and responses to the communication system : Damle, V.M., "Communication of Modern Ideas", in Desai, A.R., (ed.), *Rural Sociology in India* (Bombay : Popular Prakashan, 1967), pp. 378-88. Other studies highlighting the use of various media of communication and effectivity in response pattern are Varma, S.P., Narain, Iqbal and Associates : *Voting Behaviour in a Changing Society* (Delhi : National, 1973), pp. 200-273; Atal, Yogesh, *Local Communities and National Politics*, part III (Delhi: National, 1971), pp. 135-279; Sirsikar, V.M., *Sovereigns Without Crown* (Bombay : Popular Prakashan, 1973).

3. This is an institution dating from antiquity, where consultation, discussion or sometimes even deliberation over topics of general importance are done. The *chopal* may either comprise the whole village or only a particular caste in the village. While on specific occasions such an assembly might formally be summoned, it might also be more or less a daily assemblage in an informal way when people, tired after day's work, get together and relax. The range of activities cover several important and unimportant ones of local interest.

addressed both to elites and citizens. They were broad enough to cover even infrequent use of these media, irrespective of the fact whether these media were used directly or indirectly. Our investigations show that the media maximally used are "urban contacts" (76.8%), followed by the radio (70.7%), *"chopals"* (55.5%), and "newspaper" (48.8%). The high response for "urban contacts" is obviously because of greater socio-economic mobility among the villagers in recent times.

District-wise, some interesting trends were identified. Newspapers are read by the largest number of elite respondents (57.1%) in Bharatpur district, while 'radio' (87.1%) and 'urban contacts' (93.5%) matter most in Ganganagar district. In the other three districts of Nagaur, Jhalawar and Bhilwara, fewer elite persons use various media of communication. Of these districts, the responses are lowest in Bhilwara, except in the case of use of urban contacts (87.1%). Another notable trend is that in Bharatpur, the *chopal* serves as an effective media of communication, to the tune of 95%. This percentage is the highest of all the districts. The only plausible explanation for the overwhelming emphasis on this medium is related to social customs and typical traditions of the area, where the *chopal* has been an effective assemblage of rural folk for a long time. Coming to citizens responses, the over-all aggregate and district-wise trends do not show variance, except in respect to less emphasis on all the media.

Further questions in this context sought to identify the intensity of interest of respondents in the type of information that they sought through a particular medium. The questions in this regard were addressed both to the elite and citizen respondents. Only the first preferences have been considered here for analysis because the responses in other categories are scanty. To begin with, we take up an analysis of the nature of information derived from newspapers. It was found that in comparison to members of the elite group, citizens were clear and straight-forward in their responses. Also, about half (48.7%) of the elite respondents who are newspaper readers fall in the 'non-response' category, which for citizens is 39.1%. Asked which news they prefer, national or State-level, 35.0% of the elite respondents answered 'none in particular', while 17.4% of the citizens gave that answer. Thus, only 16.3% of elite readers reported whether they are more interested in 'national' or 'State' level news. Of these, 10.0% had a preference for 'national' level and the rest for 'State' level news. The respective figures for citizen readers are 39.1% and 4.3%. One reason for this difference in percentage may be that the percentage readership among citizens is quite low (11.5%) and so vagueness in their replies is less apparent. It may, however, be pointed out in regard to responses both of the members of the elite group and the citizens that they may not always be able to discriminate in an effective way about levels of news.

COMMUNICATION PATTERN WITHIN PANCHAYATI RAJ SYSTEM

Our investigation has shown that citizens lag behind the elite in the use of these media, except that of the *chopal*. Now we propose to analyse the patterns of communications within the framework of panchayati raj. The focus here is on the groups with which the elites communicate on questions involving local development as well as personal affairs. That will throw light on the groups usually consulted by the elite and also on the intensity of the communication pattern. For this purpose, a structured question, with a number of alternatives, was put to elite respondents, and it was explained to them that the question sought to include both formal and informal modes of consultation. At the coding stage, these alternative categories were reduced to 5, *viz.*, institutional elite persons, officials of development administration, officials of regulatory administration, (police revenue, etc.), social circle (caste, family members, etc.) and people in general. The data thus tabulated, show that the emphasis is on members of the institutional elite group, that is, elected representatives such as sarpanch, pradhan, M.L.A., etc. That 33.5% of the elite respondents report 'very much' and another 35.4% report 'somewhat', as the extent of consultations they hold with panchayati raj elite persons, merits our attention. It is not unexpected that elite respondents in the sample, most of whom are elected respresentatives, should have greater communication with their own counterparts. Second place goes to 'people in general' with 30.5% of elite respondents indicating 'very much' and 29.9% reporting 'somewhat', as the extent of consulations they hold with the people. These responses seem to include both consultation with the people in general in a formal way (through meetings of the *gram sabha*), and consultations in informal gatherings such as the *chopal* and at temples. It might, however, be noted that the elite has not shown adequate enthusiasm for its contacts with development officials, with whom it ought to have been in closest contact. This is not a flattering reflection on the institutional and personal structure of panchayati raj, which has primarily been envisaged as a development mechanism. This becomes all the more intriguing when we recall that in the previous chapter a large number of elite respondents had reported satisfaction with the relationship with the officials.

Considering district-wise, of the total 113 elite respondents consulting members of the institutional elite group on panchayat affairs, the highest number of elite respondents (31 or 27.4%) hail from Bharatpur district alone. Jhalawar follows with 21.2% of the elite respondents. In this regard, Bhilwara lags behind of all and Nagaur and Ganganagar districts come in between. Neither levels of development nor caste composition appears to be an adequate explanation for this trend. Perhaps what is more relevant is the legacies of erstwhile patterns of land relations. Both Bharatpur and Jhalawar fall in the *khalsa* category[4] while Nagaur and Bhilwara have had an experience of the *Jagirdari*[5] system. In the absence of intermediaries, the former system tended to be much more open, and consequently intra-elite group communication was less hindered. Ganganagar also falls under the *Khalsa* system, but the population there consists of immigrants from Punjab, forming comparatively a new society. Hence, intra-elite linkages and intra-elite communication might not have developed to an extent comparable to its level of

4. *Khalsa* land is directly owned by the ruler or the State with no intermediaries between the owner and the cultivator. Usually land revenue is fixed in cash and collected by State officials.

5. *Jagir* is a land grant from the State to someone in lieu of his service or special relationship with the ruler. Thus an intermediary is created between the State and the cultivator. He is known as *Jagirdar* and would collect land-revenue usually at exhorbitant rates, though he would pay only a fixed amount to the State. Besides, the *Jagirdar* by virtue of law or sheer force of personality, would exercise adjudicative and developmental functions also. Thus, he would be an intermediary in almost all societal relations.

development. It should be noted that development officials are consulted most in Jhalawar district (with 33.9% of the elite respondents so reporting), followed by 23.2% in Ganganagar. However, respondents of Jhalawar reported, by and large, that a particular Vikas Adhikari was extremely enthusiastic about developmental programmes and he along with his other team-mates established intimate contacts with the village folk. It was natural that with officials being readily and informally accessible, there was greater communication between the elite and development officials. While consultations with officials of regulatory administration follow no clear pattern, consultations with social circles are held to a maximum extent in Bharatpur district, followed by Nagaur. Both areas are Jat dominated, and Jats form a close-knit community. Consultations with the people in general follow the pattern of responses identified in the case of the institutional elite.

Analysing the respondents' reaction position-wise, it was found that institutional elite persons are consulted by a very high percentage of elite respondents in all the positional categories. Similarly, other categories are less sought after by all the positional categories. However, in comparison to other positional groups the elite in the category 'sarpanchas etc.' communicate more with the institutional elite, with development officials, and with the people in general. This should not be surprising as this group hails from the upper strata of society in socio-economic terms. This group also enjoys considerable administrative powers under panchayati raj. The greater resourcefulness of this group ensures greater accessibility to the institutional elite and development officials as well as to the people in general. Officials of regulatory administration and social circle are consulted by 'panchas etc.' and reputational elite persons alike. The *patwari*, a key official in the village, belongs to the regulatory administration. If the sarpanch, pradhan etc. (high-position elite members) are in consultation more with development officials and other institutional elite, the lower level elite persons rely on contacts with the *patwari*, who is easily available to them and whose role impinges on their day-to-day life. For the same reason, social groups are consulted much more by the panchas and the reputational elite members.

It appears that the ability to communicate and hold consultation with others is largely determined by the resources of a person, whether in terms of position held or socio-economic status enjoyed. A history of having *jagirdari (or non-jagirdari)* system also plays a vital role in habit formation and appears to determine the patterns of communication. It was found that sometimes officials of development administration are also not immune to feudal influences.

In the course of field study an attempt was also made to ascertain whom elite respondents would consult in personal matters. The persons most sought after for consultation are friends, relations and castefellows : 54.9% of the elite respondents consult them 'very much' and 20.7% do so 'somewhat'. Next, in order of preference are members of the institutional elite group. On the other hand, consultation with officials is not very popular. As already seen, even in matters of public importance, there is a discernible gulf between officials and the local elite. In personal matters the elite, by and large, relies even less on officials. Further, it was found that communication with moneyed groups, former jagirdars and the *Mahajan* class, is at a low ebb and this somewhat explains their loosening grip over the common man who also has contempt and apathy torwards them on account of their exploitative deeds.

From a position-wise analysis of the same data, we find that the lower level institutional elites, 'panchas', etc. are more involved in personal consultations with other functionaries, with the exception of those in development administration and in the police. Nearly 79.4% of the 'panchas' do so. Besides, 46.0% of the 'panchas' hold consultations with institutional elite members as well. On the other hand, 57.8% of the upper level elite ('sarpanchas' etc.) hold consultations with a wider social circle including relatives, neighbours, etc. and 43.7% with institutional elite members. The sarpanchas 'consult' more with development and police officials than the 'panchas' do. This clearly indicates the greater accessibility of the 'sarpanch' to both types of officials. The cause of their greater accessibility to development officials is their closer association with them on account of their functional affinity. The cause of their greater accessibility to police officials should be judged in the context of the oft-repeated allegation of the people that these elite persons have sometimes acted as the contactmen of the police. This, however, needs substantiation.

An analysis in relation to age, education and caste background of respondents was also done. This was based on data where only positive ('yes') replies were taken into consideration. Our conclusion is that the higher the level in terms of education and caste, the greater the prospects of people feeling confident in having effective communication with panchayats. This is true for both elite and citizens.

Another question concerned techniques the respondents would like to adopt in order to get development schemes accepted. Possible techniques were identified in a structured question. It was addressed only to those of the elite and citizen respondents who had positively expressed their confidence in getting development schemes executed by their panchayats. Respondents were also asked the extent to which they would like to make use of the technique perferred. The replies show that the highest number of elite respondents (43.3%) have a general preference for building up support among people through campaigning in its favour prior to placing a scheme before the panchayat. Another 25.0% of the elite respondents would resort to the technique if the situation demanded. Thus this group of elite respondents would first weigh the prospects of popular support and would then persuade the panchayat to accept a particular scheme. Among those who would seek specific support prior to placing a scheme before a panchayat, 39.0% would generally prefer prior concurrence of the 'sarpanch'. The support of the ward-panch and panchas representing other wards is also treated as an effective help by a good number of elite respondents. Thus 29.3% of the elite respondents would seek support of the ward-panch and 27.4% the sport of panchas of other wards. However, not many elite respondents would seek support from panchayat samiti and caste leaders to get their scheme accepted, the respective percentages in the two categories being 8.5 and 12.8.

The responses of citizens in the same context, by and large, support the main trends already identified. There are, however, variations. One such variation is that in comparison to the elite, fewer citizens (24.0% as against 43.9% of elite respondents) have a general preference for assessing and ensuring popular support. Still fewer citizens (16.5%) feel confident enough to strike a direct deal with the panchayat. Similarly, only 1.5% of the citizens show a general preference for ensuring panchayat samiti level support for getting a scheme accepted by the panchayat. Another 26.5% think of adopting this technique only sparingly. A larger number of citizens are inclined to rely upon panchayat-level elected representatives in this regard.

A third part of the question aimed at ascertaining the reasons for the negative reply to the first part of the question, *i.e.*, why they feel that they are incapable of getting a scheme accepted by the panchayat. The reasons advanced by both elite and citizen respondents in this regard reveal that, while many in the elite attribute the reasons to the outer world, a lesser number would also blame themselves. Thus 56.9% of the citizens, as against only 16.0% of elite respondents, attribute their inability to get a scheme accepted to their being 'of little significance'. Explaining this the respondents would state, "we are illiterate" or "we belong to the lower strata"; and therefore, nobody would consider what they have to say. Another 3.4% of the citizens report their inability owing to 'want of leisure'. It appears from the reasons stated that the confidence of the citizens is not as much as that of the elite. They seem to suffer from inferiority-complex, which arises from such facts as their being illiterate, poor or of low caste status, which set the limits of their ability to communicate with the decision-makers at the panchayat level. A large number of members of the elite, on the other hand, attribute their failure to external factors such as corrupt officials, indifferent elected representatives or factional politics.

The foregoing responses were elicited by a hypothetical question which asked whether the respondents could effectively communicate in order to see a village improvement scheme through. The finding was that the elite is more resourceful than the masses in this regard. From a hypothetical we moved on to a specific situation. A question, therefore, was put as to whether the respondents actually drew the attention of the decision-makers at the panchayat level at any time to some specific issue. Since the purpose was to ascertain the elite-mass communication pattern, the question was confined to citizens only. The responses to this question showed that 38.5% of the respondents had actually put forward a scheme for the approval of the panchayat. Thus the respondents actually communicating with the decision-makers at panchayat level are only a few, since 6.5% of the citizens felt they could get a scheme accepted if they had one to offer.

To ascertain the effectivity of the "message" that the people communicate to the elite for getting approval of a village improvement scheme, another part was attached to the main question. It read : "Did you succeed in your efforts ?" It was addressed to only those respondents who had put forward a scheme to the panchayat. The response pattern to the question when analysed showed that only a third (35.1%) reported success in their efforts. The highest percentage of these respondents is, again, from Nagaur district (44%). May be several of these citizens were affiliated to the faction that also controlled the decision-making apparatus of the panchayat.

An analysis of the reasons given by citizens for success in their efforts to get approval of schemes by the panchayat also brought out certain interesting patterns. The most important factors in this context appeared to be the use of institutional channels ; for instance, securing prior approval of the 'panchas' or the 'sarpanch' of the panchayat concrned. It will be recalled that our earlier analysis showed that citizen respondents preferred to put forward a scheme through the panch and sarpanch (members of the institutional elite group) to using official channels. The responses in the present case only confirm the earlier trend that institutional elite persons would carry more weight in a panchayat than others. Secondly, it is also interesting to note that caste support was found to be of some consequence only in Nagaur, mainly because factionalism and the caste distribution of people would have a distinct correlation there.

Another part of the question aimed at ascertaining the reasons for the failure of certain citizens in getting a scheme accepted by the panchayat. This question was addressed only to those citizens who had reported the failure of their attempt. About a third (34.0%) attributed their failure to the apathy of institutional elite persons who would show "no consideration for what the common man said."[6] It is a sad comment on the system's working that a considerable number of respondents who dared to communicate a scheme felt frustrated and were left high and dry. The response, "no consideration for what the common man says", is damaging enough. Another reason related to the popular feeling doubting the system's efficacy. Except for the reason "want of financial resources", for which the State government was largely responsible, other reasons directly related to the issue of the PR, systems efficacy. Whether due to the prevalence of factional politics or to the indifference of the 'sarpanch', they amounted to less of faith in the system's efficacy. It is only when people are assured of the system's efficacy that their participation in planning and organization of developmental efforts can be elicited in a manner to give meaning to the concept of 'people's plan'.

Thus far we have been discussing the communication pattern between elite and masses in the form of pushing through a village improvement scheme by citizens at a personal level. Now we propose to take up discussion of the communication pattern between citizens and elite at a public forum. For that we have picked gram sabha meetings. The query addressed to the citizens in this regard read : "Did you ever speak about any matter in the meetings of gram sabha ?" The responses received are revealing. As Table 6.1 shows, only 18 (9%) out of 200 citizens interviewed, replied in the affirmative. Ten of these 18 responses (55.6%) came from Bharatpur district alone. Nagaur follows, with a contribution of 5 (27.8%). It may also be added here that these two districts also reported a greater degree of party identification among citizens which, in turn, may account for their participation in *gram sabha* meetings.

The above pattern of responses is corroborated by the answers of elite respondents, though the question addressed to

6. By indifference of the sarpanch, as the field reports show, the respondents mainly meant either of the two things : the proposed scheme related to the village other than that of the sarpanch or that the scheme might not leave enough money to be pocketed.

TABLE 6.1

Whether Citizens spoke at a Gram Sabha Meeting

District	Yes		No		Total	
	No.	%	No.	%	No.	%
Ganganagar	2	11.1	38	20.9	40	20.0
Nagaur	5	27.8	35	19.2	40	20.0
Bhilwara	–	–	40	21.9	40	20.0
Jhalawar	1	5.6	39	21.4	40	20.0
Bharatpur	10	55.6	30	16.5	40	20.0
Total	18	100.0	182	100.0	200	100.0

them was different. It read : "Do you feel that people enthusiastically take part in the gram sabha meetings ?" Elite respondents interpreted 'enthusiasm' in the sense of attendance in gram sabha meetings ; they were, therefore, not giving primacy to making such a forum an opportunity for a dialogue between the people and panchayati raj functionaries. The table shows that more than 50% of the elite respondents feel that people are 'not much enthusiastic' or 'not at all enthusiastic' about *gram sabha* meetings. While 34.1% of the elite respondents found people suficiently enthusiastic, only 15.4% reported that people are highly enthusiastic.

District-wise, in Bharatpur, Jhalawar and Ganganagar, nearly half to two-thirds of the elite respondents feel that popular enthusiasm is sufficient or at a high level, with Bharatpur leading. In Nagaur, the elite response pattern (Table 6.2) is at variance with that given by citizens. In the latter case, Nagaur's contribution was more than 25% (Table 6.1). This variation shows the gap between elite and mass thinking. Obviously, party factionalism and the resultant blinkered perspectives have adversely affected the response pattern of the elite. Economic backwardness in Bhilwara has, by and large, resulted in reactions of indifference to the gram sabha.

Receptivity to Communication

After analysing channels of communication which receive or supply information, both in general and specific contexts, it is also important to look into the amount of information absorbed at the receiving end. In other words, the extent of receptivity of elite and citizens needs analysis.

To assess the nature of information flowing to rural areas and the extent of its receptivity, a number of questions were addressed to the respondents. The first question sought to enquire into the extent to which respondents were informed of the particulars of contestants for Vidhan Sabha and Lok Sabha elections. Since a period of 3 years had elapsed after the last general elections, the information sought was also a test of the respondents' capacity of retention and recollection. It was realized at the time of preparing the schedule that an average citizen might not be able to remember several details after three

TABLE 6.2

Extent of Popular Enthusiasm about Gram Sabha Meetings

Districts	Highly enthusiastic		Sufficiently enthusiastic		Not much enthusiastic		Not at all enthusiastic		N.R.		Total	
	No.	%	No.	%	No.	%	No.	%	No.	%	No.	%
Ganganagar	–	–	5	16.1	3	8.1	–	–	1	50.0	9	9.9
			55.6		33.3				11.1		100.0	
Nagaur	1	7.1	1	3.2	10	27.1	3	42.8	–	–	15	16.5
	6.7		6.7		66.7		20.0				100.0	
Bhilwara	–	–	4	12.9	8	21.6	2	28.6	–	–	14	15.4
			28.6		57.1		14.3				100.0	
Jhalawar	5	35.7	11	35.5	8	21.6	2	28.6	–	–	26	28.6
	19.2		42.3		30.8		7.7				100.0	
Bharatpur	8	57.1	10	32.3	8	21.6	–	–	1	50.0	27	29.7
	29.6		37.1		29.6				3.7		100.0	
Total	14	100.0	31	100.0	37	100.0	7	100.0	2	100.0	91	100.0
	15.4		34.1		40.7		7.7		2.2		100.0	

years, and so this question was addressed only to elite respondents. Particulars sought from respondents covered : number of candidates in the constituency of respondent, their names, parties, and the election verdict.

While coding, a four-point scale—high, medium, low, and zero categories—was evolved to measure the level of political information of respondents. For calculation, the scores per contestant were : name—1, party—2, result—1. The total scores per candidate thus obtained are 4. This was multiplied by the total number of candidates in a constituency. The total scores thus got were treated as a standard measure for calculation of high, medium, low, and zero levels of political information of a respondent in the following manner :

High   = 67% and above of total score ;
Medium = 34% to 66% of total score ;
Low   = 1% to 33% of total score ; and
Zero   = 0% of total score.

Tables 6.3 and 6.4 present the data thus processed.

An overall analysis of Table 6.3 shows that 34.1% of elite respondents have a 'high' level of political information about contestants for the Vidhan Sabha seat ; 42.7% have a 'medium' level information and another 11.0% have a 'low' level information. Thus 12.2% of elite respondents are left in the category of 'zero' level. Considering the constraints on effective media of communication in rural areas, as seen in the second section of this chapter, the overall picture is not disheartening.[7] However, it needs to be underlined that the elite generally receives information in this regard not only from the commonly used media of communication, but also from the campaign process itself. It is usual for all the candidates to

---

7. To compare, we might refer here to inferences drawn in Varma, S.P. and Narain, Iqbal *op. cit.*, pp. 138-139. This study included similar questions about Vidhan Sabha elections, which were put to the general electorate. The inference, drawn was : 15% achieving high level and 44.1% and medium level of information. With regard to inferences about Parliamentary elections, the results were worse : 12.7% attaining high level and 24.3% medium level. We might also consider the fact that the survey undertaken included information based on a third-phase enquiry in the panel study which was undertaken a fortnight after the election results were out.

TABLE 6.3

Level of Information of Elite Respondents in regard to Contestants for Vidhan Sabha Seat in 1967

District	High No.	High %	Medium No.	Medium %	Low No.	Low %	Zero No.	Zero %	Total No.	Total %
Ganganagar	6 / 19.4	10.7	22 / 71.0	31.4	1 / 3.2	5.6	2 / 6.5	10.0	31 / 100.0	18.9
Nagaur	30 / 90.9	53.6	— / —	—	2 / 6.1	11.1	1 / 3.0	5.0	33 / 100.0	20.1
Bhilwara	3 / 9.7	5.3	24 / 77.4	34.3	1 / 3.2	5.6	3 / 9.7	15.0	31 / 100.0	18.9
Jhalawar	7 / 20.6	12.5	16 / 47.1	22.9	6 / 17.6	33.3	5 / 14.6	25.0	34 / 100.0	20.7
Bharatpur	10 / 28.6	17.9	8 / 22.8	11.4	8 / 22.8	44.4	9 / 25.7	45.0	35 / 100.0	21.4
Total	56 / 34.1	100.0	70 / 42.7	100.0	18 / 11.0	100.0	20 / 12.2	100.0	164 / 100.0	100.0

approach members of the elite group in the area. Many a time candidates, being local, have close links with rural elites, quite a few of whom also come forward to campaign for one candidate or the other. One would expect the personal contact with a candidate to leave a lasting imprint on the minds of elite persons about the particulars of the candidate concerned.

A district-wise consideration of the table brings out the role of personalities involved in the contest in getting the respondents informed. Thus Nagaur leads with 90.9% of elite respondents in the 'high' category. It may be recalled here that the Ladnun Vidhan Sabha constituency to which all but 4 of the respondents belong[8] witnessed a straight contest in the 1967 elections. The Congress candidate was Ram Niwas Mirdha, former Speaker and renowned leader. His only rival, the pradhan of the samiti, was also a popular leader in the constituency. Thus it was natural for elites to recall vital information about both the candidates. In Ganganagar, most of the elite respondents interviewed belong to Raisinghnagar reserved constituency. All the candidates belonged to scheduled castes, and it was gathered that they had inadequate linkages with the dominant elite of upper and middle castes. Hence, in this case, the percentage of elite respondents in the 'high' category is much lower than in Nagaur. In Bhilwara, besides the types of personalities involved in contest, general backwardness would have also influenced adversely the retentive capacity of elite respondents. Thus here 9.7% had a 'high' level information which is the lowest figure of all the districts. Besides being socio-economically backward, the area has had comparatively less known contestants. The Congress candidate was an outsider. Respondents were confused about the party identification of his main rival. He was an independent who later joined and contested as an SSP candidate. Respondents identified his party in three ways, viz., he is an independent; he is a Swatantrite[9] and he is an SSPite. Similarly, the Congressite in the Jhalawar area under study was almost a newcomer to the major part of the constituency. His main rival (the Janta Party candidate), who won, cashed in on the popularity and actual participation of Raja

8. Even these 4 happened to be pradhans or zila pramukhs and 3 of them were highly educated.
9. Swatantrite carries two meanings in Hindi: first, the name of a party, secondly, an independent.

Harish Chandra (now deceased).

Table 6.4 presents data about the level of information of candidates for the Lok Sabha seat. The general pattern is not different, with the exception that the number of respondents in the upper level category is much lower. Thus, as against 34.1% respondents with a "high" level of information about candidates for Vidhan Sabha seat, only 6.7% have a high level of political information about candidates for the Lok Sabha seat. The table confirms the trend identified earlier that where personalities involved in the contest are renowned, they are apt to affect the amount of information received and retained by respondents. Thus, in Nagaur, among the contestants for Lok Sabha, besides three minor candidates, there were two renowned candidates: Onkar Singh (Congress) and N.K. Somani (Swatantra), well-known in this area respectively, as 'Khinwasar Thakur' and 'Bangar Seth'. Similarly in Bharatpur, two personalities were involved: Raj Bahadur (Congress), a sitting M.P. and a Central Minister, and Brijendra Singh (former Maharaja of Bharatpur). It can, therefore, be said that the involvement of personalities in Nagaur and Bharatpur was a determinant of the fact that greater number of elite respondents appears in the category of 'high' and 'medium' levels of information. In other areas under study, where all or some of the candidates were comparatively unknown, the percentages are on the low side.

Tables 6.5 and 6.6 deal with the same data in relation to age and education of respondents. Considering the data first in relation to age, it will be evident that the age-group '30-50' is better placed than the other two groups in this regard. A much larger percentage of this group falls in the 'high' and 'medium' categories both for Vidhan Sabha and Lok Sabha candidates than those of the other two groups, *i.e.*, below 30 and above 50. As seen in preceding analyses, this group is more active and participative, it also occupies higher level posts and is much more informed.

Table 6.6 brings out the role of education as a determinant of the level of information. While 53.3% of the elite respondents of 'above matric' category show a 'high' level of political information in regard to contestants for the Vidhan Sabha seat, only 37.4% of the elite respondents of 'matric and below' category and 19.2% of the illiterate category do so. In contrast,

TABLE 6.4

Level of Information of Elite Respondents in regard to Contestants for Lok Sabha Seat in 1967

District	High		Medium		Low		Zero		Total	
	No.	%	No.	%	No.	%	No.	%	No.	%
Ganganagar	–	–	16 51.6	20.8	5 16.1	16.1	10 32.3	22.2	31 100.0	18.9
Nagaur	6 18.2	54.5	22 66.7	28.6	1 3.0	3.2	4 12.1	8.9	33 100.0	20.1
Bhilwara	–	–	8 25.8	10.4	14 45.2	45.2	9 29.0	20.0	31 100.0	18.9
Jhalawar	3 8.8	27.3	11 32.4	14.3	7 20.6	22.6	13 38.2	28.9	34 100.0	20.7
Bharatpur	2 5.7	18.2	20 57.1	26.0	4 11.4	12.9	9 25.7	20.0	35 100.0	21.4
Total	11 6.7	100.0	77 47.0	100.0	31 18.9	100.0	45 27.4	100.0	164 100.0	100.0

TABLE 6.5

Level of Information by Age-group of Elite Respondents in regard to Contestants for Vidhan Sabha and Lok Sabha Seats in 1967

Age-group	High		Medium		Low		Zero		Total	
	Vidhan Sabha	Lok Sabha	Vidhan Sabha	Lok Sabha	Vidhan Sabha	Lok Sabha	Vidhan Sabha	Lok Sabha	Vidhan Sabha	Lok Sabha
Below 30	—	—	5	5	4	—	3	7	12	12
			41.7	41.7	33.3		25.0	58.3	100.0	100.0
30 to 50	40	10	40	48	3	20	9	14	92	92
	43.5	10.9	43.5	52.2	3.3	21.7	9.8	15.2	100.0	100.0
Above 50	16	1	25	24	11	11	8	24	60	60
	26.7	1.7	41.7	40.0	18.3	18.3	13.3	40.0	100.0	100.0
Total	56	11	70	77	18	31	20	45	164	164
	34.1	6.7	42.7	47.0	11.0	18.9	12.2	27.4	100.0	100.0

TABLE 6.6

Level of Information by Literacy Status of Elite Respondents in regard to Candidates for Vidhan Sabha and Lok Sabha Seats in 1967

Educational group	High		Medium		Low		Zero		Total	
	Vidhan Sabha	Lok Sabha	Vidhan Sabha	Lok Sabha	Vidhan Sabha	Lok Sabha	Vidhan Sabha	Lok Sabha	Vidhan Sabha	Lok Sabha
Illiterate	8 19.1	–	15 35.7	9 21.4	10 23.8	9 21.4	9 21.4	24 57.1	42 100.0	42 100.0
Matric and below	40 37.4	10 9.3	49 45.8	56 52.3	7 6.5	21 19.6	11 10.3	20 18.7	107 100.0	107 100.0
Above Matric	8 53.3	1 6.7	6 40.0	12 80.0	1 6.7	1 6.7	–	1 6.7	15 100.0	15 100.0
Total	56 34.1	11 6.7	70 42.7	77 47.0	18 11.0	31 18.9	20 12.2	45 27.4	164 100.0	164 100.0

93% of elite respondents in the 'matric and below' category have a 'high' level of information about particulars of candidates for the Lok Sabha seat as against 6.7% of the 'above matric' category. The table also shows that education does not automatically ensure receptivity and retention of information. Otherwise, the number of elite respondents in the 'above matric' category having high level of information would not have been confined to just one.[9]

A study in the context of caste structure was also made. It was found that upper caste elite persons have an above average share ; middle caste elite persons have a below average share ; while the level of information of lower caste elite persons is insignificant. As many as 72.2% of the lower caste elite strata show a zero-level of information when asked about contestants for the Lok Sabha seat.

Another question addressed to respondents in order to assess the level of political information concerned the acquaintance of respondents with important national and State level personalities. In all, a list of 39 names was provided to respondents and they were asked to identify the position held by each of them. The names in the list included only those important personalities as had been in the current political news, and it was expected that every conscious citizen ought to be acquainted with most of them.   The response pattern is not encouraging. A good number of respondents knew just two names: Mrs. Indira Gandhi among national leaders and Mohan Lal Sukhadia among State leaders. Many respondents could only say they were familiar with a particular name, but were not able to identify the office occupied by the person; or, some would say: Indira Gandhi is a *badshah* (emperor) or a *maharani*. While coding, a four-point scale was evolved for assessing the level of political information. The scores were allotted in the following manner :

Acquaintance with the name	—	1
Acquaintance both with name and office	—	2

9. It may be added that one person of the 'above matric status' who reported complete ignorance of particulars of candidates for Vidhan Sabha seat migrated to the area in the post-election period.

Besides, the names were classified into two groups : 'national' and 'State' level leaders, having 22 and 14 leaders, respectively. For acquaintance with national leaders the maximum score could be 44 and for State level leaders, the maximum score could be 28. Consequently, the level-rating was done as under :

Pattern of Level-rating

Level	Score range for national leaders	Score range for State leaders
High	30 and above	20 and above
Medium	16 to 29	10 to 19
Low	1 to 15	1 to 9
Zero	0	0

Table 6.7 indicates the level of information of elite and citizen respondents in regard to national-level leaders. The level of information of elite respondents is higher than that of citizens. In all, 37 (22.6%) show a 'high' level of information ; only 1 (0.5%) citizen has a 'high' level of information. Similarly, as against 6.0% citizens, 14.6% of elite respondents belong to the 'medium' level category of information. Consequently, the citizens' percentages increase in the other two lower categories, *viz.*, 'low' and 'zero'. The flow of 'current information' into rural areas is not encouraging. As seen above, even in regard to acquaintance with names and positions of personalities, about 63% of the elite respondents and 93% of the citizens are confined to a 'low' or 'zero' level of information. In contrast to this, the level of information about the particulars of contestants for Vidhan Sabha and Lok Sabha seats was far better. The main sources of information about current affairs for the village community as a whole and also for individuals, are newspapers and radio, and the latter much more than the former which are not regularly available.

TABLE 6.7

Level of Information of Elite and Citizen Respondents in regard to Knowledge about National Level Leaders

District	High		Medium		Low		Zero		Total	
	Elites	Citizens	Elites	Citizens	Elites	Citizens	Elites	Citizens	Elites	Citizens
Ganganagar	9	1	6	5	15	28	1	6	31	40
	29.0	2.5	19.4	12.5	48.4	70.0	3.2	15.0	100.0	100.0
Nagaur	9	–	8	5	16	35	–	–	33	40
	27.3		24.2	12.5	48.5	87.5			100.0	100.0
Bhilwara	5	–	3	2	23	28	–	10	31	40
	16.1		9.7	5.0	74.2	70.0		25.0	100.0	100.0
Jhalawar	6	–	3	–	20	36	5	4	34	40
	17.6		8.8		58.8	90.0	14.7	10.0	100.0	100.0
Bharatpur	8	–	4	–	16	30	7	10	35	40
	22.8		11.5		45.7	75.0	20.0	25.0	100.0	100.0
Total	37	1	24	12	90	157	13	30	164	200
	22.6	0.5	14.6	6.0	54.9	78.5	7.9	15.0	100.0	100.0

District-wise, the pattern is on expected lines. In Ganga-nagar, the highest percentage (29.0%) of elite respondents has a 'high' level of information and another 19.4% has a 'medium' level. Nagaur closely follows Ganganagar with 27.3% of the elite in 'high' and 24.2% in 'medium' level categories. Bharatpur stands next. In Jhalawar and Bhilwara the perecentages of elite respondents belonging to 'high' and 'medium' levels are much lower in comparison to other districts. The percentages for Jhalawar district are : 17.6 for high and 8.8 for medium levels. In Bhilwara 16.1% have a high level and 9.7% have a medium level of information.

The level of information of citizens of elites about State level leaders is shown in Table 6.8. In the aggregate, it will be seen that 33 (20.1%) of the elite respondents and 1 (0.5%) citizen respondent are put in the category of 'high' level of information and 25.0% of elite and 8.5% of the citizens are in the 'medium' level category. Another 47.0% of the elite and 75.0% of the citizens have a 'low' level of information. The remaining 7.9% of elite respondents and 16.0% of citizen respondents are in the 'zero' level category. A comparsion of the data with Table 6.6 shows that a slightly higher percentage (up by 2.5%) of elite respondents enjoys a high level of information in regard to particulars of national level leaders, while a greater percentage falls in the category of a 'medium' level of informa-tion about State level leaders. Consequently, at lower levels ('low' and 'zero' combined) of information about State level lead-ers, we find a smaller percentage (55%) of the elite than we find in these categories in regard to national level leaders (63%).

A district-wise view of the data brings out some minor varia-tions as compared to the previous table. Thus, in the districts of Ganganagar, Nagaur, and Bhilwara, slightly fewer elite respondents have a 'high' level information about State level leaders in comparison to the percentage of elite respondents having a 'high' level of information in regard to national level leaders. This slight decrease may be due to the fact that the mass media of information, cover mainly national news, while more of State news comes through inter-personal media of communication, such as the M.L.A., pradhan, or other local political figures.

TABLE 6.8

Level of Information of Elite and Citizen Respondents in regard to Knowledge of State Level Leaders

District	High		Medium		Low		Zero		Total	
	Elites	Citizens	Elites	Citizens	Elites	Citizens	Elites	Citizens	Elites	Citizens
Ganganagar	8 25.8	1 2.5	7 22.6	4 10.0	15 48.4	27 67.5	1 3.2	8 20.0	31 100.0	40 100.0
Nagaur	7 21.2	—	15 45.4	9 22.5	10 30.3	31 77.5	1 3.0	—	33 100.0	40 100.0
Bhilwara	4 12.9	—	9 29.0	1 2.5	18 58.1	27 67.5	—	12 30.0	31 100.0	40 100.0
Jhalawar	6 17.6	—	7 20.6	3 7.5	16 47.1	32 80.0	5 14.7	5 12.5	34 100.0	40 100.0
Bharatpur	8 22.8	—	3 8.6	—	18 51.4	33 82.5	6 17.1	7 17.5	35 100.0	40 100.0
Total	33 20.1	1 0.5	41 25.0	17 8.5	77 47.0	150 75.0	13 7.9	32 16.0	164 100.0	200 100.0

The analysis of the data in relation to age-groups, literacy, and caste-status, brings out a trend similar to the one delineated in the earlier table. Here also, the middle age-group and higher caste and higher literacy status groups contribute more to the categories of 'high' and 'medium' levels of information than others.

Another question was addressed to elite respondents to ascertain the amount of information flowing into rural areas in the context of panchayati raj. The purpose was to analyse the extent to which the elite keeps itself informed of the constitutional pattern as well as changes in the panchayati raj pattern. The question read : "What changes have been introduced since the last election in the procedure of election of panchayati raj functionaries such as sarpanch, pradhan and pramukh?" Information expected from the question involved a time factor since the changes were incorporated in the Panchayat Samiti and Zila Parishad Act, 1959, following the recommendation of the Sadiq Ali Committee, which submitted its report in 1964. The changes had the result of panchas being included in the electoral college for electing the pradhans and sarpanchas being included in the electoral college for electing pramukhs. Earlier, only sarpanchas and pradhans were included in the electoral college for electing pradhans and pramukhs, respectively. The election pattern of the sarpanch was left intact.

The replies are covered by Table 6.9. It is clear that less than one-third (31.7%) of elite respondents are correctly informed of the changes in the modes of election of various panchayati raj posts. About 28.0% of the respondents gave incorrect replies and 40.2% reported themselves to be ignorant of the procedural changes.

A consideration of the above data, by districts, shows that the highest percentage of correct replies came from Nagaur (39.4%), followed by Ganganagar (38.7%) and Bhilwara (35.5%). It is surprising that the incidence of correct replies is low in Jhalawar and Bharatpur. In case of Jhalawar, it can be explained that the overbearing influence of Harish Chandra (late Maharaja of Jhalawar), who enjoyed more or less unchallenged leadership in the district, might have reduced political competition and hence interest and involvement of the members of the electoral college

TABLE 6.9

Awareness about Changes Introduced in the Procedure of Elections to Panchayati Raj Bodies

District	Correctly informed No.	%	Wrongly informed No.	%	Reported as unaware No.	%	Total No.	%
Ganganagar	12	23.1	7	15.2	12	18.2	31	18.9
	38.7		22.6		38.7		100.0	
Nagaur	13	25.0	10	21.7	10	15.1	33	20.1
	39.4		30.3		30.3		100.0	
Bhilwara	11	21.2	1	2.2	19	28.8	31	18.9
	35.5		3.2		61.3		100.0	
Jhalawar	9	17.3	13	28.3	12	18.2	34	20.7
	26.5		38.2		35.3		100.0	
Bharatpur	7	13.4	15	32.6	13	19.7	35	21.4
	20.0		42.9		37.1		100.0	
Total	52	100.0	46	100.0	66	100.0	164	100.0
	31.7		28.1		40.2		100.0	

to a certain minimum level, and as a result, not many panchas and other members constituting the electoral college felt the impact of the changes. Coupled with this was the factor of general backwardness. Altogether, many members of the elite group were simply not acquainted with the latest changes and some could not recall the events in sequence correctly. For Bharatpur, however, no plausible explanation can be offered for the trend, as this district, by comparison, is better placed than the rest in terms of literacy percentage and the extent and intensity of various media of communication.

Emerging Trends

We can venture to identify certain board trends in regard to the patterns of communication and its media in rural areas. Five trends deserved to be mentioned here:

First, it can easily be seen that the village community is gradually giving up its insulated character. The use of radio together with urban contacts, as one of the media of gathering information, is popular ; village *chopals* are also serving as effective forums of discussion ; newspapers are a little less popular among citizens. But considering the level of illiteracy among rural people and difficulties in maintaining a regular supply of newspapers, this is hardly surprising.

Second, with regard to channels of communication within the framework of panchayati raj, it would seem that while a large number of members of the elite group prefer to consult institutional elites or villagers in collective form over affairs of public importance, they prefer to draw upon social circle (caste, friends, etc.) over affairs of personal importance. In contrast, relations, very few of the elite respondents prefer to have consultation with officials over matters either of public or of personal importance. This shows that the bureaucratic elite has failed to evoke a sense of confidence both among the elite persons and the citizenry. Further, the fact that development officials are contacted less by the low level institutional elite (panchas etc.) and reputational elite persons, shows that the officials, by and large, still stick to their officious attitude.

Third, it also seems that information which flows both through mass and inter-personal media has a greater prospect of absorption than that which comes exclusively through mass media. This is evident from the fact that there are more elite respondents having 'high' and 'medium' levels of information in regard to particulars of contestants than is the case with information about national and State level personalities.

Fourth, the survey also indicates existence of a gulf between the elite and the masses *vis-a-vis* the extent of use of various media of communication as well as patterns of inter-group communication. The gulf appears to be wider in less developed districts. It is also clear from the data that this gulf does not appear to be so pronounced in the psyche of the people as it is in their actual bahaviour. Thus even less than two-fifth of citizen respondents have tried to draw the attention of panchayats to village improvement schemes. Very few citizens actually have used the form of the *gram sabha* for communicating their ideas to the governing elite. The citizens do not seem to be optimistic about the prospects of the panchayati raj system.

Finally, the patterns of communication have been found to vary with the areas under study. Thus, in the more developed districts of Ganganagar and Bharatpur, officials are consulted more. On the other hand, in Nagaur one witnesses a greater upward flow of communications from citizens to the elite. And in that, the fact that Nagaur has a background of political articulation may be a factor. Similarly, the assumption that local candidates tend to be more popular and consequently, more likely to win popular support, is confirmed by the trend observed in Nagaur.

7

PARTY IDENTIFICATION AND
POLITICAL LINKAGES

THE LINKS POLITICAL actors have with political parties and with important personalities in a political system, are likely to contribute substantially to their influence structure. This seems to be more so in the case of the elite, already a privileged group in one respect or the other. A political actor with close links with higher-level functionaries may not only influence decision-making processes in a general way but also in a specific way, should the need arise. It is in this context that linkage politics has come to occupy a key place in the study of decision-making processes.[1]

An attempt is made here to study the patterns of political linkages as well as the party identity of elite persons in rural areas. An effort will also be made to analyse how the linkages are put into operation to get something done, especially at the panchayat samiti, district, and State levels. Finally, we will examine the impact that these linkages have on the working of panchayati raj institutions.

An analysis of the patterns of political linkages, however, cannot be undertaken in isolation from the context of the areas and elites concerned. In the context of Rajasthan, the development of political linkages is mainly a post-integration phenomenon. Earlier, poor media of communication, ineffective mobility, political confusion resulting from the existence of as many as 22 principalities of the erstwhile Rajputana and, lastly, the adverse effect of the feudal system on the

1. Studies making the point in India's urban context are Rosenthal, Donald B., *The Limited Elite : Politics and Government in Two Indian Cities* (Chicago : The University of Chicago Press, 1970) and Jones, Rodney, "Linkage Analysis of Indian Politics", *Economic and Political Weekly*, VII (25) June 17, 1972, 1195-1203.

growth of political consciousness were factors that did not prove conducive to the evolution of linkages. It might be recalled that during feudal days, the linkages were either absent or were of a unidirectional character, flowing from upper to lower level, and not the other way round. Linkages were particularly inadequate at the rural level. The psychic make-up of the political actors had also been not conducive to political linkages in the pre-panchayati raj period. We have already portrayed the reactions of members of the elite group to the important question of whether they considered membership of a political party essential for the success of anybody in public life. Only 32.9% of the elite respondents said that party member-ship was essential ('very necessary' plus 'necessary'); while 26.8% gave a negative response ; and, 25.6% were non-committal, hold-ing that membership made no difference. The remaining elite respondents were unable to reply to the question in either way. Thus, the majority of the elite believes that party membership is of little consequence for success in public life. This atti-tude can hardly be considered as conducive to forging of poli-tical linkages.

Pattern of Party Identification

Let us begin with a discussion of patterns of the party identification of elite respondents. Questions on whether the members of the elite group are formally members of a political party (and, if not, whether they show any preference for any party) or whether they decry identification with a party in any manner have been put both to elite and citizen respondents.

The first question read : "Are you a member of any of the organizations enumerated below ?" The structured question also listed, besides political parties, caste associations and professional organizations. However, the replies, by and large, elicited the names of political parties only. Hence only the pattern of party-identification is being discussed here. Table 7.1 presents replies received from elite and citizen respondents. It will be obvious that in the aggregate, as well as in each district, fewer citizens than persons of the elite status are party members. The elite thus has an edge in the sharing of political resources

TABLE 7.1

Membership of a Political Party by District

District	Yes		No		Total	
	Elite	Citizens	Elite	Citizens	Elite	Citizens
Ganganagar	14	4	17	36	31	40
	45.2	10.0	54.8	90.0	100.0	100.0
Nagaur	19	17	14	23	33	40
	57.6	42.5	42.4	57.5	100.0	100.0
Bhilwara	21	6	10	34	31	40
	67.7	15.0	32.3	85.0	100.0	100.0
Jhalawar	21	4	13	36	34	40
	61.8	10.0	38.2	90.0	100.0	100.0
Bharatpur	24	11	11	29	35	40
	68.6	27.5	31.4	72.5	100.0	100.0
Total	99	42	65	158	164	200
	60.4	21.0	39.6	79.0	100.0	100.0

over the citizens as it has in social standing, wealth, education and the use of various media of communication.

A district-wise analysis brings out certain interesting trends. As against 21.0% of the citizens, 60.4% of the elite respondents have identified themselves as belonging to a party. The highest percentage (67.7) of membership among elite respondents is in Bharatpur, while the lowest (45.2%) is in Ganganagar district, though it is comparatively a more developed area. Since Bhilwara closely follows the Bharatpur pattern, it appears that economic development and an urge for association with a party have no direct co-relation. Actually, identification with a party is an indicator of the fact that people think of parties as serving their collective and/or individual interests or are helpful in their political career. If such a feeling or urge is wanting, people will not tend to become members of any party. As shown in chapter 5, 22.6% of the elite respondents in Ganganagar said that party membership was essential for a successful public man. Considering this figure against the aggregate figure of 32.9% for all the districts one may argue that the low salience of party membership explains the fact that the lowest percentage of elite respondents identifying themselves with a party, is in Ganganagar. On the other hand, in Bharatpur, where 34.3% of the elite respondents treat party membership as essential, the extent of party identification for elite respondents is 68.6%. Another factor can also be held accountable for this trend in Ganganagar : at the time this study was undertaken, all the major political parties, including the Congress, were in disarray following a big peasant agitation launched in the district nearly 6 months earlier. Though the Congress has had a comparatively greater hold in the district, the elite persons there generally showed sympathy for one of the opposition political parties. In spite of divided loyalties they would not openly admit that they had links with any opposition party, as they were afraid that they would incur the displeasure of the ruling party.

In contrast, elite respondents felt no such inhibition in Bhilwara, a Congress-dominated area. More or less the same holds true for the district of Nagaur, where they also openly admitted the fact of their association with the Congress. We would like to suggest by way of a descriptive hypothesis here that where there is one-party hegemony at State, district and block levels, the elite does not hesitate to disclose its party identification, but where there is asymmetry they are reluctant to do so. Jhalawar offers a case in point where the BKD dominated at the block level, the Congress at the State level, and the district was divided between these two parties.

We also obtained data about party identification in relation to the generational background of elite and citizen respondents. The largest number of members of the elite and citizen groups who claim party membership are from the middle age-group (30-50). The percentage figure for elite respondents is 66.3 and for citizens 23.2. The old age-group (above 50), follows among both elite and citizen respondents ; the respective percentages are 51.7 and 20.8. With 50.0% of elite respondents and 17.0% of citizens claiming party identification, the young age-group is placed last. This only confirms the trend discussed elsewhere that the middle age-group is more mobile and active and, therefore, more involved in political processes than others.

A correlation of this data with the caste background of respondents brings out anticipated trends in the case of elite respondents though not so much in the case of the citizens. While 70.0% of elite respondents of the upper caste group are members of a political party, the percentages for middle and lower caste groups are 58.9 and 41.2. But the corresponding pattern in the case of citizens, shows a reverse order. Thus, 26.2% of lower caste groups as against 18.8% of upper caste citizens and 19.4% of middle caste citizens are members of a party. The only plausible explanation for this is that a large chunk of lower caste people, due to their enthusiasm for the Congress, have reported their membership in the party. An analysis of data on membership of other political parties by caste status also confirms this surmise.

A consideration of the same data in relation to literacy status shows that, as one moves up from the illiterate to the literate, larger percentages of respondents, both elite and citizen, tend to be identified with a party. The only exception is that no citizen in the 'above matric' category identified himself with a party. Actually, the solitary citizen respondent who belonged to this group stated that he was non-partisan. Thus, one can say that in rural Rajasthan literacy and party identification are correlated.

We now turn to analysis of the data in relation to positional status of elite respondents (Table 7.2). Once again, the data follow an expected pattern. The 'sarpanchas etc.' group leads with 78.1% of them claiming party membership. For elite respondents in the 'panchas etc.' category, the figure is 58.7% and for reputational elite members it is 32.4%. This might be ascribed to the degree of mobility and the influence the elite has come to acquire within and outside its village. Members of the elite group in high positions have more of political aspirations and are keen to acquire more influential positions and, consequently, they tend to develop a more intense identity with political parties than their counterparts in other categories.

TABLE 7.2

Membership of Political Parties by Position of Elite Respondents

Position	Yes		No		Total	
	No.	%	No.	%	No.	%
Panchas etc.	37	37.4	26	40.0	63	38.4
	58.7		41.3		100.0	
Sarpanchas etc.	50	50.5	14	21.5	64	39.0
	78.1		21.9		100.0	
Reputational Elite etc.	12	12.1	25	38.5	37	22.6
	32.4		67.6		100.0	
Total	99	100.0	65	100.0	164	100.0
	60.4		39.6		100.0	

Both elite and citizen respondents were asked to specify the political party to which they belonged. It was found that nearly 75% of the respondents belonged to the Congress. The aggregate share of other political parties was almost negligible. For example, the B.K.D. elicited the support of only 9.1% of the elite respondents. District-wise, Bhilwara contributes the highest percentage of members to the Congress party—25.7% of the total 74 members of the Congress. The contribution of other districts in order is : Bharatpur 23.0%, Nagaur 20.3%, Jhalawar 16.2%, and Ganganagar 14.8%. It may be mentioned here that the last two districts were most affected by the formation of a separate political party (first called the Janta Party ; it afterwards merged with the Bharatiya Kranti Dal) by Congress dissidents in Rajasthan.[2] In Ganganagar, though the Congress did not suffer reverses in 1967, still it lost a good measure of organizational support. This also explains why a substantial number of elite respondents in Jhalawar (6 out of 21, *i.e.*, 28.6%) belonged to the B.K.D. Surprisingly, the Jana Sangh, which has been regarded as an entrenched political party in Jhalawar, does not appear to command support of the rural elite. The same is more or less true of the S.S.P. in Bharatpur and of the Swatantra in Nagaur districts in which these parties achieved major electoral successes in 1967. Either those opposition political parties had earlier benefited by anti-Congress votes or they had failed later to prevent the erosion of their strength.

Correlating the data with background variables of age, education, and caste, we find that significant patterns emerge only in relation to caste. It is clear that an overwhelming number of all the caste-groups are identified with the Congress, but this tendency is more pronounced in case of lower castes. Thus 85.7% of the elite respondents and 81.2% of citizen respondents of lower castes have identified themselves with the Congress as against 74.7% of the elite respondents and 73.7% of the citizens doing so in aggregate terms. It might be said that the bases of non-Congress political parties are of greater magnitude among upper castes, and these parties have gained no worthwhile sustenance from the lower caste groups.

Citizen and elite respondents (who had replied that they belonged to no political party) were further asked : "Suppose

---

2. Two major leaders of Congress splinter group also belonged to these districts : Kumbha Ram Arya to Ganganagar and Raja Harish-chandra to Jhalawar. This accounts for the waning influence of Congress in these districts.

you are asked to join a political party, which political party would you prefer ?" The responses are collated in Table 7.3. Here we have grouped the preferences for all the non-Congress political parties together under the head 'Non-Congress Parties' because there are scanty data for individual parties. The bulk of the answers belong to the category : 'no party to be opted for'. By this some meant that no party comes upto their expectations, while others took the position that they were not interested in party politics ; 55.4% of the elite respondents and 64.6% of the citizen respondents hold this opinion. In the next category are those non-party members who would like to join Congress ; 32.3% in the elite category and 27.2% in the citizen category. Very few favoured non-Congress political parties.

District-wise, it appears that the largest percentage of those who would opt for no party, is found in Jhalawar district. It might be mentioned here that after the demise of Raja Harish Chandra in 1967, both the Congress and non-Congress political parties found themselves in disarray. Further, while the tide of anti-Congressism, as seen in the party's debacle in 1967, had created a new situation, non-Congress political parties failed to consolidate the gains of the 1967 elections. Hence the people did not really have the choice to opt for party alternatives. It should, therefore, not be surprising if the members of the elite group also show a preference for 'no political party'. On the other hand, in Bharatpur, a substantial number of elite respondents (27.3%) took the position that they would opt for non-Congress political parties, most notably the SSP, which has a foothold in the district. However, citizen respondents (nearly 45%) would prefer to join the Congress in this district, while an equal percentage of citizens (which is much below the average for all the districts) took the position that they would not like to opt for any political party. It appears that the Congress, having suffered a major defeat in 1967 in the district, found itself disowned by the elite and, therefore, appealed to the common man over the head of the elite.[3] In

---

3. However, on the eve of the 1972 assembly elections, the elite also began to rally to the Congress as is evident from the victory of Congress candidates with a comfortable margin.

TABLE 7.3

Parties of which the Elite and Citizen Respondents would like to become Members

Districts	Congress		Non-Congress political parties		No party to be chosen		Total	
	Elites	Citizens	Elites	Citizens	Elites	Citizens	Elites	Citizens
Ganganagar	7 41.2	7 19.4	2 11.8	5 13.9	8 47.0	24 66.7	17 100.0 26.2	36 100.0 22.8
Nagaur	6 42.9	6 26.1	3 21.4	1 4.3	5 35.7	16 69.6	14 100.0 21.5	23 100.0 14.6
Bhilwara	5 50.0	10 29.4	—	1 2.9	5 50.0	23 67.7	10 100.0 15.4	34 100.0 21.5
Jhalawar	2 15.4	7 19.4	—	3 8.3	11 84.6	26 72.2	13 100.0 20.0	36 100.0 22.8
Bharatpur	1 9.1	13 44.8	3 27.3	3 10.4	7 63.6	13 44.8	11 100.0 16.9	29 100.0 18.3
Total	21 32.3	43 27.2	8 12.3	13 8.2	36 55.4	102 64.6	65 100.0 100.0	158 100.0 100.0

the remaining districts of Ganganagar, Nagaur, and Bhilwara, a good number of members of the elite group and citizens seem to prefer joining the Congress, though, comparatively, the preference of the elite has a lead over that of the citizens. It also appears that the Congress is determined to regain its hold in Nagaur which it had lost in 1967 elections.

Responses, both from elite and citizen respondents, were also sought to the query : "For what reasons you will like to join a particular party ?" This question was addressed only to those respondents who were non-members and had also expressed their perferences for a particular party. 'The programme of party' is a consideration for the largest number of elite respondents (55.2%), while 'past performance of party' is a consideration for the largest number of citizen respondents (44.6%). It was found that by past performance citizen respondents mostly meant the works or activities of development organized by a party for a particular local area. This is followed by the consideration that a particular political party is also the 'ruling party'. Since a ruling party is better placed to offer benefits and patronage to a community as well as to individuals, this becomes an effective determinant, as vouched by 13.8% of elite respondents and 19.6% of the citizens.

District-wise, in Ganganagar, the party-programme appeals to all but one of the elite and as many as 41.7% of the citizens. The number of elite respondents indicating preference for a political party in other districts is not significant, except in Nagaur where 4 of 9 (44.4%) advance 'party programme' as a consideration. In contrast, the past performance of a political party is a consideration for an overwhelming number of citizens in Nagaur and Bhilwara districts (71.4% and 72.7% respectively). Recall that in these districts and particularly in Nagaur, the Congress has faced swift ups and downs and the electorate has not consistently supported the Congress candidates. In Jhalawar and Bharatpur 40.0% and 31.3% citizens respectively take the position that they would opt for the ruling party. Both these districts in 1967, broadly speaking, rejected the Congress, and consequently suffered deprivation of various developmental benefits. This realization seems to have influenced the decision of the citizens to favour the ruling party.

Fewer respondents, both elite (27.6%) and citizen (23.2%) would opt for non-Congress political parties. Also, elite and citizen respondents (62.5% and 23.0% respectively) prefer non-Congress political parties on programmatic considerations. The inference is that the Congress appeal is not entirely owing to programmatic considerations and there are other lures that it seems to offer. Our data reveal that a major determinant is its continuance in office as the ruling party, enabling it to extend benefits and patronage to its supporters. The responses in the category of 'past performance' may have been somewhat motivated by the same consideration ; it may be recalled here that 55.8% of the citizens prefer the Congress on account of its past performance. It is also interesting to note that 23.0% of the citizens also identify non-Congress political parties as being "in office". The explanation is that, though no political party other than the Congress has succeeded hitherto in capturing power in Rajasthan, non-Congressmen have been returned at local levels in several cases. The reference to non-Congress political parties obviously relates to their being in power at the local levels. Respondents obviously failed to distinguish between a political party capturing power at the State and local levels.

Another question concerning aversion to party identification was addressed to those elite and citizen respondents who were neither members of, nor had preference, for any political party. The responses show that out of 164 only 36 (22.0%) of the elite respondents were neither members of any political party nor had any inclination to join ; while 102 of 200 citizens (51.0%) fall in this category. The number of people in this category is highest in Jhalawar, both among elite (30.6%) and citizen (25.5%) respondents. Ganganagar closely follows Jhalawar. It has been found that respondents of this area have failed to appreciate the instrumental utility of a political party which may be due to the fact that in Jhalawar and Ganganagar districts, party organizations were, at that time at least, in disarray.

When asked to give reasons for their being averse to political parties a very high percentage (58.4% of the elite respondents and 54.9% of the citizens) failed to do so. Perhaps this is not so much by design as by chance ; they have had no opportunity of purposive contacts with any political party. This also shows how political parties have failed to create and cultivate their image in rural areas. The cases of Jhalawar and Ganganagar further bear this out. In Jhalawar 100.0% of the elite respondents and 69.2% of the citizens in this category gave no reasons for their commitment to stay uninvolved. In Ganganagar, on the other hand, only 25.0% of the elite respondents and 41.7% of the citizen respondents gave no reasons. It is noteworthy that in Ganganagar 37.5% of the elite respondents and a little of the citizen respondents, took the position that they were averse to party politics *per se*, and 37.5% of the elite respondents and 20.8% of the citizens had no faith in any political party. In other districts, the responses have been so few that any attempt to make worthwhile comparisons would be futile.

To sum up, a much larger proportion of the elite than of the citizenery is identified with a party. It has also been seen that higher the position of a person in the panchayati raj hierarchy, the greater the prospects of his becoming a member of a political party. Persons of the elite status usually enjoy a strategic position in regard to influencing policy-making organs, not only at the district level but also at the State level. They owe this position in part to their being member of a political party ; holding a position is also an incentive for becoming a party member. Among non-member respondents, it was found that a good number of the elite and citizens would prefer the Congress if asked to join a political party. The reason is ascribable to the ruling party status of the Congress, and the consequent levers of benefits and patronage it might command.

Pattern of Political Linkages

Political linkages are expected to add to one's area of influence as they enhance one's leverage in decision-making organs. Further, the intensity of linkages with high-ups should have a bearing on the leverage one would come to acquire. And yet, as already reported, these links in rural areas are still in a nascent phase. How they evolve in the future will have considerable bearing on the politics of the State at various levels.

LINKS WITH ELECTED OFFICE BEARERS

A structured question was put to elite respondents to ascertain the extent of the links with elected office bearers. They were asked to specify whether they were well acquainted with the functionaries enumerated in the schedule : panch, sarpanch, pradhan, zila pramukh, M.L.A., M.P., and chairman of the cooperative society. Our concern was just to ascertain the extent of respondents' links with the person representing their respective areas. This question was not applicable in the case of those who themselves occupied a post under reference. Table 7.4 summarises the responses to this question. It will be seen that highest percentage of respondents (88.4) report an acquaintance with panchas. As we move upwards, the acquaintance-incidence shows a declining trend, only 44.5% of the elite respondents reported an acquaintance with M.Ps. Inferentially panch, sarpanch, and pradhan are more accessible, whereas zila pramukh, M.L.A. and M.P. are less so. The reason is not far to seek ; lower-level functionaries are not only local people, they are also more frequently "seen" and "heard", whereas quite often M.L.As. and M.Ps. are persons planted from elsewhere and visiting the area rather rarely.

District-wise data in this regard have been presented in Table 7.5. Except for acquaintance with the M.P. and zila pramukh, Ganganagar district has the highest percentage of respondents having links with the given set of representatives. The comparatively high level of development and mobility, which characterise Ganganagar district might be responsible for this trend. Also, certain situational factors appear to be significant here. Thus it was a coincidence that the pradhan of the panchayat samiti selected for study happened to belong to the panchayat under study. Hence it is natural for a high number of respondents (90.3%) to show an acquaintance with the pradhan. Similarly, the chairman of cooperative society happened to have been in office for a long time and so a very high number of respondents (87.1 %) were acquainted with him. On the other hand, the Ganganagar parliamentary constituency, being a reserved one, is naturally represented by a scheduled caste M.P. Though the person concerned has been continuously returned since 1952, many sarpanchas were not even conversant with his name. Surprising as this might seem, it can

TABLE 7.4

Whether Elite Respondents are Acquainted with a Given set of Functionaries

Acquaintance with	Yes		No		N.A./N.R		Total	
	No.	%	No.	%	No.	%	No.	%
Panch	145	88.4	—	—	19	11.6	164	100.0
Sarpanch	131	79.9	1	0.6	32	19.5	164	100.0
Pradhan	119	72.6	19	11.6	26	15.8	164	100.0
Zila Pramukh	87	53.0	67	40.9	10	6.1	164	100.0
Member of Legislative Assembly (MLA)	94	57.3	48	29.3	22	13.4	164	100.0
Member of Parliament (MP)	73	44.5	69	42.1	22	13.4	164	100.0
Chairman of Coop. Society	106	64.6	21	12.8	37	22.6	164	100.0

TABLE 7.5

Percentage of Total Number of Respondents Acquainted with Given Functionaries

Acquaintance with	Ganganagar	Nagaur	Bhilwara	Jhalawar	Bharatpur	Total
Panch	90.3	90.9	90.3	85.3	82.9	88.4
Sarpanch	87.1	84.8	83.9	76.5	68.6	79.9
Pradhan	90.3	72.7	67.7	61.8	71.4	72.6
Zila Pramukh	58.1	60.6	48.4	47.1	51.4	53.0
Member of Legislative Assembly (MLA)	77.4	72.7	48.4	52.9	37.1	57.3
Member of Parliament (MP)	45.2	66.7	35.5	38.2	37.1	44.5
Chairman of Cooperative Society	87.1	57.6	61.3	58.8	60.0	64.6

be explained by noting that the elite of Ganganagar largely hails from the middle castes, and seems to believe in getting work done directly through administrative channels (and in that too on the basis of their financial resources) depending much less on its politicians. In Nagaur, on the other hand, political activities have a comparatively longer and more intense history. Consequently, 66.7% of the elite respondents have specified a linkage with the M.P. of the area. In addition, the M.P. concerned happens to belong to a well reputed industrial family of the area and has had contacts with the people. The M.P. is a popular figure and keeps himself in constant touch with the common man. Acquaintance with the chairman of cooperative society gets the lowest response in Nagaur. As already reported, factionalism in the panchayat selected has been quite intense and the chairman himself was an important leader of a faction. Several respondents belonging to the other faction reported that they were not on speaking terms with the chairman. The weak pattern of responses in the districts of Bharatpur, Bhilwara and Jhalawar conforms to the expected pattern due to the comparative backwardness and the distance from samiti and/or district headquarters of the panchyats under study.

A position-wise analysis of the same data has also been attempted. A number of elite persons occupying upper level positions in the panchayati raj set-up had linkages with higher level functionaries. Thus, 84.4% of the members in the 'sarpanch etc'. category (this category includes sarpanchas, pradhans zila pramukh, M.L.A., etc.) are acquainted with the zila pramukh, 75.0% with the M.L.A. and 70.3% with the M.P. The corresponding figures for elite persons in the category of 'panchas etc.' confined largely to village level activits, are 36.5%, 44.4% and 31.7%, and for reputational elite members, 27.0%, 48.6% and 21.6%. The higher intensity of linkages of elites in the category of 'sarpanchas etc.' with upper level functionaries shows that horizontal linkages are more intense than vertical linkages. The responses also bear out that among the elite of the two lower positional categories ('panchas' and reputational elite members) the larger number of respondents are acquainted with the M L.A. and fewer know the zila pramukh. This brings out the significance of the functional aspect of the relationships. The zila pramukh, being head of an advisory and coordinating institution, is not considered an effective contact. An M.L.A., who is expected to have State level linkages and, therefore, can get things done much more expeditiously, is preferred. The case is slightly different with those in the category of 'sarpanchas, pradhans etc.' Associated with higher tiers of panchayati raj institutions, they are likely to be more acquainted with the zila pramukh in comparison to the elite in lower positions. Once again, it is obvious that horizontal linkages are far more conveniently forged, as borne out by the fact that panchas and reputational elite persons are closer to panchas and sarpanchas. Further, upper level elite persons come quite close to members of the lower level elite in being acquainted with lower level functionaries. It might be noted that owing to cases of 'non-responses' and 'non-applicable', the percentage figures of higher level respondents having acquintance with the sarpanch and pradhans, have come down appreciably.

If we briefly consider this data in relation to variables of age, caste and education, it becomes obvious, once again, that a larger number of respondents in the middle age-group, upper castes, and literate sections have linkages with the elite at the higher level.

Table 7.6 presents the answers to a further question : "How did you get acquainted with given functionaries ?" This open ended question, was addressed only to those elite respondents who had reported acquaintance with a set of given functionaries. A number of important trends emerge. First, an acquaintance with panchas, sarpanchas and the chairman of cooperative society, is, by and large, the result of social contact, such as being a friend or relation, sharing a common neighbourhood or caste affiliation. These three factors taken together were considered by respondents to be far more effective in establishing acquaintance with panchas (71.0%), sarpanchas (71.7%), and chairmen of cooperative society (72.7%), than other factors. Among the social factors, the overwhelming contribution is that of the locality and neighbourhood. Caste affiliation and friends and relations are not considered significant factors by elite respondents. Similarly, political factors,

TABLE 7.6

Ways in which Elite Respondents got Acquainted with a set of Given Functionaries

Acquaintance with	Friends and relations	Locality/ neighbour- hood factor	Caste affili- ation	Both being active in politics	During election campaign	Having similar profession	Others	Total
Panch	7 4.8	95 65.5	1 0.7	32 22.1	1 0.7	5 3.4	4 2.8	145 100.0
Sarpanch	16 12.2	73 55.7	5 3.8	20 15.3	3 2.3	8 6.1	6 4.6	131 100.0
Pradhan	12 10.1	25 21.0	4 3.3	46 38.7	13 10.9	9 7.6	10 8.4	119 100.0
Zila Pramukh	13 15.0	10 11.5	—	27 31.0	11 12.6	8 9.2	18 20.7	87 100.0
M.L.A.	11 11.7	16 17.0	4 4.3	25 26.6	19 20.2	4 4.3	15 16.0	94 100.0
M.P.	10 13.7	4 5.5	2 2.7	15 20.6	26 35.6	2 2.7	14 19.2	73 100.0
Chairman of Coop. Society	8 7.6	65 61.3	4 3.8	14 13.2	1 0.9	3 2.8	11 10.4	106 100.0

like 'active in politics' and 'active during election campaign' do not play any significant instrumental role in this regard. It seems that the closer contacts usually prevalent in rural area and the informality of relations, are responsible for the emphasis on the importance of social factors. The instrumental role of the political factor at the village level is meagre because the needs, as well as opportunities, for political "give and take" are somewhat limited. Second, in the case of acquaintance with pradhans, zila pramukhs, M.L.As and M.Ps, political factors were considered to be far more effective. Elite respondents report political factors to be instrumental in establishing links with these four categories of functionaries and the respective figures are 49.6%, 43.6%, 46.8% and 56.2%. There too, the intensity of political factors is comparatively not as high as that of social factors in the case of panchas and sarpanchas. Third, it is interesting that more than one-third of the elite respondents have reported that they came to be acquainted with the M.P. of their area only during the course of the election campaign. Lastly, the pursuit of similar professions is not a significant factor in establishing contacts.

LINKS WITH PARTY LEADERS

In order to assess the intensity of political links, another question put to elite respondents sought to ascertain whether and how they come to develop links with party leaders. The question was confined to district and samiti level leaders because it was presumed that village level elite respondents were not likely to have effective links with State level leaders. The state of political communication in rural Rajasthan being what it is, it was found that most respondents failed to identify correctly the names of political leaders and parties. The question, therefore, addressed to elite respondents specifically enquired of them whether they happened to be well acquainted with any of the samiti or district level leaders of a political party. It was left to respondents to decide for themselves the persons they considered leaders of samiti and district level importance. Those who replied in the affirmative were further asked to specify names along with the party affiliation of leaders. As regards the first part of the question, 102 out of 164 (62.2%)

elite respondents reported that they were acquainted with samiti and district level leaders, while 13.4% replied in the negative and the remaining 24.4% did not respond. District-wise, Ganganagar had the highest percentage reporting such links (24.5%). The comparatively high level of development in this district explains the response. However, Bharatpur presents a somewhat intriguing picture (14.7%). This district has had not only a more consistent tradition of political activities, but a fairly intense competitive level of politics also. Leftist forces have been quite active there. The only explanation for Bharatpur's low response in this regard seems to be that the Deeg panchayat samiti covered by our study happens to be at some distance from the district headquarters, and also, the panchayat selected for study is distant from both the samiti as well as the district headquarters.

Regarding the number of leaders with whom acquaintance was specified by elite respondents, it was found that 35.3% of the respondents claimed acquaintance with one or two leaders, while 51.0% knew 'three to four' leaders and the remaining 'five and above'. District-wise, Ganganagar leads, where the respondents claim acquaintance with 'three to four' (26.6%) and 'five and above' leaders (38.5%). On the other hand, Bharatpur trails in responses to this question also, with 7.5% and 7.7% of total respondents, respectively showing acquaintance with 'three to four' and 'five and above' leaders. The reasons given to explain the response pattern to the earlier question also hold good here. Nagaur, Jhalawar and Bhilwara follow Ganganager, in that order. It seems this pattern is an index of the level of political activities and general development in these districts.

As noted earlier, respondents were asked to give the names of political leaders and their respective political parties. However, while coding we took into account only the first three names of leaders and the political parties with which they happened to be affiliated. In all 102 elite respondents specified their identifications as shown in Table 7.7. We should therefore, have received 306 names of leaders. However, in 79 cases (25.8%), party affiliations were not specified. The reason seems to be that respondents failed to give three names ; or, if they specified all three names, they failed to recall the party-affiliation of leaders with whom they claimed acquaintance. In the cases of second and third specifications, non-responses go up.

Of the leaders with whom acquaintance was claimed, 142 belong to the Congress. This comes to 46.4% of total expected replies, or 62.6% of total replies when non-responses are excluded. Other political parties did not come anywhere near the Congress. The Bhartiya Kranti Dal is next (with 9.5% of total expected responses), followed by Swatantra (6.9%) and Jana Sangh (3.3%). Perhaps the last two political parties have not been able to extend their activities and influence in rural areas. In any case, the response pattern of the rural elite strengthens this impression.

Table 7.8 deals with the data in regard to patterns of party affiliation district-wise. Here we have taken into consideration only the aggregate data obtained after the summation of preferences enumerated at first, second, and third places and elimination of the cases of non-response. Bharatpur leads in having links with the Congress (83.3%), followed by the Socialists (16.7%). The emergence of the latter is a significant pointer. Also, the failure of other political parties to cultivate the elite is only too obvious.

Other districts which follow in their preferential support for the Congress are Bhilwara (78.2%), Nagaur (59.2%), Ganganagar (56.1%) and Jhalawar (47.6%). It may be worthwhile to recall here that in Ganganagar, Nagaur and Jhalawar the Congress did not fare well at the 1967 elections. Also, the emergence of the influence of the B.K.D. in these districts is obvious by the responses—15.2%, 14.3% and 28.6% respectively. However, the responses also confirm that the Congress continues to enjoy an edge over all the other political parties in all the districts under study.

Lastly, elite respondents were asked to specify factors which were instrumental in their getting acquainted with leaders at the district and samiti levels. We received 227 replies. The data show that "active involvement together with the party leaders in politics" receives the highest number of responses (25.6%). If we add up other political factors, such as

TABLE 7.7

Party Affiliation of District Leaders with whom Acquaintance has been Indicated

Order of preference in recording acquaintance	Congress	Swatantra	Jana Sangh	Communists	Socialists	B.K.D.	Non-party man	N.R.	Total
First	69	3	3	3	4	12	—	8	102
	67.7	2.9	2.9	2.9	3.9	11.8		7.9	100.0
Second	47	11	3	3	4	6	2	26	102
	46.1	10.8	2.9	2.9	3.9	6.0	1.9	25.5	100.0
Third	26	7	4	—	7	11	2	45	102
	25.5	6.9	3.9		6.9	10.8	1.9	44.1	100.0
Total	142	21	10	6	15	29	4	79	306
	46.4	6.9	3.3	2.0	4.9	9.5	1.3	25.8	100.0

TABLE 7.8

Party Affiliation of District Level Leaders with whom Elite Respondents are Acquainted, by District

Districts	Congress	Swatantra	Jana Sangh	Communists	Socialists	B.K.D.	Non-party man	Total
Ganganagar	37 56.1	7 10.6	1 1.5	6 9.1	3 4.5	10 15.2	2 3.0	66 100.0
Nagaur	29 59.2	7 14.3	4 8.2	—	—	7 14.3	2 4.1	49 100.0
Bhilwara	36 78.2	5 10.9	—	—	5 10.9	—	—	46 100.0
Jhalawar	20 47.6	2 4.8	5 11.9	—	3 7.1	12 28.6	—	42 100.0
Bharatpur	20 83.3	—	—	—	4 16.7	—	—	24 100.0
Total	142 62.6	21 9.3	10 4.4	6 2.6	15 6.6	29 12.8	4 1.8	227 100.0

membership of the ruling party, co-membership of panchayati raj institutions and co-workership in an election campaign, the total goes up to 53.4%. This is a considerable response, especially since non-political factors are mentioned in 29.9% cases of the total responses only. Thus the impact and significance of political factors is only too obviously recognized.

Party-wise analysis of the same data brings out no significant trends. As far as non-Congress parties were concerned, political factors continued to play a more effective role than informal factors, such as 'friends and caste consideration' or 'locality considerations'. The only exception is that of Jana Sangh, in which case 'friendship and relationship' and locality considerations played a role to the tune of 20% and 30% of responses respectively. This only confirms that the Jana Sangh has not 'politically' touched the core of the rural areas. The non-political factors explain the affiliation of the elite to the Congress to a far greater extent than political factors.

Instrumental Uses of Political Links

Another interesting aspect of the study of linkage politics is the instrumental uses of political links. In this context one might study the effectiveness of political links at various levels. In the context of Rajasthan, three broad levels (other than the panchayat from where most members of the elite group begin their career) can be identified : the panchayat samiti, district or zila parishad, and State levels. The nature of returns, in terms of benefits and rewards, might be either personal or public. In order to ensure as little bias as possible, the question put to respondents read : "Did you ever feel the necessity of getting either some personal or panchayat work done at panchayat samiti level ? If yes, how did you get it done ? Was it done directly ? Or indirectly, through someone else ?" Similar questions were repeated for district and State levels also. The assumption here was that one will get work done through someone with whom he feels closer.

Table 7.9 presents the responses received from elite respondents in regard to whether or not they had got something done at panchayat samiti/district/State levels. In the table only 'affirmative' replies from respondents have been collated. As one moves up from samiti to higher levels, the percentages of elite respondents who had got some work done at various levels, goes on decreasing. Thus, while 48.8% of the respondents identify personal work and 49.4% panchayat work which they had done at samiti level, 34.3% have had personal and panchayat work done at the district level, and 23.2% and 27.4% respectively have had personal and panchayat work done at the State level. District-wise, Jhalawar leads in responses specifying both personal and panchayat work to be done at all levels. This is somewhat surprising considering one earlier finding that, compared to the districts of Ganganagar and Nagaur, fewer members of the elite group have had links with panchayati raj functionaries and local leaders of various political parties in Jhalawar. However, there might be some explanation for this in the fact that the question addressed to respondents implied a cumulative coverage of time as against other questions which concerned current situation. Thus we should recall that the late Raja Harish-chandra of Jhalawar, who was a senior minister in the Rajasthan Cabinet until 1966, had wide links down to the village level, and local leaders unhesitatingly used to come to Jaipur (capital of the State) or Jhalawar (district headquarters) to get work done through him. In fact, people in Jhalawar in general and elite respondents in particular, recalled many such instances and also regretted his untimely demise. In other districts, several respondents openly regretted that ministers had now become almost inaccessible. Ganganagar, Nagaur and Bharatpur can more or less, be placed on an equal footing in the context of responses to this question. The differences, slight as they are, seem to be resultant of situational factors at a given time. Thus in Nagaur, from where quite a few figures of State level importance have come up, the respondents seem to have been encouraged to contact State level leaders instead of meeting samiti or district level officials.[5] Bhilwara stands at the lowest end in this respect also. The comparative isolation

5. The argument is strengthened by what officials of Ladnun panchayat samiti of Nagaur district had to say in course of informal chats. They told the research team that sarpanchas and other leaders of this area would prefer to go to Jaipur for getting a school opened, a primary school teacher transferred, or for such other minor favours.

TABLE 7.9

Percentages of Elite Respondents in each District who had Personal and/or Panchayat Work at Various Levels

Districts	At panchayat samiti level		At zila parishad level		At State level	
	Personal work	Panchayat work	Personal work	Panchayat work	Personal work	Panchayat work
Ganganagar	45.2	61.3	41.9	29.0	19.4	25.8
Nagaur	42.4	48.5	36.3	42.4	30.3	30.3
Bhilwara	35.5	38.7	6.5	19.4	12.9	9.7
Jhalawar	67.9	67.9	44.1	47.1	23.5	44.1
Bharatpur	51.4	31.4	40.4	31.4	28.6	25.7
Total	48.8	49.4	34.3	34.3	23.2	27.4

and lower level of development of the area are the likely factors for such a response.

A position-wise analysis of the same data brings out the fact that more of the higher level functionaries get work done at all the levels. A closer examination further brings out two other trends. First, at the samiti level, the difference between percentages of various positional groups is not as marked as it is in the case of various groups at district and State levels. For example, 62.5% of the elite respondents in the category of 'Sarpanchas etc.' reported that they have had panchayat work done at the samiti level ; 64.1% at the district level ; and 59.4% at the State level. The corresponding figures for elite persons in the category of 'panchas etc.' are 44.4%, 14.3% and 6.3% respectively and for reputational elite members 35.1%, 16.2%, and 8.1% respectively. Second, the members of the elite in the higher category lead in getting personal work done at the samiti level and panchayat work done at the State level. Perhaps this shows that, while their personal work could be done at local level, they had to approach higher level authorities for works like the opening of schools and hospitals, the sinking of wells and the like. Though the district administration can also sanction such things, it seems that persuading State level authorities was considered less troublesome, because the bureaucratic process at the district level was more time-consuming and less amenable to pressures of local level leaders, while political contacts with ministers at the State level might eventually smooth the flow of benefits. The second part of the question sought to identify the persons through whom respondents tried to get the work done at various levels. It was addressed to only those elite respondents who had given an affirmative response earlier. From the responses it was seen that at the panchayat samiti level, by and large, members of the elite group had a tendency to approach directly the authorities concerned and get the work done, especially personal work (73.8%). The corresponding percentage for those having panchayat work at samiti level was 55.5%. Approaching officials through elected panchayati raj representatives was another important channel for getting work done at the samiti level. Thus the pradhan or a powerful sarpanch of the samiti would be approached. From the responses it is clear that whereas lower positional elite persons seek the help of others, members of the upper positional elite group depend on getting the work done directly. It becomes obvious that the latter have wider linkages with, and influence upon, panchayati raj officials.

The responses pertaining to a direct approach for getting work done are progressively reduced in number as we move to upper levels. Thus 46.4% and 37.5% of the total of elite respondents who had personal or panchayat work at the district level, respectively, said that they attempted to get personal and panchayat work done directly. The corresponding figures for work to be done at State level are 26.3% and 20.0%. Moreover, fewer respondents sought the help of panchayati raj representatives for getting panchayat work done at district and State levels. Consequently, one can identify a progressive increase in the percentages of seekers of ministerial help in getting something done, as one moves up to upper levels. While none seeks ministerial help at the panchayat samiti level, nearly 14.3% seek it for both personal and panchayat works at the district level, and 21.6% and 35.6% seek it for personal and panchayat work respectively, at the State level. Links with party leaders, mainly belonging to ruling party, are also considered effective in getting work done at the State level. It is also interesting that replies under the head 'others' in this regard have included such responses as : "sought help of relations of elected representatives or of officials"; "neither directly nor through somebody else ; we get the work done directly, by bribing officials" and the like.

Motives Behind Extension of Support

Our analysis so far has considered the instrumental uses of upward linkages by members of the lower level elite. The utility of these linkages does not have to be unilinear. It should not be wholly unexpected that members of the local elite group expect something as a reward for services rendered and help extended.

With this in mind, we addressed two separate questions to elite respondents asking them to specify the support they had extended in the last elections (in 1967) for Vidhan Sabha and

Lok Sabha, and the reasons which prompted them to do so. Tables 7.10 and 7.11 summarise the responses.

Table 7.10 shows that a considerable number (20.7%) of elite respondents have not sided with any contestant in the elections. Of the remaining 130 respondents who had offered active help, 57.7% had extended support to Congress ; and 20.8% to the independents. It might be noted that independents happened to be mostly former Congressmen, who left the party when party tickets were denied to them. The Swatantra party received support from 16.2% of respondents and Jana Sangh from only 2.3%. District-wise, one notes that the Congress has had support of nearly all the elite groups in Bhilwara, while it had a dominant share of elite support in the Ganganagar district. In Nagaur it was evenly matched in strength with Swatantra party. In Jhalawar and Bharatpur, the Congress organization appears to be crippled by defections, and a substantial number of members of the elite groups in both districts reportedly extended their support to independents. About one-third of the positive responses in both these districts favoured the Congress. Three elite respondents in each of the two districts report that they extended support to the other non-Congress parties, to the Jana Sangh in Jhalawar and to the Socialists in Bharatpur,

Table 7.11 presents the data on patterns of support available to contestants for the Lok Sabha seat. It is interesting that the number of non-supporters is on the high side. While 20.7% of the elite respondents did not extend support to anybody in the Vidhan Sabha elections, 29.9% did not do so in the case of elections for the Lok Sabha. Similarly, though support for Congress goes up for Lok Sabha elections as compared to Vidhan Sabha elections in percentage terms, in actual numbers the support base gets shrunk. Similarly, with the exception of the Jana Sangh, all other opposition political parties lose some of their supporters. In the case of the Jana Sangh, the increase in support is owing to the responses received from Jhalawar district alone. There the contestant was the erstwhile prince of Kota who had recently left the Congress along with the former ruler of Jhalawar. The former contested as independent on the Jana Sangh symbol, and was supported by the latter. Since both these princes have wider bases and

TABLE 7.10

Political Parties Receiving Support by Rural Elite Respondents in Elections to the Vidhan Sabha Seat

Districts	Congress	Swatantra	Jana Sangh	Socialists	Independents	Total	To none/N.A./N.R.	Total (Grand)
Ganganagar	20	6	–	–	1	27	4	31
	74.1	22.2			3.7	100.0	12.9	100.0
						87.1		
Nagaur	15	14	–	–	–	29	4	33
	51.7	48.3				100.0	12.1	100.0
						87.9		
Bhilwara	24	–	–	1	1	26	5	31
	92.3			3.8	3.8	100.0	16.1	100.0
						83.9		
Jhalawar	8	1	3	–	12	24	10	34
	33.3	4.2	12.5		50.0	100.0	29.1	100.0
						70.9		
Bharatpur	8	–	–	3	13	24	11	35
	33.3			12.5	54.2	100.0	31.4	100.0
						68.6		
Total	75	21	3	4	27	130	34	164
	57.7	16.2	2.3	3.1	20.8	100.0	20.7	100.0
						79.3		

TABLE 7.11

Political Parties Receiving Support by Rural Elite Respondents in Elections for Lok Sabha Seat

Districts	Congress	Swatantra	Jana Sangh	Socialists	Independents	Total	None N.A./N.R.	Total (Grand)
Ganganagar	18 90.0	–	–	–	2 10.0	20 100.0 64.5	11 35.5	31 100.0
Nagaur	14 48.3	15 51.7	–	–	–	29 100.0 87.9	4 12.1	33 100.0
Bhilwara	22 100.0	–	–	–	–	22 100.0 71.0	9 29.0	31 100.0
Jhalawar	7 33.3	–	14 66.7	–	–	21 100.0 61.8	13 38.2	34 100.0
Bharatpur	9 39.1	–	–	1 4.4	13 56.5	23 100.0 65.7	12 34.3	35 100.0
Total	70 60.9	15 13.0	14 12.2	1 0.9	15 13.0	115 100.0 70.1	49 29.9	164 100.0

links, the Jana Sangh image was also elevated. District-wise, the pattern is more or less similar to that discussed in the context of the previous table. The only exception is the emergence of the Jana Sangh. But, again, the candidate concerned was really an independent who cashed in on the Jana Sangh symbol and support.

A comparison of the two tables brings out some significant trends. First, one can clearly see that contestants for the Lok Sabha seat have less capability to mobilize the elite in rural areas to work for them than do have the prospective MLAs. This might be owing to the fact that Lok Sabha constituencies are about eight times as large in Rajasthan than Vidhan Sabha constituencies, and effective links are not always easy to maintain. The capability would have been still weaker but for the fact that candidates for the Vidhan Sabha and the Lok Sabha worked in close cooperation since the two elections were linked. Second, some sort of fragmented support is visible more in the case of contests for the Vidhan Sabha than those for the Lok Sabha. As shown in the table, in all five districts, which cover roughly five Lok Sabha constituencies, the Congress either has no potential opposition, or, where it is challenged with some determination, opposition forces centre round a particular common candidate. Lastly, members of the elite group are either for the Congress or for rightist political parties, Swatantra and Jana Sangh. The parties of the left, Socialists and Communists, do not have much in the way of support bases in rural areas.

Why rural elites supported a particular party in election was the burden of the next question, which we have analysed above.[6] In short, the largest number of elite respondents supported the Congress because it was the party in power : 21.5% for Vidhan Sabha and 24.4% for the Lok Sabha elections maintain so. Among other factors specified were "candidates belonging to one's own party", "protest vote" and so on. Socio-traditional factors do not appear to have had a significant role as motivating factors. This is true of factors like caste affiliation, relations, village consensus and feudal impact. Cumulatively, such responses might look formidable, but each

6. See Chapter IV.

of these individually is not really effective.   At best, wherever such considerations have been at work, they cut across political and party links.

Linkages and Political Interference

In the foregoing analysis, a brief attempt has been made to assess how far political linkages influence the working of panchayati raj institutions.   It has often been alleged that the pathetic situation in which panchayati raj finds itself today is the result of the political backing of the rural local leaders and frequent political interference from upper levels, specifically the State government.   Keeping these views in mind a hypothesis was formulated, the main part of which (as already spelled out in the first chapter) read : "It is not the involvement of the rural elite in local politics which hinders the healthy growth of democracy at the grass roots level ; the malady lies in the political linkages of the rural elite with the district and State level elites."

One part of the hypothesis has already been discussed in preceding sections.   It was seen that when it came to the issue of links with the district level party leaders or to the issue of extending support to contestants for the Vidhan Sabha and the Lok Sabha seats, members of the rural elite group in greater number have shown a preference for those belonging to the ruling party—'ruling' mentioned specifically.   This section attempts to analyse the other part of the hypothesis : whether members of the upper level ruling elite group oblige members of the lower level elite-strata in return for the latter's support, by influencing the working of panchayati raj.   The question addressed to the elite respondents in this regard read : "Will you specify, from your experience, if political interference from above affects the working of panchayati raj institutions ?   If yes, in what ways ?"   This question was meant not so much to probe into the actual state of political interference as to enquire about the perception of the problem by elite respondents.   Thus it is quite possible that respondents might be overrating or underrating the impact of political interference and the consequent state of affairs in regard to panchayati raj.   However, as our concern here is primarily elite behaviour, it can be argued that even responses predominantly weighed with perception are significant.

Table 7.12 presents responses in this context : 56.7% of the elite respondents deny that such interference exists at all. Another 28.7% claim ignorance in this regard. Thus only 14.6% state that political interference does affect the working of panchayati raj. It should, however, be recalled that political interference is alleged to exist mostly at panchayat samiti or zila parishad levels. Thus those of the elite, such as panchas, reputational elite persons etc. who are not in touch with these institutions, might be ignorant of the existence of political interference. More significantly, those elite persons who belong to the ruling party are not likely to confess for obvious reasons that political interference exists.

District-wise, in Bhilwara and Bharatpur such interference is denied, or ignorance about it is claimed by all but two elite respondents. Ganganagar contributes 33.3% of elite respondents to the total of those identifying political interference as harmful to the cause of panchayati raj. Nagaur and Jhalawar stand at 25% each. Of these three districts, where the phenomenon of interference has been identified, the panchayat samitis under study in Ganganagar and Jhalawar districts had, at the time this study was undertaken, non-Congress pradhans, while in Nagaur factionalism was both rampant and vocal. That might explain to some extent the pattern of responses. It was observed that 25.0% of 24 elite respondents blamed the pradhan for encouraging political interference. It was alleged that a pradhan would withhold or delay the grants for a particular work in a panchayat if its sarpanch belonged to a rival party. Three elite respondents in Ganganagar, two elite respondents in Bhilwara and one in Jhalawar made such complaints. Two elite respondents, one each in Ganganagar and Jhalawar, alleged that the State government would withhold or delay grants if the pradhan belonged to a non-Congress political party. However, limited in numbers, these observations cannot be lightly dismissed. Other ways of interference come to 33.3% of the total responses and 62.5% of these come from Nagaur. It should be recalled, even at the risk of repetition, that the district has had intense factionalism and the working of panchayati

TABLE 7.12

Whether Interference from Above affects the Working of Panchayati Raj Institutions

Districts	Yes, it does affect		No, it does not		N.R./D.K.		Total	
	No.	%	No.	%	No.	%	No.	%
Ganganagar	8	33.4	17	18.3	6	12.8	31	18.9
Nagaur	6	25.0	12	12.9	15	31.9	33	20.1
Bhilwara	2	8.3	25	26.9	4	8.5	31	18.9
Jhalawar	6	25.0	19	20.4	9	19.1	34	20.7
Bharatpur	2	8.3	20	21.5	13	27.7	35	21.4
Total	24	100.0	93	100.0	47	100.0	164	100.0
	14.6		56.7		28.7		100.0	

raj institutions obviously was thereby adversely affected. We came across many such examples. In one case, a local business-man offered to donate buildings for a hospital and school. Since the sarpanch of the panchayat wherein the buildings were to be constructed belonged to the faction other than that of the pradhan the latter saw to it that sanction for the opening of the hospi-tal and school was withheld. In another case, primary school facilities were also withdrawn at the instance of the pradhan because the sarpanch belonged to a different party.

Summary

The above analysis of patterns of party identification, poli-tical linkages, and their instrumental uses brings out some interesting aspects of elite behaviour. It has been seen that in comparison to citizens, many more of the elite would identify themselves with one party or the other. Among the elite, those in the category of 'sarpanchas, etc.' identified in greater num-ber with a political party than the panchas or reputational elite members. Since a majority of the upper positional elite belongs to a high social and/or economic strata and educational back-ground, it represents a segment of society which holds socio-economic superiority and enhances its prospects of access to political power and also helps it to become politically resourceful. This becomes self evident when one finds that the Congress overwhelmingly dominates the list of political parties preferred by the elite as well as by citizens. Further, while developing political linkages with higher level elites, the local elite would concentrate on those who belong to Congress. Actually, as we found in the study of instrumental uses of political links, party leaders, particularly ministers hailing from the area concerned, prove quite helpful in getting work done at State and district levels. In the absence of these links, many of the elite may not even think of getting work done at the State level.

Only one-fourth of the elite respondents interviewed report-ed having some personal or panchayat work at the State level. The reason seems to be that members of the lower level elite group lack perspective and high status, and they are also farther away from centres of power. A very high percentage of persons of the lower level elite are not well-acquainted with

MLAs and MPs. They do not have worth-while opportunities to come into contact with upper level elected representatives, while the sarpanchas and pradhans enjoy such opportunities, since the MLAs and MPs are associated with panchayat samitis and zila parishads.

While a large number of members of the rural elite group are eager to extend support in elections to those belonging to the ruling party, the higher level functionaries, in turn, extend patronage in individual and collective form. But, simultaneously, they also try to delay or withhold grants for panchayats whose elected leaders belong to another political party or faction. This is true both for State and panchayat samiti levels. Sometimes, high level functionaries obstruct the functioning of panchayati raj institutions by instructing local party workers not to allow them to function in peace.

Another important point to be noted in this regard is that in the development of political links, political factors are considered more effective than social factors. Responses also show that factors such as "being co-worker of a party", "membership of some institutions" or "acquaintance earned during election-campaign", are more helpful in developing political links with both elected representatives and local party leaders than social factors like friends, relations, caste fellows and the like.

8

THE EMERGING PROFILE

MEN ARE BORN equal, but some are born more equal than others. This dictum well sums up the concept of elite as well as the rationale of the concept. A wide range of scholars, both conservatives and radicals, including Marxians, have started from this premise and built up the whole edifice of their thought and theories around the phenomenon of inegalitarian social structure. They disagree, however, on such issues as the extent to which social inequalities are functional (if at all) ; the extent to which the process of elite formation is a factor in the perpetuation of social inequalities ; the extent to which the elite strata are indispensable ; the manner of tackling the phenomenon of social inequalities and containing its pernicious effects ; and what kind of new value-orientation in elite persons is necessary for this purpose and so on.

Viewed against this perspective, two major issues concern us in any study of an elite in society. One relates to the structure of the elite group and the other to the orientations of its members, in terms of values and cognitive perspectives. Both operate as factors of cooperation and conflict prevalent in a polity and consequently can be held accountable for various turns and events influencing developmental processes. Nevertheless both are different. The structural aspect may be held more or less as a "given" in society, in terms of bases of stratification, though its forms may change. Values, norms, roles and cognitive orientations are relatively dynamic and as such can be treated as "variables" in elite studies.[1] If this is so, one may hopefully manipulate and reorient in a desired

---

1. For a detailed elaboration of the proposition, though in a slightly different form refer to Lenski, Gerhard, *Power and Privilege : A Theory of Social Stratification* (New York : McGraw-Hill, 1966). See particularly the first four chapters.

manner the values and norms of elites in society, though elites cannot be completely isolated from the social structure that they represent.

It will be wrong to assume that panchayati raj sought to eliminate the local rural elite in quest of equality ; in fact, it aimed at using the elite as an agent of change and as a mobilizer of people in various developmental processes. Thus the panchayati raj system had a place for the elite, particularly in terms of leadership roles and in the context of developmental functions and powers. This does not mean that the transformation of rural social strata was not held as an objective. The very term 'community development' implied a quest for an egalitarian social order. But owing to the legal structure of panchayati raj, as it finally emerged, and difficulties involved in the task of structural transformation, one has a feeling that in the final analysis at best secondary importance was attached to this objective. The focus of our enquiry has been whether or not, and to what extent, the rural elite has emerged as a catalytic agent of development and as a model and instrument of social transformation. As the hypotheses elaborated in the first chapter suggest, the role of the elite was not conceived of as an isolated phenomenon. The role of the socio-economic milieu, the bureaucratic structure, and other external factors aiding or constraining elite performance, were also included in the study.

Before attempting an overview of major findings and delineating a theoretical perspective for the future, two explanations about the nature of hypotheses and the enquiry conducted to test them will not be out of place here. One is that the hypotheses of the study have a ring of negativism about them. By the time we undertook the enquiry, a feeling had grown that panchayati raj had failed. All quarters seemed to have realized it. Moreover, the analysis undertaken to test the hypotheses revolves around data gathered through questionnaires, and is, as such, confined to the perceptions of the elite and of citizens. The time and financial resources at the disposal of the study team were far too meagre to allow probes in depth using participant observation and other techniques. Nevertheless, as the preceding chapters bear out, we have tried to supplement and balance the findings through observations in the field and comparative reflections where possible.

Testing the Hypotheses : Elite Structure

Let us now turn to examine whether the study corroborates or rejects the hypotheses with which we started.

RECRUITMENT AND CIRCULATION

It was hypothesized that the emerging rural elite, particularly the institutional leaders under panchayati raj, "are not different from the traditional rural elite." The specific indices used in the form of sub-hypotheses to test the main hypothesis related to educational, social, economic, and generational background of the elite. It is borne out by our study that all these variables play more a conjunctional than an exclusive and independent role, though the social and economic variables play a relatively more deterministic role. This again needs to be qualified. At lower levels of the three-tier system of panchayati raj the social status and caste affiliation of the aspirants to office, tend to help them achieve positions of power to a greater extent than in other cases. In all the districts most of the panchas thus belonged to numerically strong castes in their wards. At places we found that the aspirants from traditionally entrenched but numerically minority castes, even if they were prosperous and commanded respect, lost to aspirants from the majority castes of even moderate means. But at upper levels, (*i.e.,* at the level of Pradhan, Zila Pramukh, and, to a large extent, at sarpanch level also), economic status has been of greater consequence. It seems that a greater caste solidarity prevails at local levels, while social pluralism increases as the area of operation widens as one ascends to higher levels. Thus the consolidated majority support automatically available at local levels is not forthcoming at higher levels, where one has to manipulate and build up a majority coalition, and there economic position comes as a great help. The efforts to build up a majority coalition are also helped by support from upper levels—a fact that our study did not probe in depth, though it is borne out by field observations. And yet upper level support is only effective in the context of existing political cleavages where they can tilt the balance but cannot create alternatives.

Thus the rural elite is predominantly a socio-economic elite. As cited earlier also this finding lends support more to

S.C. Dube's idea of dominant individuals than to Srinivas's concept of dominant castes.[2] It may, however, be pointed out here that education has yet to acquire a decisive role in the making of the rural elite. It is true that according to our data members of the elite group at higher echelons are more educated than those at lower echelons. But education in their case is a function of economic status. In the field we did not come across cases where educated persons with moderate means held higher elective posts. Even considerations of age circumscribe the role of education. A single illustration will bear this out. In the base panchayat selected in Ganganagar district, a Sikh leader educated just up to the middle standard was made sarpanch, but his son, who had a master's degree in two subjects, was not. Here age gets precedence over education, which otherwise plays a limited role. Thus the positional elite in our study is, by and large, dominated by the middle age-group, while the members of the reputational elite come overwhelmingly from the old age-group.

Thus it appears that socio-economic, educational and generational factors play more a conjunctional than exclusive role, and socio-economic factors have a greater weightage than the rest. This trend is also corroborated by several other studies particularly pertaining to India.[3] But it differs from trends described in some of the studies of elites in developed countries. For example, in the study of New Haven in United States, Robert Dahl noted a trend from "cumulative" to "dispersed" inequalities.[4] But in India various studies, including the present

2. See Chapter 2.
3. See Chapter 1.
4. *Cf.*, : "In the political system of patrician oligarchy, political resources were marked by a cumulative inequality : when one individual was much better off than another in one resource, such as wealth, he was usually, better off in almost every other resources—social standing, legitimacy, control over religious and educational institutions, knowledge, office. In the political system of today, inequalities in political resources remain, but they tend to be non-cumulative. The political system of New Haven, then, is one of dispersed inequalities." Dahl, Robert, *Who Governs ? Democracy and Power in an American City* (New Haven : Yale University Press, Paperback 1965), p. 85.

one, portray a situation of cumulative inequalities.[5]

This trend should not be taken as a confirmation of our overall hypothesis that the present rural elite is not very different from the traditional elite. Actually the broad affirmation made above needs to be qualified in several ways.

First, as the analysis of the responses of reputational elite members to questions about present and former members of the elite with substantial influence (Chapter 2) shows, the present day members of the elite group are more educated and more prosperous than former ones. While this may in part reflect the general tenor of development in the country since independence, it is certain that better education and economic status are bound to affect elite behaviour and perspectives. Thus, if not in terms of structure, the present elite is different from the traditional one in respect of its orientations.

Second, the situational context in itself is an important variable. For example, in Ganganagar, the take-off of agriculture from a subsistence level has resulted in the hegemony of peasant proprietors within panchayati raj institutions, from the village to the district level. But this is not true of other districts. There the members of the elite group, especially those who occupy positions at the panchayat samiti and zila parishad levels, have other occupations, even if they hail from peasant castes. Thus a combination of legal practitioners and landlords in Bharatpur and Nagaur, of businessmen and landlords in Jhalwar, and of businessmen and legal practitioners in Bhilwara are in control of positions at higher levels. Nevertheless all are professional politicians, because they have a long-standing record in politics and have reached the higher echelons of power through experience gained at lower echelons.

5. An exception can be found in the work of André Béteille, who notes a shift from cumulative to dispersed inequalities in Sripuram village of Tanjore district in Tamilnadu. But his data do not make clear whether Béteille understands the two terms 'cumulative' and 'dispersed' and the process of differentiation in the same sense in which Dahl has used them. Béteille himself is pessimistic about the future of backward classes. But Dahl's 'ex-plebs' are said to have wielded power and enjoyed its fruits. For details see Béteille's works, *Caste, Class and Power* : *Changing Patterns of Stratification in a Tanjore Village* (Berkeley: University of California Press, 1955) and *Caste Old and New— Essays in Social Stratification* (Bombay : Asia Publishing House, 1969).

Third, though in terms of social and property bases there is not much change in the elite structure, there is certainly a change in the norms governing the acceptability and legitimacy accorded to elite persons. As the citizens' responses make clear,[6] elite persons have to be more than father figures if they are to exercise influence. They should represent and articulate the peoples' interests. It is a different matter if present-day members of the elite group fall short of the peoples' expectations and norms. At any rate, this indicates a shift (and at places even a breakdown) of the traditional system of the patron-client relationship in village India. Finally, as the case of Nagaur district shows, intensive factionalism tends to erode the bases and capability potential of the elite to influence behaviour or play a critical role in institutional decisions.

Altogether, it can be maintained that caste status and property continue to be the resource bases of the elite system, though with a difference.[7] Caste status does not count today as much in a ritualistic sense as in terms of numerical strength. Similarly, property still matters, but property holders are different. They are no longer the old jagirdars, but are peasant proprietors. There is also a change in orientations, though it is difficult to say how much this change will accelerate the process of differentiation of elite strata, let alone the question of giving a fillip to the levelling-up process. One's doubts gain strength from the fact that members of the institutional elite in the lower economic and political stratum have a low level of ambition and they even propose to drop out in the next political contest.[8]

THE RURAL ELITE AND CITIZENS : NEED OF NEW BRIDGES

A number of studies, some of which have been surveyed in

6. See Chapters 2 and 4.
7. In this formulation we have not taken into consideration the trend indicating change in aristocratic and cultural bases of the elite, which is more or less complete except in Bhilwara, a backward district, where it is still in a partial form. This aspect has been left out, since in the ultimate analysis, aristocracy and culture are outward manifestations of property as the base of elite influence, and property has already changed hands. As the tenancy reforms did away with landlordism, aristocracy, along with its cultural overtones, disappeared.
8. See, particularly Chapter, 3.

our study, show that members of the elite group are themselves dominant individuals or belong to the dominant strata of society and occupy a superior position in relation to citizens. It was on the basis of the findings of earlier studies that we also chose to explore the pattern of elite-citizen relationships, comparing their socio-economic status and the possible extent of communication between the two. Confirming the hypothesis, we found that there were greater similarities within the elite than there were between the elite and citizens.[9] As the study of the locational factor suggests, members of the elite group have more resources than the citizens, in social, economic and political terms. Further, the dominant role of the economic factor is also shown by the fact that members of the elite group are invariably better placed in economic terms, not only in relation to citizens in general, but also in relation to citizens of their own caste. Thus the elites of upper, middle, and lower castes are financially better placed than the respective citizens of these castes. In brief, we can repeat the earlier finding that inequalities are cumulative.

As a result of their higher social, educational and economic status, the elite is also a better recipient of the flow of political information outside. Its members make greater use of the newspaper, radio, and even urban contacts. Naturally, the members of the elite group are politically more conscious and informed than the citizens. Finally, elite persons are better placed in their potential to forge political linkages.

The greater resources of the elite group notwithstanding the problem of communication between the elites and the citizens is not so acute. When asked whether they feel confident enough to put forward and get a village improvement scheme accepted by their panchayat, 61.5% of 200 citizens replied in the affirmative. The corresponding percentage for the elite responses is 80. This is not too wide a gulf. Moreover, 38.5% of the citizens also pointed out that at one time or the other they had put forward an improvement scheme. Another 21.5% said that

9. This formulation is being made only in relative terms. Otherwise the elite has its own system of stratification. As seen earlier, those who are at the top in the social system have been elevated to the highest posts in the panchayati raj system also.

they actually had not thought on those lines.[10] It should not be forgotten, however, that a substantial minority of citizens would not do so, precisely because they lacked faith in panchayati raj leadership. Thus we should not conclude that the gap in socio-economic status had erected a Chinese wall between the elite and the citizens. There are several channels like *chopals* where the informal pattern of communication does prevail between the elite and the citizens. In spite of changes in the wake of development, the functional utility of the *chopal* has not been diminished. It may be recalled here that a good number of citizens, in their reply to the question of how they would get a scheme accepted by the village panchayat, observed that they would do so by personally approaching the ward panch and the sarpanch.

What is lacking, however, at the local rural level, is the growth of formal institutions providing a platform to the villagers to enable them to acquire greater confidence, have a more effective voice, and thereby a more meaningful participation in the management of local affairs than what they have today. These formal institutions can be the gram sabha, local units of political parties, a farmer's club, and the like. However, as our data bear out, these institutions are in poor shape in rural areas. Even the gram sabhas, a key institution in the panchayati raj system, are hardly used as forums of expression of popular opinion. Extension services as well as local party units need to pay attention to the vacuum here if democracy is to have some foundation at the grassroots level.

INSTRUMENTAL USES OF VERTICAL POLITICAL LINKAGES

The linkages that the rural elite develops with the district/ State level elite are a political resource that help build up and, more important, preserve the elite structure at the village level. The linkage may prove to be both functional and dysfunctional not merely for the elite structure but also for their orientations and behaviour. We had, therefore, hypothesized that "it is not the involvement of the rural elite in local politics which hinders the healthy growth of democracy at the grass roots level ; the malady lies in the political linkages of the rural elite with the district and State level elite." It was

10. See chapter 6.

further hypothesized that the upper level elite supports its counterpart at the rural local level, even overlooking its defaults and rescuing it, at the cost of community interests, to build up and buttress its own bases.

To begin with, it can be said that members of the rural elite group have good links with members of the upper level elite strata. Sarpanchas, pradhans and zila pramukhs, etc., who have a more effective say in panchayati raj affairs than the panchas, and who have been more mobile also, are better placed in this regard. Nearly 70 % to 85% of them have links with one category or the other of elite at the district and State levels. Further, it is also borne out by the study that in the forging and development of these links political factors, such as affinity as co-party workers and contacts necessary to meet the demands of elections, play an important role. But more important than the links is the phenomenon of instrumental uses of these links. A large number of elite respondents do support candidates for Lok Sabha and Vidhan Sabha elections because they have been sponsored by the ruling party. In return, they naturally expect help in getting their own and institutional work done. This contention comes into bold relief when we find that, while only 20% of the elite respondents have had personal or panchayat work done directly at the district or State level, the rest have relied on the help of a minister or made use of political influence in some other form. Again, it has been seen that the evolution of links is a function not so much of the degree of development but of the nature and intensity of political activities and the presence of an amiable personality or personalities at higher levels who are easily accessible to members of the local elite group. In this regard Nagaur and Jhalawar have been at one or the other time better placed than the rest of the districts, including Ganganagar.

We are in a twilight zone as far as the responses on the functionality/dysfunctionality aspects are concerned. The responses to some questions suggest that the instrumental uses of political links may not be detrimental to larger community interests. For example, only 14.6 % of the respondents have corroborated the phenomenon of political interference which is also treated in more than one case as a corrective measure.

Still one may feel that this is not a total picture. The Janus may have another face and yet, since the respondents themselves are a party to it, that face may remain *incognito*. The suspicion is strengthened not only by the responses of 14.6% of the elite respondents who confirm the phenomenon of political interference, but also by the silence observed by as many as 28.7% of the elite respondents on this score. But more revealing in this context are the informal observations of officials who point out that as a *quid pro quo* for electoral support, the upper level leadership condones the acts of ommission and commission of local leaders. This is particularly noticeable in respect to complaints against panchayati raj representatives who embezzle vast amounts of money, do not hold panchayat meetings regularly, do not get the budget approved by proper authorities, take arbitrary decisions with no regard to the majority opinion, and so on. In this way, the growth of norms, the evolution of a net work of institutionalized roles, and democratic structures at local levels receive a setback. Thus the hypothesis is not unequivocally rejected. Still for want of sufficient evidence, we leave it open.[11]

THE RURAL ELITE AND DEVELOPMENT ADMINISTRATION : STRUGGLE FOR ASCENDENCY

An allied aspect which again overlaps the boundaries of structure and orientations concern the pattern of relationship between the rural elite and the developmental bureauracy. We may recall here the hypothesis that "there is maladjustment between elected representatives and officials under panchayati raj." It was elaborated by way of sub-hypothesis that maladjustment was due to historical (*i.e.*, feudal), psychological, and social factors. These factors could affect the structuring of the political and the administrative elites, and generate inhibitions on both sides, thereby perpetuating the gulf between

---

11. More evidence supporting the hypothesis is amply available in Grover, V.P., *Panchayati Raj Administration in Rajasthan* (Agra : Laxmi Narain Agrawal, 1973). For a comparative study encompassing Rajasthan, Maharashtra, and Madras, see Iqbal Narain, *et al.*, *Panchayati Raj Administration, Old Controls and New Challenges,* (New Delhi, IIPA 1970).

the elected representatives and the officials. For example, the feudal psyche of the officials, which made them assume a patriarchal role, combined with the socio-educational distance between them and the rural elite would account for maladjustment between the two. Broadly speaking, this hypothesis can be taken as confirmed. But in cases where members of the rural elite group are equal or surpass the officials in socio-cultural (including educational) and economic status, urban outlook, and behaviour, they have an edge over the officials. There the officials at times feel inferior to, and toe the line of, elected representatives. But this qualification only confirms rather than negates the formulation that relational patterns are largely a function of the structuring of two elites.

It may also be added in this context that in course of informal interviews with the officials, it was found that they are full of contempt for members of the panchayati raj elite group and charge them with thwarting development efforts and hindering the normal functioning of administration. Some major allegations against elected representatives have been that they do not accept (in fact resist) 'sound' advice from the developmental bureaucracy ; that they indulge in corrupt practices ; and that they bask and thrive under the political umbrella, and through manoeuvrings and political pressures paralyse administration. Informal interviews, the elected representatives would not admit that they are looked down upon by officials or that they are not listened to. But in the course of informal chats, when the respondents feel assured that their remarks will be treated as off-the-record, they would narrate stories which would confirm the formulation made here. The same pattern is reflected in the analysis of responses describing official-non-official relations. The data show that there is a consensus that relations between key officials and elected representatives under panchayati raj are not tense ; some maintaining that they are very cordial. But when we tried to explore whether smooth communication channels exist between the officials and non-officials, a totally different pattern of responses would emerge. It may be recalled here that less than 10% of the elite respondents would frequently consult the development officials in matters related to panchayat work while another 24% spoke of having consultations only 'sometimes'.[12] Consultations on personal matters were even fewer. This may be due to the members of the elite group or the areas, having a low level of education and administrative experience, and failing to have *rapport* with, or assert themselves against, the officials. Thus the panchas lag behind sarpanchas, pradhans, pramukhs, and M.L.As. in their *rapport* and consultations with the developmental bureaucracy. Similarly, the poorly developed districts of Bhilwara and Jhalawar trail behind the developed district of Ganganagar.

Thus we came across both situations—one in which the officials ignore the low-placed representatives, and the other, where the officials are dominated and over-ruled by the relatively better placed rural elite. While the maladjustment is partly due to differences in socio-economic status, it is also the result of lack of proper orientation in terms of internalization of systemic goals and values. As the discussion of role-perceptions in our study shows, the elite has a limited perspective about the goals of panchayati raj. Similarly, the officials gave an impression in informal interviews that they can manage things better independently of the people's representatives, little realizing that they failed to do so when they were all-in-all in the pre-panchayati raj period. They also appear not to have imbibed the underlying philosophy of panchayati raj and community development.[13]

Testing the Hypotheses : Elite Orientations

To study the motivations, orientations and behaviour of the rural elite, the key hypothesis that we worked with was that the rural elite under panchayati raj was more interested in politics than in the fulfilment of developmental obligations. A sub-hypothesis suggested that the rural elite pursued personal or factional interests more than community interests as it was

12. See chapter 6.
13. See chapter 5. These points are even more neatly and boldly brought out in the context of Rajasthan in other studies like *The Pattern of Rural Development in Rajasthan* (Jaipur : Evaluation Organizations, Government of Rajasthan, 1960) ; Mathur, Kuldeep, *Bureaucratic Response to Development* (Delhi : National, 1972) ; and in the context of Uttar Pradesh in Kothari, Shanti and Roy, Ramashray, *Relations Between Politicians and Administrators at the District Level* (Delhi : IPA and the Centre of Applied Politics, 1969).

primarily concerned with the preservation and expansion of its support bases. We did not expect the rural elite to be *apolitical*. For, if it is to exercise political influence it must play politics. What we wanted to know, however, was whether its members could take a complementary view of politics and development or pursue the former to the exclusion of the latter.

ELITE ORIENTATION : A COMPLEMENTARY VIEW OF POLITICS AND DEVELOPMENT

The analysis of the data in the preceding chapters, especially in chapter 5 shows mixed results in this regard. There is a wide consensus among members of the elite that panchayati raj has been only partially successful, though some maintain that it is a total failure. But not all agree that panchayati raj functionaries are in any way responsible for it. Only 18.2% of the elite respondents attribute the poor performance of panchayati raj to selfishness of, and corruption among, members of the rural elite group. Another 20.4% point to factional politics as the cause of the failure, while 29.9% blame the apathy of State government. District-wise, there is not much difference in the response pattern, except that a larger percentage (39.3%) of elite respondents in Nagaur identify factional politics as the basis of failure of panchayati raj, while in Bhilwara, at least at the level of perception the problem of factionalism is almost nil. The study of factors motivating members of the elite to take to public life, as attempted in chapter 3, corroborates the same trend. While only 12.8% of the elite respondents admit to selfish motives, 57.3% mention village-service and another 12.8% refer to the quest for popularity. Among citizens the respective percentages in regard to these motivations are 49.5, 21.0 and 10.5. Again, Nagaur stands apart in the identification of selfish motives in larger percentages ; otherwise, there are not many district-wise variations on this score.

We also tried to discover whether members of the elite group are suitable agents of social change. The study does not provide an answer straightway in terms of 'yes' or 'no' to this query. Actually, social change in India's rural areas has two dimensions. One relates to the emergence of rural society from its subsistence level and insulated and static character. The other concerns the minimization of inequalities so that more homogeneous and participant communities emerge. With regard to the first we can repeat what we said earlier in the context of the first hypothesis : that the citizen's concept of local notables is changing. They want to see in them not just a patriarch, but a representative as well. They should both articulate and meet their demands. An elite falling short of this expectation will lose its influence. Thus it hardly matters whether members of the rural elite group are development-oriented or not. Under the tremendous pressure building up within a rural society in the throes of modernization, the development-orientation is going to become a value, a criterion to judge whether one is of the elite group or not. The identification of this subtle trend does not necessarily contradict the earlier finding that the members of the rural elite are obsessed with politics and are motivated by personal or factional interests. Politics is bound to be there wherever there is a question of allocation of scarce resources. The point which is being made here is that it is wrong to take always a dichotomous view of politics and development.

As far as the second dimension is concerned, the emergence of a rural elite has certainly not meant the minimization of inequalities. As the analysis of locational factors in chapter 2 and 3 and of benefits accruing from panchayati raj in chapter 5 show, people at the lower strata are very handicapped and feel deprived of various benefits, let alone the question of their rising up the ladder of elite position. Moreover, the impressions gathered through informal discussion with various groups in the field also suggest that the upper strata as well as the rural elite resist efforts at re-stratification and remapping of land relations. For example, the peasant castes are opposed to the allotment of land to people belonging to scheduled castes and tribes on the ground that they would thus become short of manual labour on their own fields.

It appears that while panchayti raj functionaries are much concerned with factional, if not personal interests, the extent of the pernicious effects of this involvement is subject to local variations. But perhaps involvement in factional politics cannot be avoided in a democratic polity ; nor it is necessarily anti-developmental, though its excess naturally increases costs, in terms of peoples' mobilization for development, as we found in Nagaur. The State-level leadership and developmental bureaucracy have to share the blame in this regard too.

Production Vs. Civic Amenities : No Dichotomy

The testing of an allied hypothesis that members of the rural elite group are more 'civic amenities oriented' than 'production-oriented', has been a rather arduous job, because a majority of the respondents failed to differentiate the two concepts neatly. More often than not they used the overarching term 'development' to cover the two concepts. While speaking of 'development' they talked of the need of *Khuranja* (pucca village streets), lighting, electricity, sanitation, irrigation, loans, and so on. If the survey team tried to illustrate the point by citing examples, the respondents would take the position that they needed both, which also seems to square with the objective reality in rural India. We may even argue that civic amenities *vs.* production is perhaps not a very realistic formulation. Indian villages, by and large, need both, though some may emphasize civic amenities more, while others stress production to a greater extent.

Some sort of differentiated response pattern on this issue can be seen in the context of the question dealing with the attributes of an ideal panchayat in chapter 5. If we add both first and second preferences indicated there we find that 41.5% of the elite respondents would like an ideal panchayat to concentrate on a civic amenities programmes and 37.2% on production-oriented programmes. But a still higher percentage expect an ideal panchayat to impart justice honestly. Responses of citizens in this respect favour civic amenities, with a percentage of 46.5, followed by production-orientation (37.5%) and imparting of justice (31.5%). Thus there is a slight tilt in favour of civic amenities programmes. The need of a village, and not so much its level of development, is a variable here. For example, in Ganganagar, a comparatively developed district, there were more responses favouring civic amenity programmes than in other districts, since even in prosperous communities in Ganganagar street lighting, drinking water facilities, etc., were not properly provided. On the other hand, in a backward district like Bhilwara, where production-oriented programmes have not made much headway, members of the rural elite group lay stress on these programmes.

Thus it is the situational context which explains whether the elite is production-oriented or civic amenities-oriented. Members of the elite group though unable to make a distinction between production and civic amenities, still tend to emphasize that which they find most wanting in their own situation. It will thus be perhaps wrong to assume, as we did while formulating the hypothesis, that a segmental view of the two as an attribute of the rural elite, or as an index of the aspirations of the rural populace, is possible. A complementary and not segmental view may help in delineating a realistic profile of the rural elite.

A Perspective for the Future

What future awaits the rural elite ? Pareto would have answered : "the graveyard". For him history is the graveyard of aristocracies. The governing elite, owing its position to lionlike qualities, degenerates and is replaced by those who have acquired or are in the process of acquiring lion-like qualities. Marx has linked the phenomenon of influence and replacement to the nature of the forces of production and technological advancement. Dahl, however, under the influence of pluralist thought, finds the concept of elite itself to be a misnomer and treats it as non-operational, because one is unable to trace the threads of decision making to particular group of people, particularly in the context of industrial or developed democracies. His contention is that with the growing democratization, the centres of decision-making and sources of influence get diffused.[14] Do we, then, assume that as technology helps produce surpluses and democratization penetrates downward, the elite in rural areas will fade away ? A number of other studies, made in the context of developed democracies, do not lend support to the view that sources of influence cannot be traced, or that elites are on their way

---

14. The trend of argument seems to run althrough Dahl's work *Who Governs ?* cited earlier. For a concise and theoretical plea, see his arlicle, "A Critique of Ruling Elite Model", *American Political Science Review*, LII (2), June 1958 : 463-69.

out.[15] Further, as Giovanni Sartori points out, the aversion to the concept of elite is due to its origins in anti-democratic thought and this still haunts and clouds our perception about the place of elites in a democracy. Etymologically speaking, elite means 'worthy of choice' and so the concept may be understood in terms of 'leading minorities'.[16] Our position is that democracy does not necessarily involve the elimination of elites ; the challenge facing it poses the issue of their re-structuring and re-orientation. Elites have so far survived in developed countries and the question of their 'withering away' appears to be utterly premature in developing societies. Our poser in the context of the third world should therefore be : "What is the direction of change in the structure and orientations of elites and can the direction of change be taken as an earnest for the compatibility of elites with a democratic polity ?"

WIDENING OF ELITE STRATA

In the comparison of members of present and past, reputational or influential, elite groups, some notable trends emerged. One was that in all the districts, except Nagaur, the number of the elite persons identified as influential is greater now than it was in the past. Even in regard to Nagaur it can be said that the decrease in number has not been the result of the shrinking of elite strata because of concentration of resources in fewer hands ;

15. *Cf.*, An observation by Riesman "Ruling Class Theories Applied to Contemporary America seem to be spectral survivals", in *The Lonely Crowd*, p. 232, quoted by Sartori, G., *Democratic Theory* (Oxford, 1965), p. 132. The author of the *Lonely Crowd* who puts forward a 'veito group' theory and thereby leans on the side of pluralistic theory concedes the element of domination particularly at the local level. C. Wright Mills, in his work *The Power Elite* (New York : Oxford, 1956), offers a strong refutation of pluralistic theory. For a review of the controversy and for a defence of the concept of 'elite', see Prewitt and Stone : *The Ruling Elites : Elite Theory, Power and American Democracy* (New York, Harper & Row, 1973). See also Baltzell, E. Digby, "Who's Who in America" and "The Social Register" and Kaufman, Harold, "Prestige Classes in New York Rural Community" in Bendix, Reinhard and Lipset, S.M. ed., *Class, Status and Power : A Reader in Social Stratification* (Free Press, 1965). Bachrach, Peter : *The Theory of Democratic Elitism : a critique* (Boston : Little, Brown and Co., 1967 and Bachrach, Peter and Baratz Morton : Decisions and Non-Decisions : An analytical Framework, *American Political Science Review* 57 (3), Sept. 1963 : 632-42.

16. G. Sartori, p. 112.

it has rather been due to the intense factionalism that reduced the influence of the socio-economic notables and thus inhibited the process of their emergence as a power elite. It may also be recalled here that the largest additions to the elite strata were found in Ganganagar. The additions have a qualitative significance as well because the minority castes also get a share in this process of the widening of the elite strata.[17] Some doubts may be cast on the validity of this generalization when it is recalled that people at the lower strata have been less ambitious and even felt like dropping out in the next elections (Chapter 3). But this trend is likely to be offset by two factors. First, one witnesses the phenomenon of the increasing independence of lower strata from clientle and vassal status. Second, political resourcefulness, both in terms of consciousness and linkages, is on the increase and is being increasingly shared by people in the lower strata. It is common knowledge that in the wake of universal adult franchise, the lower strata are coming into their own and making their presence felt. Again, Ganganagar can be treated as model for the future here.[18] Of course, the process of restratification is not going to be smooth but it cannot be denied that positive indications of this trend are already there.

SECULARIZATION AND CLASS CONSCIOUSNESS

Religion and rituals used to be part and parcel of Hindu life and every facet of social behaviour was guided by them. The division of labour, the system of distribution, wages, and orientation toward work were all regulated by *Dharma*. Above all, the system of stratification itself was sanctified by religion. To a large extent now this is all changed. Instead of the *jajmani* system (some sort of clientle relationship), there is

17. See Chapter 3.
18. In this regard the course of development is likely to follow the pattern of Punjab and even Andhra and Gujarat, where labour is comparatively in short supply, rather than that of Tamilnadu, Kerala or Bengal where labour is in surplus and where lower strata, despite their political organisations, have no leverage in bargaining. A useful insight into the process of the accommodation of new groups is provided by the data presented by O.P. Sharma in *Emerging Pattern of Rural Leadership in India.* (mimeographed) Ph.D. thesis submitted to the Indiana University in 1966. For comparative purposes see Myron Weiner's Study of Kaira (Gujarat) district in *Party Building in a New Nation* (University of Chicago Press, 1967), pp. 69-129.

now a bargaining system. Similarly, status differentiation on the basis of politico-economic achievements rather than ascription, is very obvious. Old patterns of hegemony are changing. In no district does a priest hold a reputational or elective position. In the base panchayat in Nagaur, first sarpanch was a village *purohit* and a Brahmin scholar. But in the next election he did not contest. Finally, a significant change that would affect the basis of traditional stratification is noticed in terms of attitude towards socio-economic inequalities. The *karma-phal* theory is no longer accepted and thus one's social status is not seen as the result of one's karma in a previous life. The pattern of responses, especially from lower strata, suggest a realization that inequalities are man made.[19] This is in part obvious from the profile of role expectations from panchayati raj in general and panchayats in particular drawn by the citizens, and is in part based on informal discussions and field observations. Discussions in chapters 3 and 6 also highlight the trend that patterns of life which have a sanction in the caste system are not *ipso facto* accepted ; there is, in fact, growing resistance to them, particularly under the impact of growing class consciousness.[20]

FROM AUTONOMY TO INTERDEPENDENCE IN RURAL POLITICS

Another trend that has already been set afoot is that the rural communities are coming out of their self-imposed isolation and are consequently losing their island-like autonomy. By this we do not mean that rural communities are losing their

19. This trend can well be generalized for the whole of India. *Cf.* : "Indeed, the new technology inadvertently challenges the underlying rationale of the traditional religious ethic of sacrifice and 'renouncing all attachments to the fruits of action.' Poverty and unrewarded effort are beginning to be perceived as remediable by man, and rooted in differential access to resources which are necessary for exploiting the opportunities created by modern science . . ." Frankel, Francine R. *India's Green Revolution* (Princeton : University Press, 1971), p. 202.

20. This does not mean that caste-structures have been displaced by class-structures. This just reflects a change in the psychic make up, though its potential implications in the redrawing of the contours of social stratification cannot be denied. Some of these implications have been discussed by Rajni Kothari in his introduction to *Caste in Indian Politics* (Longman 1970). Also see André Béteille, *Caste : Old and New. op. cit.*

significance or relevance ; in fact, they are now assuming added importance in terms of linkage politics and as the bed-rock of political support structures. This is the result of the growing interdependence of State, district, and panchayat level leadership, for which ample evidence is contained in our analysis of patterns of political linkages in the preceding chapter. The upper level leadership approaches the local rural elite for electoral support and in return offers patronage or deprivation, depending on response of the latter to the overtures of the former. In this regard what is important is the phenomenon of linkages, or their function in terms of the sharing of mutual benefits. Societal or organizational interests, according to our evidence, get secondary importance at best. Finally, when we come to instrumentalities, we find that caste or occupational affinities are an important factor in the development of linkages. Though a number of respondents feel that in developing vertical linkages the sharing of a common political platform or political experiences matters most, this itself quite often turns out to be a function of caste and occupational affinity. Thus, though caste is no longer a sanctifying agent, it does help in the forging of linkages and the distribution of benefits.

Two implications of the process deserve mention here. One is that the village no longer remains an all-embracing community to which the total life of its inhabitants is confined. This may encourage socio-economic and political mobility on the one hand and weaken the sense of identity of the elite with their village on the other. Second, the village can no longer be treated as a self-sufficient unit for political analysis.[21]

RURAL ELITE AS A MODERNIZING AGENT

The statement that the members of the rural elite group act in their enlightened self-interest and that, left to themselves, they will not be interested in directing the processes of social

21. The rationale of village as a unit of analysis has been for long a controversial issue. The linkage aspect adds a new dimension to this controversy.

change, does not require the marshalling of any evidence.[22] It has been argued that the elite is more modernistic than modernizing.[23] Our finding, however, is that on account of the tremendous pressure for change, members of the elite group just cannot ignore their role as agents of modernization. Chapters 4 and 5 which examine the nexus of influence and role of elite members *vis-a-vis* panchayati raj, bring out the accent on developmental roles. Elite persons, anxious to have and maintain a wide network of influence, have to assign priority to developmental roles. It may also be added here that they alone can play this role as they are nearest to the rural folk, not merely in terms of geographical proximity but also in terms of basic similarity in life patterns.

The bureaucracy, however, feels, as our field observations show, that members of the rural elite group are indifferent to their developmental roles, which is not entirely true. If they could be involved in the planning process to a greater extent, they would take to the developmental role more earnestly than they do today.[24] It is, however, in the logic of the process of re-structuring and re-orientation of rural leadreship that they should increasingly accept developmental roles and thereby, openly and assuredly, become agents of modernization.

DEMOCRATISATION, EGALITARIANISM AND THE IMPENDING PARTICIPATION CRISIS

The advent of universal adult suffrage with the grant of

22. Our own study contains enough evidence in this regard. Reference can also be made for similar findings to Mathur, M.V., Iqbal Narain, *et al.*, *Panchayati Raj in Rajasthan : A Case Study in Jaipur District* (New Delhi : Impex India, 1966). The same applies to State legislators also. For details, see Sisson, Richard, and Shrader, Lawrence, *Legislative Recruitment and Political Integration : Pattern of Political Linkage in an Indian State*, (Berkeley : Califoenia, 1972).

23. Beteille, André *Caste, Old and New., op. cit.*

24. For a discussion of some theoretical dimensions of the problem see Iqbal Narain, "The Administrative Challenge to Panchayati Raj", *Indian Journal of Public Administration*, July-September, 12(3), July-Sept. 1966, 564-73. The problem of dialectical relationship between imperatives of centralized planning and of local autonomies finds a good treatment in Valsan, E.H., *Community Development Programmes and Rural Local Government* (London : Praeger, 1970).

equal legal status to all on the basis of "one man, one vote", in the wake of the country's independence started a levelling-up process. Further, as different interests got articulated and factionalism became more pervasive, political majorities acquired a coalitional character built around promises of a just socio-economic and political order than obtained on the eve of independence. This explains to a great extent why cultural and aristocratic elites had to withdraw from the arena of competitive politics. Used to non-competitive and coercive practices, the traditional leadership found itself incapable of withstanding the compulsions of democratic politics and courting popular support. Thus it had to give way to new leadership which was skilled in persuasive techniques and could work for developmental benefits, both of which go a long way in building up political majorities. Change on this pattern was noticed in all the districts, Bhilwara being the last to follow suit. This also accounts for the broadening of the elite structure and the change in its orientations to which a reference has already been made elsewhere.

While on the one hand the implications of the levelling-up process are becoming obvious, the rural communities, already bred in an environment of inequality, are faced, paradoxically enough, with the prospects of growing inequalities on the other. This is particularly happening under the aegies of the "Green Revolution" which has so far not come to Rajasthan in any considerable measure. Given the low level of development and vast potentialities of untapped resources, rural tensions born out of a growing urge for egalitarianism in the wake of democratisation on the one hand, and increasing inequalities under the aegies of the "Green Revolution" on the other, may not arise in Rajasthan in the near future. But the possibility cannot be ruled out altogether. The examples of West Bengal, Bihar and Tamilnadu can be cited as cases in point. In these States, the democratic process has received a set-back, in part because of rural tensions. The only hope lies in the dispersal of various sources of power so that the ruling elite does not become oppressive and partisan in its quest for self-perpetuation, or in what Dahl has called a shift from cumulative inequalities to dispersed inequalities. Though even then oligarchic tendencies may remain, competitive oligarchies may keep the process of democratisation alive and may even lead to its meaningful fruition in the establishment of an egalitarian social order and the emergence of a democratic elite. One can, however, not be over-optimistic. The experience so far in other Indian States has been that the interests and values of the rural elite at the grassroots level, convey and coincide with those of the political and bureaucratic elites at higher echelons, providing a cushion and buffer to each other and uniting them all against the demands and pressures of the lower strata for meanigful parti-cipation in the political process and the consequent sharing of power and its fruits.

Epilogue

We have no prescriptions to offer. We, however, still feel that if democratisation is to imply socio-economic and political change and result in an egalitarian society, it will not help to apply a measuring rod for evaluating the rurals elite which is different from the one used for the elite at other levels, and there-by malign the members of this group, as if they were the only sinners. The fact of the matter is that we just cannot conjure up two different worlds—one urban and the other rural in the study of the elite. The rural elite is not to be treated as an isolated phenomenon ; it is, in fact, part and parcel of a living and interactive elite continuum from the bottom upwards and *vice versa.* If we want to restructure and re-orient that elite, we have to view it as such and that too against the backdrop of the Indian polity in its totality and of India's socio-economic structure, with all its diversities, contradictions, and dilemmas. Then alone it will be possible to evolve a set of uniform values and norms for elite behaviour and performance at all levels, which is the crying need of the hour.

INDEX